Advance Praise

"*Steps* is a powerful personal story about the resilience and perseverance of an Irish immigrant family who initially found their way to Port Deposit, Maryland during one of most volatile eras of American history, the late 1800s. By tracing these family roots for over four generations, this story navigates the evolving of a family from poverty to prominence in education, labor, and politics. The personal nature of local stories like these are imperative to bringing to life the timeline of American history that is often over generalized. Dr. Bolgiano compels the reader to consider the ways that American society and the laws that governed the land affected people's lives in real space and in real time. More importantly these local narratives illustrate the power of the people in shaping their own identities and their own destinies despite any opposition. The influence of the Susquehannock tribe, the resilience of black populations in bondage as well as freedom, the determination of women to self-identify and be empowered, and the strength of the working class are all undeniable. Because of *Steps*, these voices are now acknowledged and will be heard."

> — Tiffany Packer, Ph.D., Lecturer, Dept of History, Towson University

"Author Barbara Bolgiano's remarkable work has both restored and enriched our collective understanding of our immigrant ancestors. By presenting the Murray family and their labors as granite quarrymen and blacksmiths, she has put the role of our simple Irish ancestors, and their transformative work in a young America, on full display. We also benefit by a fully developed presentation of their role and place among community life in Port Deposit, a burgeoning river boom town that transitioned from a ferry spot to a valuable port by putting to use nearby abundant natural resources. We learn well of the desperate Irish laborers who arrived during the Great Hunger, and performed difficult work that benefitted the major cities and towns of the region. Thanks to Barbara for this valuable aid in understanding our heritage in deeper ways."

—Luke F. McCusker III, Managing Director, Irish Railroad
  Workers Museum

"Following *Steps* narrative and photos, I became well acquainted with the town's changes throughout history. As I read, the town came alive and began to feel like home and its residents became like family. Port Deposit is now on my bucket list and when I visit, I will already be familiar with its founders and the generations of people who cared about its future. Not only will I appreciate its present day persona, but I'll understand the quality and toil the granite workers left behind in the surviving granite buildings. *Steps* left me with a lasting impression of Port Deposit and Cecil County. I know when I visit it will feel like coming home."

—Patricia Hopper Patteson, Author of *Kilpara, Corrib Red* and
  Hearts Apart

"A drive through the main street of Port Deposit today reveals a sleepy town of no special interest except that the town is defined by steep cliffs on the east side and the Susquehanna River on the west side. These topographical features makes Post Deposit a "one-street town" and consequently one is inclined to ascribe little significance to this little town. In *Steps*, Barbara Bolgiano reviews the town's economic history and describes the sequence of economic events and how these affected the town. However, of greater significance is her familiarity with generations of families who lived in Port Deposit and how their lives were shaped by economic events, and how their careers also affected the town's destiny. Her access to years of correspondences from family members allows you, as the reader, to witness these events. It is this attention to detail which make Bolgiano's book so fascinating. The relationship between family members; the relationship between families and their impact on the town make this book "come alive". Once you have read *Steps* you will never be able to think about "Port Deposit", "immigrants", or the "depression" the same way."

—William Paré, Ph.D., Historian and Founder, St. Patrick's Chapel Historical Society, Conowingo

"In *Steps*, a new title that presents a history of Port Deposit in the context of immigration to the town in the late 1800s and includes many stories from early generations of families, Barbara Bolgiano has provided a thoughtful, fascinating social history that offers fresh insights and understanding about this unique town. In this carefully researched work, the past unfolds while the community evolves as "newcomers and old-Maryland families blend together," creating a framework for considering extraordinary changes in this river town. The more contemporary presentation of the past is taken up in the 2nd part of the book. In this section history about specific eras, movements, and people are presented, and the stories of five generations of Murrays, who immigrated to the United States from Ireland. Dr. Bolgiano has produced a fine blend of solid research and a readable narrative in this social and family history. This title will have a place on my bookshelf, and I recommend it to anyone interested in community studies, Port Deposit history, or the stories of families who were part of the town's past, working in the quarries, enduring great floods, migration, the Civil War-era, prosperity, and much more."

—Michael L. Dixon, M.S., M.A., Historian and President, Historical Society of Cecil County

STEPS

STEPS

Barbara J. Bolgiano

with a Foreword by Cynthia Landrum

Apprentice
House Press
Loyola University Maryland

First Edition

Printed in the United States of America

Paperback ISBN: 978-1-62720-163-6
E-book ISBN: 978-1-62720-164-3

Design: Meghan DeGeorge & Jaclyn Oill
Editorial Development: Mary Del Plato
Marketing: Serena Chenery

Apprentice
House Press
Loyola University Maryland

Apprentice House
Loyola University Maryland
4501 N. Charles Street
Baltimore, MD 21210
410.617.5265 • 410.617.2198 (fax)
www.ApprenticeHouse.com
info@ApprenticeHouse.com

Contents

List of Illustrations

Foreword

On Highway 222 in between Port Deposit, Maryland and the Conowingo Dam stands a historic sign that signals the farthest north and west that John Smith traveled, as he explored the Chesapeake Bay and its tributaries in 1608. Referred to as "Smith's Falls", the sign states the following:

> In 1608 Captain John Smith ascended the Susquehanna River until stopped by the Rocks. On his map he calls this point "Smyths Fales" marking it by a "+" which he explains as meaning "Hath bin discovered what lies beyond is by relation".[i]

In 2016, the sign marks the confluence of Amish communities, a Girl Scout Camp, a hydroelectric dam, biker bars, a casino, a granite quarry, a retirement condo community, and two port city settlements that pre-date both the War of 1812 and the American Civil War. The sign also reaffirms the source of the colonial name of the falls and that the river, and implicitly the larger region, had been "discovered" by the English within a year of the establishment of the Jamestown settlement in 1607.

What it fails to communicate, is that the Susquehannock Tribe, more than likely, refused to allow Smith to travel further into the interior by exploring beyond what is today the Conowingo Dam. Unlike other tribes who comprised the Chiefdoms of the Chesapeake Bay, the Lower River Susquehannock were potentially less amenable to the English in reference to trade, tribute, and long-term alliances through marriage and/or treaties (they later aligned themselves with the Dutch and Swedish).[ii] As the "keepers" of the interior kingdoms that were hinged upon the eastern seaboard of the North American Continent, they represented the tribes who, in 1608, were willing to go to war (if necessary) rather than easily acquiesce to the attributes of European society beyond what they deemed to be mutually beneficial trade relations. In contrast, many of the coastal nations lining the Chesapeake Bay and its regional tributaries represented Native Peoples who believed, at least initially, in the potential for peace in reference to relations with international foreign powers. This philosophical divide that existed in 1608, became the central axis from which all diplomacy stemmed in reference to long-term Indian-white relations, as the Chesapeake Bay became the seat of power for the first English colonial system and later the United States. Regardless of era and/or geographic location, however, the Algonquin Confederations were bound to a prophecy that predates the Age of Exploration by a few hundred years.

According to John Phillips[iii] (Ojibwe), in 1200 A.D. (roughly) the spiritual leaders that represented the major Eastern Confederations had the same prophetic dream, in reference to a people who were coming from the East to live amongst them. After runners were sent between the tribes, the leaders of the Algonquin Nations came together in council. The central message relayed to each tribe, was that they had a diplomatic choice between the path of peace or war. If they chose the path of peace, they would survive relatively intact. If they chose the path of war, they faced almost certain annihilation. Some tribes such as the Ojibwe chose to put down their weapons, disband their warrior societies, and head to the western parameter of their homelands. Other tribes chose to take a stand and fought the invaders, rather than "walk the line" of neutrality and peace.[iv] As each tribe and/or confederation contemplated which direction to take, at the same time they inherently understood that this would be a long-term universal struggle between the path of peace or war, with all of the historic tensions and overtures between the two extremes.

Margaret Connell Szasz suggests that the initial native-European contact long pre-dated the establishment of the Jamestown Colony. Europeans had made their presence known to other coastal Algonquian at least eight decades before Jamestown. Indeed, prophecies bore testimony to the influence of this earlier contact, for according to William Strachey, Powhatan's priests had warned him "that from the Chesapeake Bay a Nation should arise, which should dissolve and give end to his Empire." A second prophecy forecast that twice the Powhatan Confederacy "should overthrow and dishearten the attempts....but the third tyme they themselves should fall into their Subjection and their Conquest." [v]

When Chief Powhatan chose to solidify his relationship with the English colonists through the marriage of Pocahontas and John Rolfe in 1614, he was attempting to steer a course of neutrality through the gauntlet of the English colonial system as it expanded from the Chesapeake Bay into the interior. As the leader of a powerful mid-Atlantic Confederation, who were the caretakers of the coast and spirit realm that they represented, Powhatan was fully cognizant of the diplomatic tone that he was establishing with this international alliance between two individuals of equal social standing who belonged to the "anointed class" of their respective parent cultures. The Susquehannock, however, chose not to align themselves with the English Crown at this time in their effort to stem the tide of colonization, as intimated by John Smith when he recorded what he encountered after he sailed up the river from the bay.

Prior to 1608, the confluence of the Susquehanna River and the Chesapeake Bay was where the Susquehannock, Lenni Lenape, Iroquois, Piscataway, Nanticoke, and Powhatan Nations (among others) had lived unhindered since the other side of memory in their respective kingdoms by the sea. As the "People of the First Light", they represented the coastal confederations of tribes who greeted the morning light in the east as the sun traveled west on its daily rotation. As tribes who defined themselves by water, they navigated their canoes from one settlement to the next throughout the bay and its coagulating network of interior river systems.

The Tidewater Nations were loose confederations of paramount chiefdoms, with a werowance (district chief) answerable to the head chief. Each town had a ruler (also called a werowance) who answered to the district chief.[vi] The towns themselves were settlements that consisted of scattered palisaded longhouses, that were interspersed with cultivated gardens and groves of trees that partially protected them from inclement weather. Most towns were inhabited by a hundred people, and it was not uncommon for individuals of the same hamlet to live on either side of a stream and/or river. Over time, People grew accustomed to navigating the waterways that formed the central spiritual and political spine of the tribes living within the Tidewater Region.[vii]

The priests within each tribe were the sentinels who kept the solar and lunar calendars at religious centers that were marked on the horizon by petroglyphs, pictographs, and ceremonial mounds. In 2016, Priests still maintain the rituals for conjuring spirits, divining the future, raising or quelling storms, and disabling enemies with confusion.[viii] The Priests have always held tremendous influence over the leaders that they serve, because they are viewed by their respective tribes as people who "walk with power". Traditionalists living within the Tidewater Region have never ventured into any considerable enterprise, without first consulting the priests, who serve as the intercessors between the two worlds[ix] and who are posted as "watchers" along the banks of the Potomac, Severn, Susquehanna, and Rappahannock Rivers (among others) that feed into the larger Chesapeake Bay at geographic locations that are deemed to be the confluence of powerful forces. Such a location exists at the mouth of the Susquehanna River in downtown Port Deposit, Md. and is marked by a mural that lines the river with pre-contact Native silhouettes that merge the past with the present.

For the Chesapeake Bay Nations, their road to disappearance and subsequent resurrection began in 1623, after the first Virginia Massacre in 1622 and was followed by other pivotal moments in diplomacy within the region in 1644, 1676, and 1783. The most critical juncture in which their world was ruptured and turned upside down, however, was in the 19th century when President Andrew Jackson signed a Removal Bill in 1830 that forced all tribes east of the Mississippi River West to Indian Territory. The Susquehannock, Piscataway, Powhatan, and Nanticoke (among others) represented the coastal nations that remained behind by "hiding in plain view", which is what some of my relatives did on the maternal side of my family in order to maintain their long term role as "caretakers" of the Tidewater Region. By the 21st century, the tribes of the Chesapeake Bay had long been relegated to the status of "ancient civilization" that had vanished, as the colonial cell that took root in 1607 expanded and thrived as the Republic moved West, embraced the Industrial Revolution, and solidly coopted most land on the North American continent.

Evan Pritchard (Micmac) states that in Lenape belief, our souls walk towards the west when we die, traveling along the "Spirit Road", which can be seen reflected in the Milky Way at night, each footprint a shimmering star. For many Algonquin people, the act of exiting a western door face-forward is a metaphor for death itself. This was another reason for the Lenape and other coastal nations to feel unsettled about leaving their homes and land to travel west into the unknown mysteries of the frontier at critical junctures during the colonial era and the period of the Early Republic.[x] Those that remained behind perfected the art of shape-shifting their surface veneer, as they fully faced the infinite generational obstacles placed before them.

Philip Deloria (Dakota) suggests that the plotting out and exploring of the United States has for a long time meant celebrating the nation's growing power and its occasionally wise, often tragic, sometimes well-intentioned deployment of power on the continent and around the world. The celebration of national character, on the other hand, has frequently involved the erasure of such exercises of power. This story is a very different one: it is more tightly linked to destiny, to First Peoples who simply vanish, to the relativity of culture and meaning, to a long standing license to make oneself over. Americans have often been inclined to keep the narratives of American nationhood and American character away from each other. And yet, the two stories are inseparable.[xi]

The bloodlines of the tribes are still present in the landscape, through systematic inter-marriage with non-Native peoples living within the Tidewater Region and in the foothills of the Appalachian Mountains, whose ancestors either immigrated (over time) to the eastern seaboard from Europe and/or were brought in bondage after the African slave trade was first introduced into the Chesapeake Bay by the Dutch in 1619. Considered by some to be the first "gateway" between the East and the West on the North American Continent, in

2016 the pre-colonial past of Port Deposit seamlessly merges with the present, as the overlapping layers of human occupation rise up from the ground as vaporous mists of granite, brick and wood.

CYNTHIA LANDRUM, PH.D.
Seattle, September 2016
Dr. Landrum is a university professor of American History and specializes in studies of Indigenous Nations. She is the author of *The Valley of the Kings: Rehabilitation of the People of the Columbia River and Pacific Rim through Ceremonialism* and other forthcoming books.

Preface

On a summer visit to Port Deposit, Maryland in July of 2004, my aunt, Patricia Ellen Murray, took my family on a car tour of the town. This was not our first tour of "Port". Since the early 1960's when my cousins and I were old enough to stay at our grandparents' home in Port Deposit, our aunt would drive her red Chevrolet Impala alongside the town's historical buildings and the houses owned by our Murray relatives to tell us about the people and the places that made this town a special place for her.

Town Square, Port Deposit, Md.

i. Town Square, Port Deposit.
This view of Port Deposit looking south on Main Street from the Town Square shows on the east (left side), the Town Fountain, the Cecil National Bank Building and Carson's Pharmacy Building, and on the west (right side), the Winchester Hotel and the Rappaport Building.

Our Murray ancestors were immigrants to America and inhabitants of Port Deposit in the days when the town was a thriving center of trade up and down river and rail, as a key river port for the Mid-Atlantic States. The Murray family of 19th and early 20th century Port Deposit led rich and interesting lives; many lived in their entirety in the town. Hearing stories of how the river and quarry shaped the lives of our relatives, made me realize how we, who may only visit Port on occasion, are part of this family's story too.

On this particular tour, I took snap shots and recorded the oral history. Whether it was due to my age, my sons' eagerness for family connections, or a new-found appreciation for ancestral family history, the event provided the impetus for me to interview, research and record. Family albums of Murray Port Deposit revealed old photographs and new stories about how history shaped the town and the lives of my mother's family. My aunts, sisters and cousins also found interesting information about the family's role in Tome School, and my children learned that they were the sixth generation to attend St. Teresa of Avila's Catholic Church. The time period and circumstances after the Great Depression also piqued an interest. Jerome and Mabelle Murray's family moved around in the southern states before returning permanently to their home and family in Cecil County, Maryland after the United States Naval Training Center (U.S.N.T.C.) Bainbridge had been built.

The county's place in the Revolutionary War, the War of 1812, and Civil War may be known to locals, but it provided a learning experience to me, mainly through my aunt's frequent letters enclosed with historical newspaper clippings, and my perusal of local history books while on visits to Port from my home in England. Later a study of the census records of the 7th Election District of Cecil County from 1840 to 1930 brought the town's people and businesses to life. In a sense, the gradual development of Port Deposit through the ages is a model for the evolution of many small towns. Here was a town nearly self-sufficient in its resources and provisions, in its supply of food, places of employment and almost all that a household required from shoe makers to wheelwrights, and doctors to seamstresses. Through its extreme hardships, such as the periodic ice gorges, and the intense booms arising from the lucrative granite, lumber and riverside trade, the community of newcomers and old Marylanders blended together and created a very unique period.

The following pages include first, a brief history of the town, to give a feel for what it might have been like to live in "Port" in the late 19th and early 20th centuries. These have been divided into sections that define the town, such as "River and Stone", and "Ice Gorges and Floods". A more contemporary record of Port Deposit while on the car journey forms the second part. History about the specific homes and buildings include "Baseball fever", "The Underground Railroad and the Iron Foundry", and "Public Health". Interspersed are photographs and stories about the first five generations of Murrays and the people and places of Port Deposit, Maryland.

The journey of weaving these stories passed on in the venerable story-telling tradition of the Irish led to a realization of the parallels that link that period of history to the present day. The crossroads that formed in Cecil County, were a crossroads of those who had migrated westwards across the Atlantic from Western Europe at the exact point in time that those both free and enslaved in the southern states were moving northwards. The powerful economic growth that resulted from its geographic position also brought some very unique people to this riverside town who felt the call to defend the rights of these same immigrants, and grant them free education.

My exploration of McClenahan's quarry was made easier

by Nancy Roberts' compilation, *We Called It The Everlasting Granite And, By Golly, It Is* and in particular the stories about the many Murray men who worked in the quarry. Their stories and times were recollected in exacting detail by Jerome, who like his grandfather and father before him, worked there as a pre-adolescent. I learned that the quarry families were far from impoverished; on the contrary, they led rich and full lives in ways less defined by economics and more so by their sense of community in the town. Furthermore, their opportunity for work resulted in advancement for their families.

Most astonishing was a discovery that a young teenage woman, partially illiterate from missing school in a starving Ireland, who provided no fixed record of her age or year of immigration, would raise a career woman for a daughter, one who would go on to provide educational opportunities for children in Baltimore. The pattern in general repeated itself in many families, and although there was the occasional scenario of "one step forward, two steps back", their momentum was unstoppable. The Murray family were an ordinary family who simply lived in an extraordinary place, but if their stories were commonplace, their times were not. They speak to us about the forgotten values and deeds of past generations. It is a privilege to share them with you.

Barbara Bolgiano
St. Albans, August 2016

To the Murray girls

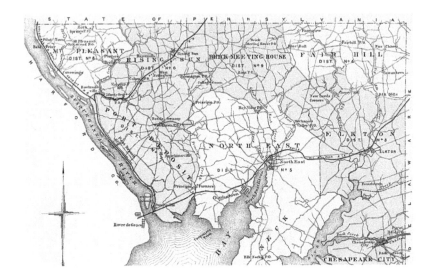

ii. Detail from map of Cecil County from the Illustrated Atlas, 1877.
*The northern sector of Cecil County is shown in this view. Courtesy of The
Sheridan Libraries of The Johns Hopkins University.*

iii. Panoramic View of the Susquehanna River above Port Deposit.
The view north of the Susquehanna River from Pinnacle Rock on Mount Ararat shows the islands from west-to-east (left to right) of Snake, Spencer, Wood and Robert's, Steele's and Sterrett. The town of Port Deposit is on the eastern (right) bank. The ruins of the Rock Run Bridge piers beyond Snake Island, and the tower of Memorial Hall of Jacob Tome Institute on the hill on the right are visible. The Conowingo Dam is just out of this view taken in 1987, taken with a Pentax-1000 camera using Kodak color film. Courtesy of Rev. John J. Abrahams III.

Part I.

A brief history of Port Deposit

Early Inhabitants

1. Native American woman on the bank of the Susquehanna River.
*Detail from an engraving by James Smither on Mason and Dixon's 1768
Pennsylvania and Maryland boundary map. Courtesy of The Library of
Congress.*

Before the banks of the Susquehanna River were colo-
nized by European settlers, the native-born Susquehannock
tribe of Iroquois ancestry lived on the islands, shore and
woodland of the thirteen-mile stretch of the Susquehanna
River between its mouth at the Perryville flats and the Bald
Friar rocks at Conowingo, so-called because of one distinctive, shiny quartz boulder in the river.

There is evidence in fact of periods of habitation of the
Susquehanna River Valley by indigenous peoples for the past

11,000 years or more.[1]

> *Most of us tend to think of the Susquehannocks as the people who had always occupied the environs of the river. After all, the river was named for them. However, [Captain John] Smith's Susquesahanockes were just the last group of human beings to inhabit these river lands before the coming of the Europeans.*[2]

We know most about those Susquehannocks that lived in these environs between the late 1500s to the late 1700s, because of their 1608 meeting(s) with the Smith touring party, as well as from the artifacts they left behind. The many thousands of stone tools and weapons documented in the early 1900s by archaeological and anthropological expeditions to Port Deposit also attest to their settlement. Between 1920, when it was sure that a dam at Conowingo would become a reality, and 1926, when its construction began, historians and anthropologists of the Maryland Academy of Sciences, the Maryland Geographical Society, the University of Pennsylvania, Princeton University, the Smithsonian Institute and Tome School all came to collect Indian artifacts from the environs of the lower Susquehanna, to document and later study.[3] Finds of hunting, skinning and cooking tools, were supplemented by the discovery of a grinding or mashing station made out of stone, for maize, bean and grain. Reports of bushels-full of objects being removed in short periods of time are probably not exaggerations, as private collectors, scientists and county residents alike wanted to track down these precious items while it was still possible.

One of their villages, the elusive Poppemetto, lay between Rock Run on the northern edge of Port Deposit to just north of the Octoraro Creek area.[4] The Susquehannocks also lived on the islands up to the water falls at old Conowingo. Archaeologists reported habitation of Palmer's [also called

Watson's or Garrett], Robert's, Snake and Vanneman Islands. With their knowledge of the signs of the tides and seasons, the Susquehannocks would have harvested large and small mammals; migratory fish and waterfowl; beaver, otter, muskrat, from the shore; and from the woods, deer and squirrel, as well as the plentiful fruit, nut and cultivated crops. Bear and "wolfe" were among the skins they wore.

The incredibly rich rock art that was found on the shore and river rocks of Bald Friar, now partly submerged in the Conowingo Reservoir (and in part destroyed by the dam construction work), was created by Algonquin-speaking inhabitants, who preceded the Susquehannock Indians. The choice of location of their rock art through the lower Susquehanna River Valley, near running water, and where earth met sky, and, the subjects of their pictorial designs, tell of their deeply spiritual connection with the earth, and the healing powers of nature. These were possibly places of meditation, for reconnecting with Nature. These earlier Algonquians lived north of the Conowingo and "Smith's Falls" and their communities extended up river into Lancaster and York counties. The remains of these and far earlier communities lie buried now deep beneath the river bed and shorelines. Time will reveal secrets to future communities about the ancient inhabitants of these shores.

Those Cecil County residents who may have been fortunate enough to find Susquehannock relics formed a deep reverence for these objects, and for those people who created them, not only for their artistry and physicality, but for their self-sufficiency, their endurance, their deep knowledge and skills, and perhaps above all, for their living in total harmony with Nature. The indigenous spirituality of the American Indians has at its heart being at one with the whole physical and geographical earth, the spiritual and living earth, including all life, and with the Creator (or Great Spirit). Although these peoples are invisible, their spirit lives on. They have preserved the abundant local environment for their children's children – ourselves, and we must now do the same. As in the Iroquois saying of the period, "In our every deliberation, we must consider the impact of our decisions on the next seven generations."

River and Stone

2. Arks and Rafts.
This painting by Grace Humphries illustrates a long wooden ark filled with goods being navigated on the Susquehanna River. Courtesy of the Port Deposit Heritage Corporation.

As the last town on the 444-mile long Susquehanna River, before it empties into the Chesapeake Bay, Port Deposit, gained wealth and culture from the abundant natural resources that were found locally as well as shipped downstream. By the middle of the 1800s, Port Deposit was a vibrant boom town, and a center of trade on the Susquehanna River.[1]

Before the installation of hydroelectric dams on the river, some boats and barges had the capability to travel upstream as well as down, to deliver lumber, coal, grain, other raw and refined materials, food stuffs, whiskey, and, eventually, granite. Many of these craft, including the long, unwieldy wooden arks, and some flat-bottomed rafts, could only go downstream, and once they reached their destination, they were dismantled at the lumber sale yards and repurposed long before the practice of recycling gained popularity.[2]

So by the time the Maryland state bill was signed by Maryland Governor Winder on December 12, 1812, changing the name of the town from Creswell's Ferry to Port Deposit,[3] it had become a port of deposit for arks and boats from as far north as its source in Cooperstown, New York. The bulk of the goods from upstream came from Pennsylvania, and were warehoused and redistributed for sailing and steam ships that came up the Bay from Baltimore, Maryland's largest city and a major eastern seaport.[4]

In 1608, Englishman, Captain John Smith, and his party of explorers, ascended the river from the Chesapeake Bay until they were stopped by the rocks of the "Susquesahanough" above the current town in the vicinity of native Susquehannock villages.[5] This rocky area of the river and its bank, a few miles upstream of the town and wharves, was key to the entry into the town for centuries, being Thomas Cresap's ferry landing (from 1729)[6] and the site of the old bridge slip-road (completed in 1815-17 by the Port Deposit Bridge Company).[7]

The creek along the north edge of Port Deposit, emptying in to the north-eastern shore of the river became aptly known as Rock Run,[8] and the small valley that it carved out as Rock Run Hollow. Running parallel to the eastern shore of the river was the 30 foot wide, 9 mile long Susquehanna Canal maintained by the Maryland Canal Company (from 1783 until about 1820).[9] Later a railroad was also built along the same side of the river, which became an important shuttle between the quarry and the town wharves.[10] A common denominator in the evolution of this development was the stone – stone in the river and steep rock walls above the river.

But these were different kinds of stone, created in distinct epochs: the river stone landed here some two million years ago, during the freeze-melting cycles of the last Ice Age, when massive flows of water were powerful enough to move and leave behind the huge boulders.[11] The granite stone beneath the earth's surface, on the other hand, formed some 250 million years before this, even before the continents fully divided from each other. It was the very slow solidification of the molten stone mixtures beneath of the crust of the earth, created when lava deep within the core of the earth boiled upwards, that caused diverse types of stone to liquefy and mix, creating eventually the very high strength and beautiful stone that is typical of granite.[12]

The U.S. Geological Surveys of the early nineteenth century provided prospectors with information about precious resources to mine and market, not unlike today's gas explorations. The 1902 Maryland Geological Survey and the 1910 U.S. Geological Survey gave practical information about each quarry, stating of the Port Deposit quarries, "The natural advantages of quarrying and shipping at this point would, indeed, be difficult to excel."[13]

While stone had been dug out of the Port Deposit quarry from at least the late 1700s for use in colonial stone dwellings, it was not until the early 1800s when the granite quarry business took off and became a mainstay of the town for the next century. Around 1816 to 1817, the stone was quarried to supply the Port Deposit Bridge construction (crossing the river above Rock Run), which in turn served to transport the quarry's stone and the town's goods southwards, and, in 1829-30, the canal owners showed an interest in the business. In 1832, Mr. Ebenezer Dickey McClenahan purchased the quarry and expanded it further.[15]

McClenahan and his managers and sons employed Cecil and Harford County residents, and experienced and novice quarrymen alike to bring granite out of the rock walls that rose two hundred feet above the river bed. African-Americans, many moving northwards, and immigrants from Italy, Ireland and elsewhere were all given jobs.[16] At one time, more than five hundred people were working at the Port Deposit quarry. Jobs to be had were those of dynamite blasters or "powder monkeys" to create openings in the rock; stone cutters, and, blacksmiths to sharpen their tools; stone masons and crushers to work the stone; horsemen, including a hostler, for caring for the horses, a farrier for shoeing them, and teamsters for driving them; derrick (or crane) operators, and transportation workers, supervisors, managers, watchmen and contractors to support the entire operation. The horses both brought the derricks to life, by turning in a circle to lift and move the blocks, and pulled 2-wheeled carts to take the stone to wagons, railway cars, arks, boats and trucks.[17] From the sons of the McClenahans, who were the proprietors, dealers and timekeepers, to the sons of the quarrymen, who were the waterboys and cart-drivers, the quarry was operational up to 14 hours a day, seven days a week,[18] eleven months a year.[19]

3. McClenahan & Bros. Quarries, Port Deposit, Md.
*Detail of a drawing published by Lake, Griffing & Stevenson in the county atlas
in 1877. The long building with black smoke coming from the chimney is the
location of the blacksmith's shops. Courtesy of The Sheridan Libraries of The
Johns Hopkins University.*

The granite from the Port Deposit quarry was highly
sought after. The texture, color, strength and geological formation featured in its unique power to transform the town.
All granite contains three rock types: feldspar, the white
part; mica, the black part; and quartz, which adds the color.
Port Deposit granite, is mainly a light gray to bluish-gray
color when freshly cut, and has a characteristic composition
with a high proportion of black mica flakes arranged in a
curving pattern,[20] which would make this stone attractive for
modern, domestic use. However, in the 19th and early 20th
centuries, the demand for stone was from the constructors
of buildings and structures built to last centuries: bridges
and tunnels, churches, mansions, even the foundation of
the U.S. Treasury. From Washington D.C. to New York City,
and many points in between, buildings were built with Port
Deposit granite, including over eighty churches and buildings in Baltimore and Philadelphia.[21] Many of the homes and

sidewalks in the town of Port Deposit were also built with granite from the quarry.

Compact, homogeneous and strong, with "a crushing strength of 85,000 pounds on two-inch cubes", this stone outperformed other granites.[22] Moreover, the smoothness of the cut surfaces, and the ability to cut out sized, rectangular blocks and transport them by river, made this granite economical to manufacture, process and sell.[23]

The McClenahans employed nearly a dozen of the Murray family, my ancestors, many of whom lived on Granite Avenue in the Rock Run area. John, Joseph, William Joseph, James, Joseph, Thomas Harry, John Patrick, Patrick Henry, and Jerome Patrick Murray were all quarrymen. Some worked as blacksmiths, but just as many were stone cutters. Murrays were also common laborers and one was even a waterboy!

While Ebenezer D. McClenahan hired half of the first generation of Murrays at the quarry, the McClenahan Brothers gave jobs to the second and third. On June 13, 1868, the deed for the quarry was passed from Ebenezer and his wife, Margaretta, to John Megredy and Robert Emory McClenahan, and it legally became McClenahan & Brother Granite Company of Cecil County.

In about 1873, at the age of 12, my grandfather's father, William Joseph Murray, son of Irish immigrants, started working as an apprentice blacksmith. At the quarry a team of blacksmiths were responsible for making and maintaining hand tools for the stone cutters. These included wedges or chisels, punches or points, mallets and hammers, and rings, for carrying the water containers or water yokes. Water and spit were used to locate "dark" seams, which could be divided into multi-ton blocks by hammering feathering wedges into such seams. This would result in natural cuts that preserved the block shapes, and allow smaller hunks to be moved, loaded and delivered.

Each blacksmith worked for a team of stone cutters, and the granite production could not happen without these teams. The same cutters would come back to their own blacksmith's shop at the forge during the day to have their tools put back into good working order. The blacksmithing was vital to the efficiency and quality of granite production; blacksmiths earned higher wages and could get work up to 11 months of the year, when some men only got work for 6-7 months. At the age of 16, William Murray, as a fully-fledged blacksmith and union member, received $1 to $1.25 per hour. (Others earned 10¢ per hour.) This was in 1877. William worked there for over five decades, and was in charge of Shop #1 when his son was a waterboy.[24]

A sketch of the quarry and company store area was made by William's son, Jerome Patrick Murray, in 1976 at the age of 78. He drew this for Nancy Roberts and her book *We Called It The Everlasting Granite And, By Golly, It Is*. Remarkably for his age, he could recall the area in some detail, although paper and pencil were always an extension of his thoughts and plans. His sketch is oriented with the Susquehanna River at the bottom, and shows the long Pennsylvania (Penna.) railroad bisecting Rock Run Creek. The McClenahan quarry area is shown on the left and the Rock Run area on the right. At the center is the location of a rectangular grist mill, labelled "Mr. Smithson's mill and house". On the left is designated the area where 12 blacksmiths shops were located (each working for 8 stone cutters), located close to the 'Fresh water Jug!', a 'derrick moving stone', and a 'one horse derrick', the derricks being adjacent to the railroad, so the stone loads could be swung out on to the railroad, river arks or wagons, and later motorized trucks.[25] The Port Deposit Store Co. is on the far right, between Susquehanna River Road, now Route 222, near the bottom of Granite Avenue labelled 'to Colora and Liberty Grove' and the railroad. Surrounding this are two hotels and the 'African Peoples Co. Store', as well as 'Frank S's 2-story building', probably the store of Frank Sargable, a German immigrant grocer in 1910, as well as the Rock Run passenger station. Across the creek there were offices and another blacksmith's shop. Also listed were three saloons at Rock Run, and in Port Deposit, 3 railroad stations, 3 drug stores, 5 doctors and 2 dentists.

Like other lifers at the quarry, many blacksmiths starting working in their late teens (some after periods of apprenticeships), and continued to work into their sixties or seventies, if able, a span of fifty years or more. The number of blacksmiths in Port Deposit increased from eight in 1860, to sixteen in 1870. They were in such demand; there were no additional blacksmith available aside from the town's industrial blacksmiths. Like a modern tradesman, a blacksmith owned his own tools, and bought his own materials. Reynolds Hardware store in Rock Run catered for them with bar iron which they could pick up on their way to work. As for the waterboys, several from Rock Run worked at the quarry up to ten hours per day, earning fifteen cents per hour. Wearing metal yokes they each carried two 12-quart buckets of water back and forth from a spring near the railroad, each serving fifty men.

— ❦ —

Having inherited the tools of the Murrays who were blacksmiths, which included her grandfather, William Joseph, and her great-uncles James Francis and Joseph, Patricia Ellen Murray donated them to the Paw-Paw Museum, at 98 North Main Street, Port Deposit. The forge and anvil used to be kept on the front porch of Jerome's home on Foundry Hollow

Road, where visitors heard that his "father could, with one hand, pick up the anvil by its horn!" The skill of a blacksmith lay in knowing the all-critical areas of thermal strength, energy store and weakness of a piece of metal, so it was vital that they could control the heat level and its proximity.

4. William Joseph Murray on his porch at 38 Granite Avenue.
This photograph of blacksmith, William Joseph Murray, was taken around 1920 when he was 59 and still working in McClenahan's quarry.

The blacksmithing tools were displayed with this label at the Paw-Paw Museum.

The forge and anvil with blacksmith tools belonged to my grandfather, William Joseph Murray (born February 9, 1861). He was born in Port Deposit and is buried in Mt. Erin Cemetery in Havre de Grace, MD. He grew up at 159 Main Street, Port Deposit. When he was 12 years old, his father was killed in a horse accident. He was apprenticed to a blacksmith. At the age of 16, he became a full-fledged blacksmith, and worked on his own. All the time he worked at the local quarry. He made tools and kept tools sharpened. His parents were from Ireland. He married Mary Ellen Murray (no relative, but also an Irish immigrant) of Port Deposit. They had 8 children and lived at 38 Granite Run, Port Deposit.

– Patricia E Murray, 10/30/07

The demand for granite stone and the market for "Port Deposit granite" were such that the McClenahan quarry operated for very long hours, under extremely hazardous conditions. The employers kept the wages low by hiring people eager for work, and the freedom-from-want that work was to give their families. African-Americans were recruited en masse from downtown Baltimore and given jobs as "laborers" by the dozen, arriving in wagons and trucks. European immigrants also arrived in large numbers. The new workers without homes initially boarded in the quarry-owned "Dirt Bank",[26] or rented a room in nearby Rock Run Hollow, if able. Many also later established their own homes in Rock Run.

Initially they were employed as laborers. Later on, they or their sons were given specified jobs, such as those of hand-driller, blaster or fireman, all of which had their hazards, but would have been better paid. In addition to the intrinsic danger of the jobs themselves, was the exposure to the bitter cold of the winter and the blistering heat of the summer. The undeniable fatigue of the workers who were on the job for at least ten hours per day[27] and 6 to 7 days a week, should also be factored into their job description.

If intense demand for Port Deposit granite led to its rapid supply, then the stone would have to be blasted, cut and shipped at a rate to meet the orders. The self-styled Rock

Run Bard who penned "Port Deposit in Verse" in 1881, gave few clues about the quarry owners but perhaps they were prophetic:

The two brothers McClenahan,
Are the first that we will mention;
They are giving work to all they can,
But profit is their chief intention.[28]

On May Day a decade later, a day full of significance for labor movements worldwide, members of the Port Deposit Branch of the Granite Cutter's Union held a strike. In a Special Dispatch from Port Deposit in the *Sun* on May 13, 1891 the headline announced: "THE QUARRYMEN'S STRIKE, Port Deposit Granite Quarry Workmen Still Out, and Their Demands".

The strike of quarrymen in the Port Deposit granite quarries of McClenahan Bros., which began May 1, continues, with no sign of yielding on either side. A large number of the men have secured employment elsewhere and gone away from Port Deposit. Those who remain unemployed have nothing to do except to meet daily and talk the situation over. More than 250 men are out of employment. They are encouraged in their attitude by the Federation of Labor, the president of which, Mr. Joseph Duncan, tried last week to bring about a settlement between the men and the Messrs. McClenahan, but without effect. Mr. John Creswell, secretary of the Granite Cutters' Union, has also visited the strikers, encouraging them to hold out, and assuring them [them] that the Federation of Labor in Baltimore would back them in every way possible. He stated that if other men were employed in their places the granite cutters would refuse to work Port Deposit stone so quarried, and that the building trades would take action in regard to it. The men who are out of work are sober and orderly, and have been so ever since the trouble began; their idleness is a serious thing

for them and for the town. The Port Deposit quarry-
men have been organized since August 11, 1890, as
a branch of the National Union in close affiliatiation
[sic] with the American Federation of Labor. They say
the wages paid in Port Deposit to quarrymen aver-
ages about $1.40 a day of ten hours, while in another
quarry of this State the men get $1.87 a day for nine
hours and eight hours on Saturday. Their demand is
nine hours for five days and eight hours on Saturday
without reduction of wages and to receive time and
a-half for overtime, with double time for night and
Sunday work. These demands were submitted in
March last to take effect May 1, and on refusal the
men stopped work and walked out. They have all been
paid off since and discharged. The employers had in
advance sent information that they could not shorten
the hours nor pay any more wages, and refused to rec-
ognise the organization or to submit the case to arbi-
tration. They were notioned [having thoughts] that
that those who stopped work would have to consider
themselves discharged and apply as individuals if
they wanted afterward to continue work under old
conditions. Amongst the quarrymen out are a num-
ber of Italians. Anticipating the trouble the employ-
ers stopped taking orders a month or two ago. When
in full operation the Port Deposit quarries were the
largest single industry hereabouts except the fisheries,
which have also stopped.

At the meeting of the Federation of Labor in Baltimore,
last evening, the president, James Duncan, made a
report upon the quarrymen's strike. After stating the
unsuccessful result of his trip to that place for the
purpose of urging upon the employers the justice of
the strikers' demands for a nine-hour day, he pre-
sented a series of resolutions asserting the presence in
Baltimore, recently, of a representative of Port Deposit
quarrying firms to make an arrangement with some
of the city officials for modifications of contracts for
stone. The resolutions, which were unanimously

adopted, request the Mayor and city commissioner "to take no part in the endeavour to starve the Port Deposit quarrymen into submission. All sister organizations are asked to assist the striking quarrymen."

The fact that this strike held for as long as two weeks, is a sign of an incredible solidarity amongst the workers and their strength in numbers. The chief negotiator for the local quarrymen was also a heavyweight. None other than the president of the Baltimore Federation of Labor, Mr. James Duncan, was in Port Deposit ready and able, and some might say, waiting, to take on the McClenahans. Duncan was also president of the Granite Cutter's International Association and he must have been incensed about the conditions of employment for the workers in Port. He also must have had substantial financial backing in the subscriptions paid by a large percentage of the branch membership.

The McClenahans, the newspaper article hinted, knew it was coming. They should have. Mr. Duncan, one of the most powerful Labor leaders in America and later to become the leader of the AFL, spent his previous Labor Day on September 1, 1890 in Port Deposit, on the first day of it being instituted in Port Deposit (which was also only the fourth Labor Day in American history). It was a major event with people from other towns filling every train. Parades through town were led by a float holding granite specimens, pulled by eight horses. Local bands took part, and four separate marching ranks were made up of quarrymen and iron molders, union and non-union alike. They passed through the McClenahan's end of town and congregated afterwards at Happy Valley Park, which was up the hill on what is now Bainbridge Road to participate in Caledonian (Scottish Highland) Games near Mt. Ararat.[29]

So although the McClenahans knew that unrest was

at foot they chose to play hardball. Eventually the restive workers with pressures from their long daily absences from home, the additional stress of providing for very large and growing families, and possibly even with concern about their own resilience, took the bull by the horn.

The strike occurred during May, a seasonal period when production normally would have been at a maximum. Despite the bosses' attention to contractual obligations, the strike hurt, and it would have hurt both sides a lot. The most important factor weighing in for the quarry workers was their unity.

On the previous Labor Day, seventy five men of the local Stonecutter's Union and 300 men who were drillers and quarrymen marched in the parade through town to the Park. Historical accounts tell us that in Port Deposit both black and white workers numbered among the rank-and-file members of the union. Many of the men essentially lived side-by-side, walked to work side-by-side, and importantly, raised families' side-by-side. They recognized what a sixty hour work week was doing to themselves and their families. In their individual quests for freedom and prosperity, they themselves had become subjugated.

As far apart from each other they were in mother tongue, color or religion, they were even *more* alike. They may have paid for their sugar in different stores, educated their children in different schools and worshipped God in different buildings, but at the end of the day, sugar was sugar, the same ABCs were taught, and it was one God who answered their prayers.

Three of the 10 known blacksmiths in Port Deposit in 1880 were Irish, and everyone knew how stubborn an Irishman could be, even a hard-working one, with the name of James Duffy or Thomas Foran or William Joseph Murray. Other stubborn blacksmiths were the African-Americans, including the experienced and loyal William Lee from Rock Run, and possibly Alfred Bell and David Bond,[30] in addition to George Lamm, of German heritage. Then there were the Marylanders: Samuel Keatley, Columbia Wilson and Trueman Smith.

Without the blacksmiths to sharpen the tools, to cut the stone, no stone could be cut. Without cut stone, there was no need for the horses to turn the wheels. The workers' demands would cost the proprietors an extra $1,265 a week in wages, while the reduction in hours would equate to 10 men lost per day. There is no evidence that a compromise was reached between the managers and the workers though. The *Cecil Democrat*, the Elkton newspaper which may have been sympathetic to the workers reported on May 9, 1891 that "the strikers number about two hundred and fifty and are nearly all citizens of the town of Port Deposit [ ] they are an industrious and hardworking and experienced quarrymen." The paper quoted that "we think it is the wish of all citizens that their differences may soon be settled and the familiar quarry whistle soon be blown to call them to work again." However, it was not settled so soon. On May 16, there was "no sign of yielding on either side." The frustration of the quarrymen and the union spilled over into the Letters to the Editor of *The Cecil Democrat*. There was now very serious trouble, and a three-way battle, as reported on June 27,

> *James Duncan, corresponding secretary of the Baltimore Branch of the Granite Cutters' National Union writes to The Baltimore American as follows:*
>
> *In contradiction of the statement given, apparently by parties interested, to the press, and published last Saturday to the effect that McClenahan Bros., of Port Deposit, have all the men they need, and twenty-five*

granite cutters (union men) cutting granite, I have to say that the firm have no union granite cutters at work, for the act of going to work makes them oppositionists. So much so is this a fact that the executive board of the granite Cutters' National Union have issued an order that, should the Port Deposit members of the union, or any member of it go to work there, pending a settlement of the quarrymen's trouble, they thereby renounce their character as a branch, and are classed in the scab list of the union, and the work of the firm scabbed until a settlement is effected.[31]

It was clear that matters were not going the way of the quarrymen, and an anonymous writer, signing his name simply as STONE CUTTER wrote from Port Deposit on July 1, 1891 on behalf of the stone cutters in rebuttal to the letter "purporting to come from James Duncan", explaining that,

We appointed a committee to wait upon the firm, and find out whether or not there was any probability of their acceding to the demands of the strikers. The committee reported back to us that there was no hope, whatever, for the strikers. Thereupon all the stone cutters in Port Deposit having been idle forty days on the ninth day of June had a meeting and decided nearly unanimously to reconsider the action of May the second, then to notify the firm that we would go to work which we did on June the tenth.[32]

Their feelings for the national union could not have been made clearer as they laid out their position, "We further claim that we have done all that could be expected of us to further the claims of the strikers, and that we are better friends of the quarrymen than those agitators who are trying to prevent them from going to work."

It would be decades before labor laws were enacted, but families were suffering, and good will at the quarry was at stake. Even though action could have been taken far earlier to prevent the stoppage, the national union acted in their own self-interest which thwarted a chance of a settlement. It was abundantly clear to all involved, nevertheless, that for forty days in the spring and summer of 1891, people-power had prevailed in Port Deposit, Maryland leading to this work-stoppage.

What had occurred in 1891 in Port Deposit at McClenahan & Brothers' Quarry was uncommon in the United States.[33] In urban areas like Baltimore, Boston, Philadelphia and New York, "manufacturers did not hesitate to employ blacks in order to undermine white labor unions".[34] This led to [the blacks] being considered as potential strike breakers. The poor Irish would have been in the same category. Tensions naturally arose between ethnic groups competing for resources.

"Nativists", from the Native American Party, with anti-immigration and anti-immigrant agendas, fomented unrest in response to the growing numbers of non-native and non-white communities.[35] The Know-Nothings, as the nativists became known, because of their secretive meetings and typical response "I know nothing about it",[36] rose to power in parts of America in the 1850s. Violence resulted between fear-ridden black and Irish communities in the big cities.

This was not the case in Port Deposit. In Rock Run near the quarry, a high percentage of people (European immigrant and African-American) were employed, so cheaper labor could not easily be found. The union also played a role. "As union-isation spread in that era", Tim Pat Coogan wrote, the Irish and blacks co-operated with each other, "both in work-sharing and, throughout a number of hard-fought strikes, in work stoppage".[37]

From newspaper accounts, this had been a hard-fought strike. Organizing the Port Deposit branch of the stonecutter's union was a collective effort by people of different ethnic groups, with the Italians, notably, collaborating in the effort.[38] The men identified strongly as quarry workers. Backing the actions of the men out of work, were their families and the fishermen. The courage it took for the striking men to forego pay, job security, and their homes (for those living in "Dirt Bank") was remarkable, but they would have been bolstered by their collective identity as "quarrymen". This strike and the organization leading up to it are evidence of their common desire for a favorable resolution.

Some workers did not return to McClenahan's Quarry, but could have sought work in some of the other quarries in and around Port Deposit, including Coulson's and Cross's quarries in Rock Run (also referred to as the Rock Run "Covered Bridge Quarry"), and the Upper Quarry on Liberty Grove Road. These produced lower quality granite, and stone for construction projects. By mid-May, "a number of the strikers have left the town", it was reported, "and are working in Wilmington, Baltimore, and Pennsylvania."[39] Granite and stone quarries were also operating in northern Baltimore County near Liberty Reservoir, where many Irish were known to have settled, such as in Waltersville (later called Granite, Md.), which is near Woodstock. These included the stone cutter, Patrick Henry Murray from the 2nd generation "Tall Irish" Murray family, and his wife Mary Ellen Bortell Murray, a local girl.

The effect of the McClenahan quarry strike had an effect on the rest of the town. "Business is depressed, fishing season is over, and everything is having a gloomy aspect."[40] By Labor Day of that year, there was happier news from the McClenahans with business becoming "quite brisk", with "between three and four hundred men employed rushed with orders."

That year, there was no mention of an invitation being extended to James Duncan to the town's Labor Day celebrations on Monday, September 7. Only Professor Webber's band of Baltimore was engaged for the occasion when all were invited to spend the day enjoying themselves at Happy Valley.[41]

The Company Store

5. The African Peoples Company Store and the Port Deposit Store Company.
The granite company's stores for African-Americans (left) and white people (second on right, with overhanging roof) were photographed in this winter flood photograph from Rock Run c.1904. Photograph provided by Rev. George Hipkins.

While only men able to cope with the physicality of the job were employed in the quarry opening itself, both women and men worked for the McClenahans in other capacities. The McClenahan "Company Store" also known as the Port Deposit Store Company, was located in Rock Run at the corner of Granite Avenue and Main Street. It served as the company store, or commissary, for McClenahan's employees, but could be used by the public, too.[42] It was up and running by 1871.

Quarry workers were paid in "script", or paper money at the store, which could be redeemed to purchase hardware,

food and household items. The books of script were in denominations from $1 to $10. When paying for goods, a person
would put their script and/or cash in a metal carrier, which
would run up to the ceiling on a wire and over to the cashier's
cage, wherein change would be returned. The store operated
for almost fifty years, closing around 1919.

A separate "African Peoples Company Store" was across
the street from this store, and can be pictured in a photograph taken during high water one winter. This as well as
the separate work areas and facilities at the quarry, and separate schools and churches in town, could be recognized as
representative of the Jim Crowism, or apartheid system that
typified southern states, during the period of Reconstruction
(1863-1877), designed to be a gradual process of integrating
the southern states into the slave-free Union, and even far
beyond.[43] Federal civil rights acts of 1866 and 1875 defined
citizenship and protection under the law, and equal treatment in public places. Much more would be needed in the
course of time.

~~~ ⟨Ɖ⟩ ~~~

Jerome Murray started working at the store during summer vacation in 1908 at the age of ten, working 14 hour days,
6 days a week for 25 cents a week. Jerome worked for Mr.
Leslie Roberts in the store, and went to Mrs. Leslie Roberts
after school to get extra teaching. Jerome drove a horse
and 2-wheeled break cart, or a horse and wagon for grocery
deliveries.

Miss Bertha Foran, the youngest daughter of Thomas
Foran and sister of John Foran, who were both blacksmiths
at the quarry, was a cashier and bookkeeper at the company
store for many years. She caught the eye and eventually

the hand of a Murray in marriage. Uncle Jim Murray, from Jerome's mother's side was also a blacksmith at the quarry, and Jim would have become acquainted with Bertha from the Foran men, as well as his own trips to the store, only a short stroll from where he lived. Both would have been considered to be "a good catch", and they had much in common, except age. Bertha was born in 1883, when Jim was a teenager.

Jerome's Uncle Will and his older brother Joe also worked at the store; so did his youngest sister, Annie. With four uncles from his father's side working in the quarry, it is likely that the Company Store was, at times, full of Murrays! Jerome used to tell some interesting, even legendary stories. One was about the company store.

I owe my life to the company store" comes to mind when I hear the term, "company store". The one in Port Deposit was owned by the granite quarry.

I worked at the company store during summer vacation. One job was to take Old Nell, the horse, and go to Rowlandville to collect eggs for sale in the store. I liked this, as it was a ride through the country, and it took a big part of the day.

Another job was to take Old Nell, go through town in the morning, and take orders. These orders would be filled and then I would return and deliver them to the houses in the afternoon. One day, I was let into the kitchen of a house on South Main Street near the Episcopal Church. Things here did not go too well. It seems that the mistress wore a wig. There she was in the kitchen with her bald head. Both the maid and I got a "dressing down" for me being there.

On Monday mornings after the weekend, it was my job to wash the green mold off the hams, pork, hot dogs and bologna, with vinegar!

The Company Store is gone now. It used to stand at the bottom of Granite Avenue on Main Street. However, a little bit of it remains for me. The back and front granite steps of the old Company Store are now the back and front steps of my home in

Port Deposit.

Jerome's wife, Mabelle, and other women, too, no doubt, learned to be savvy at the meat counter, especially with the inside knowledge of the meat-wiping practices. Mabelle would wait until someone got a cut of meat and then she would quickly get in line to get the better quality meat.

———————

The McClenahan Family owned and operated the quarry until about 1914.

There were several changes of ownership after that leading to an unsettled period for the business and its workers. World War I and the Depression brought the beginning of the end for the business as it was, as buildings made with granite were too costly to build. Workers again demanded better conditions, as during this period, hours had crept back to fourteen hours per day, seven days a week.[44] This was a sign that support from the national union to the Port Deposit branch itself had fallen off, although the local branch did remain active in the 1900s. The quarry eventually closed in 1965 after rip-rap was quarried for use in the jetties in Ocean City.[45]

Ice Gorges and Floods

6. Aftermath of the 1910 Ice Gorge.
A view from N. Main Street looking north at Rock Run. A team of twenty workers cleared the road and alleyway to the Company Store, the building on the riverside (left) with the low overhanging roof. On the cliffside (right) ice is stacked up over the walls towards the houses with a fence above the wall damaged by the ice. The Foran Family album.

Before the Conowingo Dam was built, floods and ice gorges were far too frequent for comfort in Port Deposit. Winters were more severe then, and the river would regularly freeze, sometimes forming a solid sheet varying in thickness from sixteen to twenty-two inches. With a slight thaw, the melt

would raise the river level and the ice would be
The gorges were caused when river ice met de
ice at the shallower, narrow entrance to the Ches
causing river ice and water to converge and bac
town, literally into homes and businesses. Huge
would often move houses as well as block the street and railroad tracks, and ten to twenty-five foot piles of ice completely
filled the town.

After dark on Monday, February 9, 1857, "the jam-up
began, loosening ice beating downstream with a rushing
sound. The sound was like *none can realize who have not
been present at such scene.*" The sounds of shouting from the
injured, and desperate people escaping could be heard over
the sound of the thundering ice. "The next day larger chunks
moved in and in less than two minutes [crushed] a house."[2]

Ice and water flooded houses every few years, and regularly filled entire first floors containing kitchens and utility
rooms. People coped by moving furniture to their living and
sleeping quarters on the second floor until the first floor situation had been remedied, and the furniture could be restored
to place. The stench and smell were unbearable. Others who
had drilled and plugged holes in their floors, unplugged them
before evacuating their homes to prevent walls from lifting
off the floors from the pressure of the water. Stone pavements
and sidewalks were laid in the mid-1800s to help residents
get to-and-fro when Main Street became a mud bath.

Once telegraph and telephone communication became
possible, news from Conowingo and points north in
Pennsylvania, could be used to accurately predict the scale
of the flood in Port Deposit. Warnings from Harrisburg, for
example, which is sixty five miles up river, gave residents a
five-hour window of time to move food and furniture.

On Friday, March 18, 1875, the Baltimore *Sun* reported

on the impending disaster from different locations.

> *Afternoon reports from Columbia have grown alarming, and warned us to prepare for a freshet tonight, and the rivers now rising rapidly and an immense amount of ice is passing down the river at a rate of twenty miles per hour, filling it from shore to shore. Many of the wharves and lumberyards are now flooded, and if the ice gorges below, the town will be flooded before morning. The river has risen ten feet at Conowingo, nine miles above here, in three hours, and the bridge at that place is in danger of being carried away. At Peach Bottom the rise was very rapid.*

A general dispatch at 8 P.M. from Conowingo gave the warning

> *The river has risen ten feet in the last two hours. The bridges here will doubtless go.*

And again from Port Deposit, at 10:15 P.M.,

> *River still rising, and huge masses of ice passing down with a noise like thunder. The ice is mixed with spars and parts of timber rafts, showing that there has been destruction above. ... The warehouses of David & Pugh, J.H. Rowland & Co, and J. Tome & Co., are surrounded by water, and their lumber is scattered about. ... Seventy-five timber rafts lying along the shore between here and Perryville will probably be torn to pieces and scattered.*

A second correspondent to the *Sun* from Port Deposit dispatched this report.

> *March 18, 10 o'clock P.M. – The ice continued running here at 7 o'clock this evening, and the river rose four feet in ten minutes, and has now been running rapidly ever since. The whole town is excitement, and persons are rushing with their furniture and earthly effects to the hills. The water is in the streets and across it in*

many places, and continues to rise steadily. It is also above the railroad, and men are tearing up the track in places and doing all that can be done to save their property. The train due here at 8:20 this evening could not get within a mile of the town for the ice gorge. The crisis is at hand.

The wharves and shore of the river have been crowded with spectators since the commencement of the flood, and the night being such a bright moonlit one, makes the scene one of grandeur and beauty. Some of the ice is four feet thick, and is running at a rate of a mile in three minutes. There has been no slack in it since it commenced running. It is supposed that the river is open clear to its mouth.

The situation at the mouth of the river was far from clear to those in Port Deposit, however, and fear of an ice gorge was uppermost in their minds.

11.40 p.m. – The water is still rising steadily, and it is feared the ice has gorged at Havre de Grace, and is backing the water upon the town. Business men with offices on the wharves have removed their books and valuables with the aid of boats, and all families lying in exposed places have removed to places of greater security, and are prepared for the worst. The board walk at the lower end of the town is floating, and many houses are partly submerged.

These hour-by-hour descriptions of the initial stages of a winter flood told of the desperation of the town residents, officials and businessmen. They were right to be concerned. The devastation was usually dreadful. During one ice gorge, probably in 1904, a warehouse on river shore, at the bottom of Granite Avenue, had to be taken apart and rebuilt. The builders redesigned it with a round side facing the river hoping to avoid a repeat calamity. Another gorge moved a house across from the Catholic Church onto the road. It had to be torn down and rebuilt.

In response to the devastating flood in 1910, the town's politicians pressured Congress and the War Department to remedy this intolerable situation. Continual pressure began to be put on politicians to enact government works on the river banks and to remove the rocks from the river near Rock Run. Eventually, the townspeople, businessmen and politicians agreed that the rail road bridge pylons south of town were the cause for the jamming of the ice. The ice at the B & O Railroad bridge had the appearance of mountains of ice which were piled high in the river "from fifteen to fifty feet high".

The prevention of repeat disasters was obviously a major concern of the residents, and it appears that the post-disaster handling of the ice gorges, and lack of positive action, became important and recurring electoral issues. Following two more back-to-back ice gorges in 1886 and 1887, the message should have gotten through, but whether adequate measures had been taken was another matter. The *1898* Report of the War Department's Office of Civil Engineers stated that part of the eastern bank of a submerged ridge of land began to be removed opposite Watson's Island, 3 miles below Port.[3] Other improvements included dredging the river above Watson's Island to increase its depth. However, the bridge pylons were not modified, and they would repeatedly be implicated.

In Jan 1910, at the last great ice gorge, an account from the *Rising Sun Herald* reported,

...railroad communication has been cut off and will not be restored for a week. Food in the town has become scarce and a fresh supply can not be brought in to any extent for several days. The streets are filled with ice, in some places 10 feet high. But with remarkable energy, the inhabitants have gone to work to

clear away the debris.[4]

⸺ ❦ ⸺

Jerome recalled the ice would begin to pile up in layers on the river. Then when the ice started to melt and flood, big cakes would push ashore. People would then run outside and yell, "the ice is running!" Jerome said that there was real terror. A newspaper reported as the river was rising in Jan 1873 that "people are looking in each other's faces in blank terror, and fear to give utterance to their thoughts."[5] The piles of ice would knock down trees or tear down anything in the way.[6] Almost worst of all, the ice actually forced itself into homes. Families could shiver for months, and infectious diseases became endemic during the aftermath.[7]

Just twelve, Jerome helped his boss, the Company Store manager, Leslie Roberts, in advance of imminent flooding. He said, "In those days no one got through a year without having to move the goods up because of flood. One year we moved the things in Mr. L.B. Roberts' home three times. At the time of the 1910 ice gorge we didn't move the store supplies high enough."

On January 25, 1910, the *Baltimore American* under the headline "PORT DEPOSIT IS COURAGEOUS" reported indeed that the upper part of the warehouse of the Port Deposit Store company warehouse completely washed away, but "barrels of sugar were untouched."[8]

Other incidents in Rock Run were recounted, including the escape of the Thomas family through a trap door on the roof, and an unusual happening at Jerome's great-uncle.

> *In the residence of John Bannon, also at Rock Run, the family had raised the piano, weighing nearly a thousand pounds, on trestles hoping that thereby it would escape being filled with water. When the family*

returned, the piano was found resting on the trestles, but only with two of its legs, and it seems almost a miracle that it did not go to the floor, as all signs point to the fact that it must have been carried around the room by the water.

7. Looking South on Main Street.
Workers cling to the leaning poles to restore power or telecommunications to the town after the 1910 ice gorge. They are looking south from around 130 – 140 N. Main Street. From a postcard produced by I & M. Ottenheimer, Baltimore, Md.

That year the whole of McClenahan's workforce helped the 3,000 strong Penna. Rail Road crew clear the tracks and sidings. Dynamite and steam shovels were used to move the ice. It took eight days to clear the tracks! Telephone lines came down and linesmen working for Diamond State Telephone Co., including Jack Murray from Main Street and the Postal Telegraph Co., had to work in the icy weather to install new wires and lines. A picture postcard showed workers on a power or telecommunications pole leaning at an angle of 45 degrees to the road threading new line. Families back in their homes now needed all the help they could get.

> *The rebuilding and repairing of the private residences presents the greatest problem that now confronts the people of the town. The great damage to this class of property occurred in Middletown and Rock Run, the middle and northern sections of Port Deposit. In these sections the labouring classes live. Most of them own their homes. Four years ago they suffered considerable damage from which they have not entirely recovered. Many of them declared today that without assistance they would be unable to rebuild their homes.*

The McClenahans, the town, and other people considered bringing lawsuits. A town meeting followed and the Board of Commissioners decided not to press for state or federal aid, arguing that the town would provide aid. In fact, it was people from Perryville who sent baskets of food and the County that provided 300 loaves of bread. Finally, the state cleared the sidewalks.

To prevent such regular flooding from the Susquehanna and to provide hydroelectric power, a decision was made that a dam should be built upriver from the town. Initially there were plans to build two dams, one above the Conowingo Bridge, and one further downstream closer to the town. A license for the dam construction and hydroelectric plant installation was granted by the Federal Power Commission in Washington to the Susquehanna Power Company in Baltimore in January 1925. The cost was estimated to be $52 M. The electricity generated by the plant would be used for the city of Philadelphia, and for electrifying the railroads between New York and Washington, with the first stage being the Philadelphia to Wilmington line. The financial pages of the city papers carried stories, as investors were anxious to back this safe investment project which might produce untold gains.[9]

Not all were so enthusiastic. Such was the threat to the Pennsylvania Water and Power Company operating the hydroelectric plants further up the river that a federal injunction was brought in by the Pennsylvania firm desperate to protect their supply of electricity to other areas of Pennsylvania.[10] By the time this happened, the momentum had grown for a single-dam project below the Conowingo Bridge, and there was no turning back.

Others were concerned for the communities, countryside and protection of the cultural treasures in the Susquehanna itself. The Secretary of the Smithsonian Institution wrote a letter to the Public Service Commission asking that the rocks with Indian carving be protected. The Washington, D.C., *Evening Star* reported in June 1925 on the suggestions that plaster casts or at least photographs of the heavier rocks be taken, and that the lighter rocks should be lifted to higher ground. "The carvings constitute a valuable record that should be preserved, and the Public Service Commission is asked to do all that it can to that end." Some petroglyphs and pictographs from the American Indians were removed; some treasures were found, others were destroyed, and many were buried during dam construction.

Dam building began in March 1926. Of the 3,800 workers employed on the project, many were local people. Workers from further afield stayed in temporary housing or camped nearby. When completed, it was the second largest hydroelectric station by power output in the U.S.A., only smaller than the plant at Niagara Falls. Residents in Conowingo were moved, the rail station was closed, and the Conowingo Bridge above the dam was blown up with explosives before the dam became operational. The dam, though controversial in some respects, greatly alleviated the frequency and severity of flooding of the town and stopped the ice from "running" into the streets and homes of Port Deposit.

Arrival of the Irish Immigrants

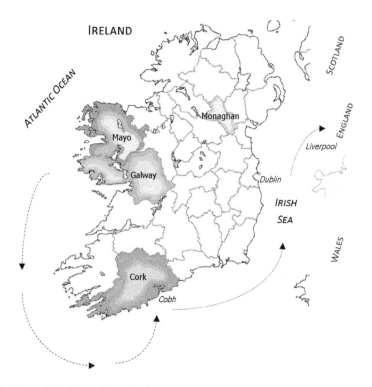

8. Map of the Counties of Ireland.
The shaded counties, mainly in the west, are those where the first Murrays to Port Deposit originated. Those counties were some of the worst affected by the Great Famine. The majority of people in post-Famine Ireland travelled to Cork, overland or by sea, and then via a boat from Cobh to Liverpool, where much larger transatlantic sailing or steamships docked.

Although there is no proof why my Irish ancestors settled in the town of Port Deposit in the middle of the 19th century, it is a near-certain fact that they came to America as a result of the devastating failure of the potato crops in Ireland between 1845 and 1851, and the sustained starvation and hardship due to the Great Famine (in Irish: *an Gorta Mór*). The suffering of the Irish people was compounded by the inhumane treatment from the occupying British. Wherever possible, entire families or individual members fled from the widespread and unfair land evictions, and the systematic repression of Catholics in Ireland.

The failure of the potato crop, due to widespread fungal infection was not the sole cause of the *famine* itself, the likes of which have not been experienced anywhere else in modern history except perhaps in China in the 20th century. Colonization of Ireland beginning in the tenth-century, following Viking and Norman invasions of both islands, was also not the main cause, although an Anglo-Saxon power base established over the Celtic peoples since that time became a contributing factor. Rather King Henry VIII's insistence on annulling his marriage with his first wife, so he could remarry (1533) and obtain a male heir was its real taproot. His break with the all-powerful Roman Catholic Church began a period of violence against the fabric and practices of the Catholic faith – the great abbeys and churches were broken up, and Britain declared that its citizens should be loyal to the English church. From 1801, Ireland was ruled by Great Britain, although the systematic repression of Catholics began in 1695.

Catholics were subject to gross inequalities, especially in the areas of landownership and tax. Irish-born Roman Catholics were to a large extent unable to own their own land, were unable to rent holdings greater than ¼ acre, and could not dodge payments of money to the ruling government to support the Protestant clergy. This disempowerment of Catholics in their own homeland, and their dependence on what could be produced on small tracts of land, made them dependent on the potato. Nature then rained the fungal spores into the rich, wet and warm summer earth and blew the buds onto the growing leaves. An infective cycle that took only a week to get into the potato was carried further and further by the wind and moist air of the Gulf Stream that came up the north Atlantic. Not only were the good potatoes wiped out, the good people nearly were, too.

BOY AND GIRL AT CAHERA.

9. Boy and Girl at Cahera.
News of the famine reached readers of "The Illustrated London News" early in 1847 when a series of drawings and stories by Mr. James Maloney entitled "Sketches in the West of Ireland" were published. This drawing was published on February 20, 1847 with an accompanying description. "The first Sketch is taken on the road, at Cahera, of a famished boy and girl turning up the ground to seek for a potato to appease their hunger." Courtesy of Ireland's Great Hunger Museum, Quinnipiac University, Hamden, CT, and the Skibbereen Heritage Centre, County Cork, Ireland.

It is now recognized that food actually produced by the Irish in Ireland during these years, including oats, oxen, sheep, swine and wheat, food which could have been fed to the starving, was exported by the British to line their coffers.

Catholics were not allowed to own land — it was seized by the British, who allowed them to become tenant farmers and punished them when the potato failed.[1] Open practice of religion was also at stake, and indeed, in Britain, Catholic Mass was forbidden until 1829. Widespread practices, and government policy by the elected, and the unelected, both British civil servant and aristocrat alike, were downright shameful. The little "relief" or charity that was provided was often impracticable, and required starving people with little energy to walk long distances to obtain grain. Some were offered the chance to live in "workhouses", where families were split apart and life was generally intolerable. It was left to charitable groups to do what they could. The Quakers were foremost in responding.

The Central Committee of Friends collected food and money from America, England, and other countries, and with the 200,000 pounds sterling they raised, roughly equivalent to 25 million dollars in today's money, they opened soup kitchens across Ireland. The first soup kitchen was opened in Cork in November 1846, and soup was made on a 200 gallon–scale basis with industrial scale boilers steaming the kitchens.[2] In Skibbereen, a small town in West Cork, soup was fed to 8,600 people every day.[3] The starving came with containers to take soup home for the hungry, and soup was sent out to the surrounding districts in barrels.

10. The Steam Mill Building at Skibbereen.
The soup kitchen in Skibbereen in West Cork fed soup daily to 8,600 people during the Great Famine. In February 1847, over 3,000 people came into the town for help.[3]

Foreign governments from North America and Continental Europe and, as far away as India and Australia, also endeavored to help. The first of many relief ships from America, the U.S.S. Jamestown left Boston and arrived in Cork harbour on the 12th of April, 1847, carrying 800 tons for the region of Munster, the south-western quadrant of Ireland. Another kind of aid was that of "assisted emigration" whereby landlords could pay for the transatlantic passage for their non-rent paying tenants. This way the paupers could leave their property without the landowners having to destroy their cottages and drive them away, often into the ditches, dirt banks and woods as was the practice.

An American who became a spokesman for human rights visited Ireland at that time. It was Frederick Douglass, who had been born enslaved in southern Maryland, and later published his autobiography, *The Narrative of the Life of Frederick Douglass, an American Slave*. He sailed across the Atlantic in the summer of 1845 to promote his book and the cause of slavery's end. He also hoped to make enough to buy his freedom. (The Fugitive Slave Act of 1793 meant that he could be returned to his slaveholder, even while living in a northern state or territory where slavery had been abolished.) The timing of his speaking tour in Ireland and Great Britain came at a formative time for the young Douglass, who was just twenty-seven. Ireland was experiencing the first of six seasons of potato blight, which peaked with the Great Famine in 1847.

Mr. Douglass witnessed unprecedented scenes. According to historical narratives, every gathering was abuzz with praise for his eloquence, and talk of the unfolding tragedy — destitution, disease, starvation and death. He is thought to have struggled between expressing his thoughts on the local situation, and staying true to his mission; after all, the Irish, he reasoned, were not in chains. But the seventy year old Great Liberator, Daniel O'Connell, an anti-slavery and independence campaigner, encouraged the young Douglass to embrace all causes for freedom from oppression.[4] Later in the trip, Douglass wrote in a letter to his sponsor from the American Anti-slavery Society,

> "I am not going through this land with my eyes shut, ears stopped and heart steeled. ..."

> "I see much to remind me of my former condition, and I confess I should be ashamed to lift up my voice against American slavery, but that I know the cause of humanity is one the world over. He who really and truly feels for the American slave, cannot steel his heart to the woes of others. ..."

> "I am not only an American slave, but a man, and am bound to use my powers for the welfare of the whole human brotherhood."[5]

Between 1841 and 1851, more than a million people died of disease and starvation in Ireland, and at least another two million left the country, emigrating to North America, England and Australia.[6] One cemetery in Dublin recorded 5,944 deaths in one year alone, and mass graves became the norm in places. In the west, bodies would be buried in fields, if possible.

People who emigrated from continental Europe in the 1800s and early 1900s often travelled to America as families, but most who came from Ireland were young people travelling in ones and twos. They left families, famine and disease in their wake, principally, cholera, dysentery and tick-borne typhus.[6] Those who immigrated were usually the sons and daughters of farmers and labourers.[7] Young unaccompanied girls were vulnerable to exploitation on all stages of the journey, even in the harbor town of Cobh,[8] pronounced "Cove", but there was little money to send others to accompany them. To maximize the chance of a family's survival, young people were sent to various different countries as well.

11. Irish Emigrants Leaving Home – The Priest's Blessing.
*By 1851, the news from Ireland was of its depopulation. The reporter from Cork
wrote "I am disposed to think that about the middle of May the great emigrational
torrent ceases to flow from these shores.... None perhaps feel more severely the
departure of the peasantry than the Roman Catholic clergy." During that year,
an estimated 250,000 emigrated, and for each affected family there was a great
loss. The drawing was of a whole village preparing to leave by the landroute on
the Kenmare Road to Cork. From "The London Illustrated News", May 10, 1851.
Courtesy of Ireland's Great Hunger Museum, Quinnipiac University, Hamden, CT,
and the Skibbereen Heritage Centre, County Cork, Ireland.*

To travel from Cork by water to Liverpool on the west
coast of England, the main port for transatlantic embarka-
tion, cost only a few shillings, or about $18 today. Money could
then be raised there, if needed for the journey to America,
which cost between £2 and £6 pounds sterling (about $170 to
$1,200 today). In Liverpool, poverty and harassment of the
travellers went in hand-in-hand.[9]

Assisted emigration, by landowners who paid for the
cheaper passage of their poor peasants on "coffin ships", was
of little assistance to their life-chances.[10] Some ships arriving in North America had up to hundreds dead or dying.
Ships destined later for the America were said to operate

at a higher standard; to regulate immigration, Congress set restrictive laws limiting the numbers of passengers allowed, and increasing the fares. Those very few who could afford standard class had their own berths, and could walk on deck. But the vast majority of passengers travelled in steerage class, and were crowded together below decks for the entire journey. The elderly and the very young were most vulnerable. Some died, others were born at sea. Many arrived filthy, starving and literally, in rags.[11] Most Irish emigrating to America arrived in New York City, where they boarded in tenements, and earned some money before moving on.

During the Great Famine, there was a 26 to 29% decrease in the population of the Irish counties where Jerome Murray's grandparents originated from, namely, Mayo, Galway and Cork in the west of Ireland, and Monaghan, in its northeast (Table 1). They came to America because of the potato famine, as young people in the decade after the first crop failures. From their own birth dates and those of their first-borns in 1856 and 1861,[12] it is likely that all four were in their teens to mid-20s when they left their homes to make the rather risky and expensive five-week journey to a new life in America.

Table 1. Emigration details for grandparents of Jerome Patrick Murray

Name	County	Year of Emigration	Age	Relation to Jerome Murray
Joseph Murray	Galway			Paternal grandfather
Mary Donnelly	Mayo	1856	18	Paternal grandmother
John Murray	Monaghan			Maternal grandfather
Bridget Bannon	Cork	about 1847		Maternal grandmother

Miss Mary Ellen Donnelly was only about 18 when she left County Mayo on the west coast of Ireland in 1856. Between 1846 and 1851, County Mayo had the highest "excess mortality rate" in Ireland.[13] In addition to those expected to die in a given year, an additional 58 people out of one hundred perished. It was not a question of "if" a family member should leave, but "when" and "how". Mary Ellen Donnelly may have initially landed in Baltimore, because within a year or so of emigrating, she became the young bride of Mr. Joseph Murray, marrying in St. Patrick's Church in Baltimore in December 1857. She was nineteen and he was five years older. Mary Ellen was probably wearing a lace shawl she was thought to have brought directly with her from Ireland, the gift that was a symbol of hope.

Miss Bridget Bannon also left her home in Cork as a teenager, and would have sailed to Liverpool from Cobh, or Queenstown as it was named by the British, before even embarking on the steamship or sailing boat to cross the Atlantic. What did she bring with her? An unrelated Bannon family of five arriving in Baltimore on a Liverpool-to-New Orleans ship in April of 1847 brought 2 chests and a bed. Many came with far less. A single person could really only manage a traveling bag and a blanket, unless they could pay for help.

Another thing they brought was their mother tongue, as the majority spoke Gaelic, or Irish, as their first language. Bridget could not read or write in English (or possibly Gaelic either), it was consistently reported, so books would not have been worth their weight. It is likely that she arrived in New York and became acquainted with Mr. John Murray there, and they may have married there in New York before moving to Port Deposit.

⌇⌇⌇⌇⌇

How did John and Joseph Murray find out about the granite quarry in Maryland? News about McClenahan's Quarry in Port Deposit would have been out in the east-coast cities, where Port Deposit granite was sought after for buildings.[14] And what would they have made of "Port" upon their arrival? The *Cecil Whig* reported that the following businesses existed in Port Deposit around 1860:

... 18 dry goods and grocery stores, 7 devoted to making and selling shoes, 3 to drugs, 14 to the sale of liquors, 2 tailor shops, 4 millinery stores, 2 stove and tinware shops, 2 wheelwright shops, 3 warehouses, 3 blacksmith shops, 6 lumber yards, a grist mill, a saw mill, a sash factory, a watchmaker's

shop, a quarry, and a tannery; besides there are three practic-
ing physicians, 2 or 3 painters, several carpenters, a number
of dressmakers, one parson and no lawyer.

This list is borne out by the census and records of the day, except for the last. This was a growing, business-minded town, and records show that it had at least one justice-of-the-peace and a magistrate.[15]

A contemporary description of the town in 1878 described it as having "extensive granite quarries, and a large trade in lumber, hay, grain and fertilizers, and an extensive foundry and machine shops." Four granite dealers, and five companies dealing in lumber and trade goods, were named.[16] In 1856, R.A. Solomon C.E, a chartered engineer, drew a map based on data from a land survey. It was of a curiously F-shaped town with a wide, $1\frac{1}{3}$-mile Public Road running down the backbone, a County Road running 90° from the main street along Rock Run on the north-west side — the top of the F, and, the "Road to Battle Swamp" running out the middle. The road that ordinarily comes out from the southern side (MD Route 222, or Bainbridge Road), turning the town into its more familiar E-shape, was totally omitted, with the words Corporation Line barely an adequate substitute, as though R.A. Solomon was working strictly to his contract. This "obliterated" part of Port Deposit, though, was included in census data from the Seventh Election District, and it would develop its own interesting geographic, naval and social history. The most interesting part of this map from a purely historical perspective was that of the riverside.

Very extensive waterfront coverage by warehousing and wharving, docking and dealerships, would feature in practically every map drawn for the next half-century. Wharf-owners often had land extending from river-to-cliff: Edwin Wilmer, R.J. Rinehart and Jacob Tome; J.J. Heckart who claimed $40,000 real estate value in 1870; and Dr. Gilmore's Heirs. This was the golden mile and every square inch of waterfront was utilized for the purpose. Other land-owners, like Joseph W. Abrahams, Rebecca Creswell Murphy, Samuel Roland, J.P. Vanneman and Cornelius Smith, were also notable, the latter simply with the cartographic designation, Corn. Smith.

One of the advertisers in 1871, Jacob Tome & Co., bought economical, long-running ad space in *The Cecil Whig*, a newspaper, established in 1841 and published on Saturdays. The *Whig* was regarded then as a Republican paper (having shed its old Whig brand), expressing pro-Reconstruction, pro-abolitionist, pro-farming sentiments, and also being for the railroads, for Western expansion and for protecting the interests of "Northern" businesses. On page 2, the local news and political page, it also slandered the views of the pro-Southern leaning Democrats that bought the *Baltimore County Democrat*.[17]

Tome & Co. advertised throughout the seasons in the *Whig* in large letters, "Deals in Hay, Straw, Grain, Coal, Guano, Lime, Bone, Plaster and Salt", curiously without any reference to their lumber trade, let alone Tome's bank, but clearly they knew their markets. This four-page, miniscule-print paper had a wide subscription, up and down the Eastern Shore, and from Philadelphia to Baltimore, and it wisely devoted page four to farming – agriculture, horses and cattle. Half its space contained money-making ads, and it cost 5 ¢ per copy, or $2.00 per year, so it not only had a wide readership, it was also affordable. And besides being influential, it would have been read, re-read, saved and re-used. Being on the thin side, many a column would have found itself too, in a farmer's outhouse.

In addition to importing goods produced throughout the

entire 27,000 square-mile watershed of the Susquehanna which floated to the warehouses, being able to source and supply grain (wheat, corn and oats), timothy hay and fertilizer (the bone, guano and lime), essentially goods from-farmer-to-farmer, with a miller or two sandwiched in between, was extremely important to the town's businesses. Not surprisingly, the Town Commissioners were all businessmen, and though they were invariably white, male and with few exceptions, born in America, their election was not always secure, especially following severe floods and ice runs. It would not be long, however, before the sons of immigrants would be making decisions as elected officials.

In the 1878 *Maryland Directory* of towns Port Deposit was described as a "bustling, thriving and quaint town, compressed by the Susquehanna against the rock-bound cliffs, which rise almost perpendicularly to the height of one and two hundred feet." Furthermore, "there is room only for two streets along the face of the river. Most of the houses on the eastern side of the main street jut against these cliffs. Some have terraces rising from the rear yards, far up the cliffs."

Most immigrants, being *economic* immigrants in that period, would board or rent, and the "dirt bank" homes provided by industry, are reminiscent of workers' cottages and terraced houses in the mine and mill areas of Great Britain.[18] Homes were desperately needed for the industrious town. The population of Port Deposit was listed as 1,008 in 1850, and the census counts would double to 1,973 in 1880, and increase by another 20% to 2,347 by 1890.

For those in a position to buy and build, lots were being sold from Rock Run to Battle Swamp Road by Mrs. Rebecca E. Creswell Murphy, a Lancastrian who made good in her marriage and family, but found herself with far too much land on her hands, owning much of the land on the north side of Main Street between Foundry Hollow and Rock Run. Acreage in Port Deposit was valued at $25-$100, the going rate for good farm land in Cecil County.

The author of a letter to the *Cecil Whig* in December of 1852 described Rock Run as having "6-8 dwellings, 2 hotels and a reputation for pugilistic exhibitions". The 1856 map of Port Deposit confirms the first aspect, and hopefully our newcomers did not contribute to the fighting that was witnessed there. As for Middle Town, the name given to the stretch of homes on North Main Street between Rock Run and the center of "Port", the author suggested that it be renamed "Mud Town" due to "the state of its delapidated houses and patched up tenements". Contrary to the picture painted by the letter-writer, these two areas of Port Deposit were actually growing and thriving and so were its residents, even if the "narrow road, lapped by water, extended through the length of the town serving for a highway when the river permitted".[19]

For all the opportunities available for immigrants to Port Deposit, it would be very unlikely if they did not encounter hostility and distrust of some kind. Governor Thomas Hicks of Maryland from 1858 to 1862 was considered by some to be a Nativist himself, because he held anti-immigrant and anti-abolitionist views. To some extent, safety would lie in numbers for the immigrants to Port Deposit.

〰 ◯ 〰

Mary Ellen Donnelly's new husband, Joseph Murray, who like her was from the west coast of Ireland, was anxious for work and found employment working for Mr. John Keaveny, a contractor for the Port Deposit and Columbia Rail Road and McClenahan's quarry. Joseph was to meet misfortune, but not immediately. John Murray, husband of Bridget, had ambitions of owning land. Both young men, whether they anticipated it or not, would acquire their greatest riches in their children.

Mary Ellen Donnelly and Bridget Bannon both married men with the surname of Murray, although their Murrays were not related to each other. Whether they were friends before Mary Ellen's son married Bridget's daughter in 1884, we cannot know, but can assume this to be the case, as they certainly had a lot in common. Both were similar ages, had at least eight children of similar ages, attended the same church, and importantly, were Irish. Their husbands and sons were employed by the quarry, their daughters learned dressmaking and needle skills, and they both remained in Port Deposit for the rest of their lives.

A fine cobweb lace shawl made of spun wool with a silk Irish crochet fringe was given to Patricia Murray as a Christmas present in December 1950. It was from her great-aunts, daughters of Mary Ellen Donnelly Murray, who lived at 159 North Main Street, Port Deposit. The letter with it said,

Dear Patricia –

We are sending you a Conormough [or Connemara] Square or shawl <u>direct</u> from Ireland. Hope you will like it.

With love and best wishes from Aunt Sarah and Ellen

Since their mother came from Ireland, it was always thought that she brought it with her on the boat directly from Ireland. This very fine and delicate shawl, would have been for a special occasion, such as a wedding or baptism. Cobweb lace pieces were displayed at the Great Exhibition in London in 1851, and in the Dublin International Exhibition of 1853.

Aunt Sarah and Ellen's letter in itself, is interesting. The spelling of "Conormough" is a phonetic spelling of

"Connemara", the rugged land by the sea in western Ireland. Familarity with correct Irish pronunciations or spellings might not come easy for daughters of those who had little schooling. The closing, "With love and best wishes from …" is typical of an Irish or British letter to family or close friends even to this day.

Bridget and Mary Ellen are both likely to have been proficient in needlework and sewing skills. Back home, money made from lace and sewing during the Famine was a great help to families and was used for buying food and necessities. The Presentation sisters in Connemara were noted for teaching these skills, and, in Cork, the Sisters of Mercy had lace-making schools. Bridget's oldest daughter, Margaret, and her Bannon nieces all became professional seamstresses, as did Mary Ellen's daughter Ellen.

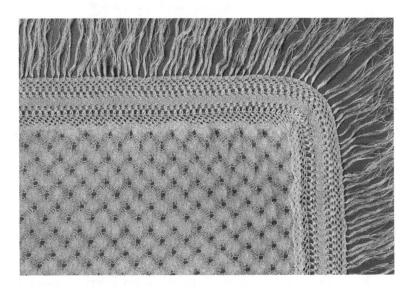

12. Detail from Mary Ellen Donnelly Murray's Cobweb Lace 'Conormorough Square'.
This delicate shawl was brought directly from Ireland by Mary Ellen Donnelly. It would have been used for her wedding and possibly for the baptism of her children. Photographed by Robert Longuehaye.

The town that the Murrays and Murrays-to-be eventually came to had already transitioned from a "Ferry" to a "Port", by the time they arrived. John and Bridget settled in the northern village of Rock Run, the site of the ferry, bridge, fishing piers and grist mill. It was a growing place of trade, homes and business. The Joseph and Mary Ellen Murray family established a home in Middle Town.

Later generation family members used to distinguish the two Murray families by referring to them as the "Short Irish" and the "Tall Irish"[20], or the "Rock Run Murrays" or the "Downtown Murrays". This was vital because of the preponderance of Anns, Ellens, Elizabeths, Marys, Jameses, Johns, Josephs, Patricks and Thomases on each side. This repetition of treasured family names was widespread amongst this generation, as it has been in other cultures. Wherever there was a risk of, or actual child mortality, names were repeated even in the same family, for example, when one child died, and the name was used a second time. Bridget and John's ninth child was named Joseph, after his brother, Joseph Andrew died a year before. Second names helped keep special names and memories alive, too. At the end of the 1800s, *five* Mary Ellen Murrays lived within a mile of each other; all five were related by blood or marriage.

John Murray, Bridget's husband from County Monaghan in the north of Ireland became a quarryman at McClenahan's stone quarry, and his sons were to follow him in the trade. At the time of the 1880 U.S. Census, the elder son of this family, Thomas, aged 24, was going to work in the the quarry alongside his father and younger brother John Patrick, aged 17. Younger boys, James and Joseph, who were 12 and 3 at that time, were to become blacksmiths. There was little opportunity for boys or girls to stay in school beyond 16. The girls in the family were Margaret, aged 22, the seamstress; Mary

Ellen, aged 18, "in service" at the McClenahan Mansion; and Elizabeth, and Catherine, aged 13 and 8.

It was around this time that John Murray sponsored John Bannon, the younger brother of his wife, to come to Port Deposit.[21] John Bannon himself had actually moved from Ireland to England after the Famine, where he married a young Englishwoman, Sarah. Together they boarded in a working class neighborhood in County Durham in North East England, while he worked with hot metal in a foundry, as a "pudler". John sailed to America ahead of the rest of his family in 1880, and Sarah came a year later with two young children, Andrew and Hannah, ages about 6 and 5, and Baby Ellen. The rented a house in "Dirt Bank" while John worked as a laborer in the quarry, and there Alice, little John and Eliza were born.[22] After 1900, John and his older son, Andrew, both moved to Rock Run, living side-by-side, just a few houses up the hill from his sister, Bridget, and her family.

A turn-of-the-century photograph of John taken with Sarah, perhaps in Mr. Alonzo Barry's studio in Port, shows a portrait of a man who had bravely endured a life of physical hardship. His right hand was larger than the left, swollen and disfigured. He probably had chronic eczema leading to lichenification, or a leathery thickening of the skin, as a result of unsafe working practices, widespread at the time. In 1900, John was 60, and still working in the quarry.

The particles of silica that the quarry workers inhaled and that got beneath their skin were occupational hazards of their job, with the risk of silicosis of the lungs and dermatitis and eczema of the skin. The most frequent injuries were probably hand injuries, though. Control measures were not introduced in the U.S.A. until the 1930s and 1940s. At the heavy stone quarries where huge blocks were extracted, guesome, fatal and life-changing injuries occured, some skull-crushing and others spine-tearing.[23]

From census records, it is clear that the sons and daughters of these Murray and Bannon families became bread winners at an early age by learning skilled trades that were in demand in Port Deposit at that time: quarrying, especially, blacksmithing and stonecutting for the men, as well as dressmaking for the women. The number one priority for the Irish diaspora was work to counteract their number one enemy, poverty. The Irish were even opposed to restrictions on child labor, such was their need for the security of work.

The newcomers would have been competing with many others for jobs, for there was a 82% increase in population in Port Deposit between 1850 and 1870, and it would keep increasing at that pace. Although this increase was partly due to industrial growth in the town which supported the settling of new European immigrants, and the additional births that came with large and growing families, there was also a significant South-to-North migration that was happening during this period. As found in many places in America, there was a crossroads in Port Deposit, a meeting place of people also separated from family, on the move, seeking a better, safer, and more abundant life.

African-American Migrations

13. Portrait of Mr. Will Baker at the Granite Quarry.
This quiet gentleman was the last person to remain living in one of the original huts at the quarry, and represents African-Americans who came to Port Deposit during different periods of history. For many years he worked the Hopkins Farm that bordered the quarry. The photograph was taken in 1982. Courtesy of Rev. John J. Abrahams III.

Even before the Civil War commenced in 1861, freed and fugitive African-Americans were on the move fleeing slavery and its oppression. The statistics speak for themselves. By 1850, there were 3 million slaves in the southern states, then 4 million by the start of the war.[24] Of these, 80,000 enslaved people lived in Maryland, and 900 in Cecil County.

Even as President-elect Abraham Lincoln entered the White House on March 4, 1861, the country was coming apart at its seams. Seven of the 33 states had left the Union. The American Civil War began a month later. From Maryland,

8,718 of the soldiers were black and 33,915 were white.[25] For all soldiers, regardless of color, fighting in the Civil War could be a one-way ticket to the grave. For the black even more so, because once trusted to properly fight, they fought the fight for freedom with their whole being, and they suffered a high mortality rate. "It has been estimated that their rate of mortality was nearly 40% greater than that among white troops."[26]

A most important factor for black Marylanders was the guarantee that any enslaved entering the war for the Union side would be guaranteed freedom at its end. Lincoln's excutive order of January 1, 1863, the Emancipation Proclamation, had not actually proclaimed that blacks in the southern border states of Delaware, Maryland, Virginia, Kentucky and Missouri would automatically be freed. Their emancipation in Maryland was only guaranteed by crucial revision of the Maryland state constitution in October 1864, led by two men from Port Deposit, John A.J. Creswell and Jacob Tome.

Cecil County had an all-important twenty-three mile northern border, the north-eastern border of Maryland with Pennsylvania on Mason and Dixon's Line. Travelling westward were the Maryland counties named Harford, Baltimore, Carroll, Frederick, Washington and Allegheny; travelling east was New Castle County, Delaware. These twenty-three miles of Cecil County were extremely important, as slaves coming up Maryland's Eastern Shore might pass through Cecil County, and it provided safe havens, and well-travelled routes. These routes along the river, through the town and country would be used for decades, even after the war ended and slavery was abolished in Maryland. Between 1916 and 1919, one million African-American people would form part of the Great Migration northwards and westwards.

Mason and Dixon's Line

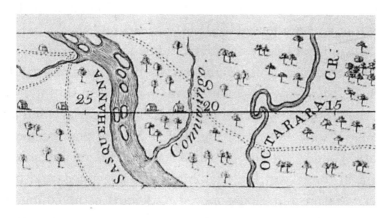

14. Mason and Dixon's Boundary Map at the Sasquehanna River, the Conniwingo and Octarara Creeks.
Mason and Dixon made a preliminary survey of this area in early May 1765, and completed it two months later. According to their journal, on April 30, 1765, after crossing the main branch of the North East River, they "sent expresses to the Commissioners to acquaint them we would be at the River Susquehanna in 12 days." The five-mile marker numbers on the map had their origin at the north-eastern boundary of Maryland with Delaware and Pennsylvania. Courtesy of Library of Congress, Geography and Map Division.

How the two surveyors, mathematicians and astronomers by trade, came to define the line of latitude that would geographically delineate freedom, that is, the boundary between Maryland and Pennsylvania, is a story worth retelling. The measuring and the marking of the ground would involve a trip across the ocean, a portable observatory, a sixteen and one-half foot surveyor's chain and plumb line, as well as a contingent of people for negotiating with the native Americans in western Maryland. Mr. Charles Mason and Mr. Jeremiah Dixon were to undertake a challenge that had confounded many before them – to mark out on the ground that which had been delineated on maps, according to the descriptions on documents of parchment: the land charter of Cecilus Calvert, Lord Baron of Baltimore (1632), the deeds of the Swedes and the Finns who purchased the Delaware lands originally belonging to the Dutch (1638), and the land grant of William Penn (1681).

Mason and Dixon started off in London in August of 1763. After arriving in Philadelphia on the 15th of November, 1763, almost exactly twelve months was required to initially verify the tri-state boundary between Delaware, Maryland and Pennsylvania. It was fitting that a granite post be placed there. Then a line fifteen miles south of the most-southern point of the city of Philadelphia was determined, and from there Mason and Dixon moved westward establishing the "fifteen mile line" all the while, keeping a meticulous diary. The snowfalls in the winter of 1764-65 halted their slow-but-steady progress, and they began again early in May 1765, laying the simpler one-mile stones and fancier five-mile posts between the two states on the true boundary line. For the purpose, they used white oolite limestone which was impervious to the weather, and could be sourced from the Cotswold hills of western England or the isle of Portland in Dorset, England. According to their agreement, the line going westward would be marked by stones cut with the letter 'P' for Penna. facing the north side, and an 'M' for Md. on the south side, and at less frequent intervals the coat of arms of the Calvert and Penn families would also be erected, each on their respective sides.

Upon reaching the Susquehanna River on Cecil County's western border with Harford County, they marked a rock in the riverbed. They repeated their measurement of the river several times, recording their celestial observations whenever the sky was clear. This was in May 1765. According to George Johnston, county historian,

> *The distance from the northeast corner of the county to the east side of the Susquehanna, as determined by them, is about twenty-three and one-quarter miles, and the width of the river, which they obtained by triangulation at that time, where the line crossed it was sixty-seven chains, four perches, and sixty-eight links.* [27]

The Cecil County boundary line of the older "deliberate, painstaking" Mason and his younger impatient partner was not completely set in stone until after they concluded their westward survey just beyond the Susquehanna River, and went back to the tri-state boundary, working their way back and making any necessary adjustments. After they completed the boundary as far as the river in early July, they "continued the line" westwards. They continued as far as they could proceed, while respecting the territory and the advice of the native American Indians in their party. After making corrections, they completed the boundary maps they were required to make. The date was December 26, 1767. It was just over four years since they started, when they were deemed to have completed their task. [28]

The political significance of Mason and Dixon's Line, as it was called at the time, was not lost on the Baltimore attorney, John H.B. Latrobe when he addressed the Historical Society of Pennsylvania (on the occasion of their thirtieth anniversary) on November 8, 1854. Having reviewed all the events that had occurred since the surveyors drew their line in the ground four score and six years before, Latrobe concluded his speech that evening in Philadelphia by expressing a hope that there would be a unification and strengthening of the nation "as cloud-shadows" from slavery's impending end passed. [29]

Here just ten miles south of Mason and Dixon's Line where the mighty river waters run before they empty into the big bay flowing southwards was the town in the county, which played its part, ready or not, willing or not, aware even, or not, that its people and culture would forever change. It is right to recall the events and peoples that defined a cross-road in the history of an American town in mid-to-late 1800s, where European immigrants who migrated west across the Atlantic met African-Americans heading north. For a time they would share the same road on their individual freedom journeys.

Churches and Schools

15. Tome Memorial Methodist Church built in 1872.
Photograph taken in 2017. Courtesy of Dorothea Henrich.

In the latter part of the 1800s, there were eight places of worship in Port Deposit, and these church communities provided supporting roots for newcomers. The original Methodist Episcopal (M.E.) Church built in 1821, now Paw-Paw Museum was the first church built in the town itself.

The builders used local granite and fieldstone. Being the only church, people of all faiths worshipped here, travelling from twenty to thirty miles away. With local granite, too, the second Methodist church, Nesbitt Hall, was built in 1837 using the measurements of Paw-Paw Hall, which were then doubled. The very grand Tome Memorial Methodist Church (1872) was then constructed by doubling the measurements of Nesbitt Hall.[1]

By 1843, African-American people comprised 23% of the population of Port Deposit, and worshipped God as a community in their own homes and buildings. In 1853, they came together to build the Howard M.E. Church at the bottom of Foundry Hollow Road (now Center Street). The 1877 map also lists a 'Colored Methodist Ch.' on the south end of town on Bainbridge Road (possibly the Cokesbury United Methodist Church), and that year the First Baptist Church would also be built further up on North Main Street. The *Cecil Whig* in Feb 1876 printed a letter from a writer who signed as Guyas Cutas listing both the African M.E. Church, ministered by Rev. P.J. Adams and the African Bethel, where Rev. Jeremiah Young preached.[2] These communities thrived, later forming several parishes, with a stone church at 196 N. Main Street later becoming the Bethel African M.E. Church (c. 1911).

Granite, too, was used for the Presbyterian Church (1872) on South Main Street. Jerome Murray's wife, Mabelle Thompson Murray, who was of English heritage, attended St. James Episcopal Church on High Street, which was built in 1871 on land donated by Jacob Tome. The location and histories of all the churches in Port Deposit can be found in the Walking Tour Guide of Historic Port Deposit available at the town museums.

The Roman Catholics, including the Murrays, also had to find premises. The Irish and Italian populations, especially, were growing. St. Patrick's Chapel at Pilot Town in Conowingo (1819) was attended by large numbers of Irish who built the canal and bridge. When possible, Catholics went to Mass there and received the sacraments of Baptism, Confession, Eucharist, Confirmation and Marriage. On their death bed, they may even have received the anointing of Extreme Unction, as it was then called. The earliest place where Catholics were known to attend Mass in Port Deposit itself was at a home of the Abrahams later called Abrahams Hall (or Building), in the center of town at 15 North Main Street. Later Catholics met in the Banking House until the building of St. Teresa's Church began on North Main Street.[3] Its cornerstone was laid in 1866 and the church was completed in time for the baptism of Mary Ellen "Ella" Murray in the summer of 1867, the fifth child of Joseph and Mary Ellen Donnelly Murray, who may have been wrapped in the treasured Connemara Square.

A rectory, or priests' house was built before the church. Some of the first pastors for the Catholic community were Rev. Lawrence Malloy from Westmeath, Ireland, who started out living in Abrahams Hall; Father John D. Carey, who travelled from Elkton; Rev. Joseph Luke Barry, Rev. Peter Paul Arnd who served from 1893 until 1901, and Father Miles J. McManus, who was a pastor during WWI and built up the community at Perry Point.[4] Some of the priests were neighbors and friends of the Downtown Murrays who lived opposite the church. From oral history of the "Murray pew" at St. Teresa's and the devout faith of Aunts Sarah and Ella, we can be sure that this parish church baptised and buried many a Murray family member.

In contrast to the grand, granite churches in the town, is the rather more plain Balderston Quaker Meetinghouse, six miles north on Liberty Grove Road in Colora. Built in 1841 of stuccoed fieldstone, for Primitive (Plain) Quakers, it now holds just one meeting per year.

16. Balderston Meeting House.
This photograph of the meetinghouse on the Colora Road at Corn Cake Row shows separate entrances for men and women. Courtesy of Rev. John J. Abrahams III.

Various rural chapels and chapel schools were dotted around Port Deposit and from some of these would have sprung independent, privately run schools, lasting only as long as the school teacher. A Mrs. Robert Evans, was the Principal of the Evandale Home School two miles north of Port Deposit in the 1870s, which was for young ladies and children. One early school "which left a strong impression on the hearts and minds of an early generation" in the mid to late 1800s was a school taught by Mrs. Miranda Beach, "a lady of cultivation and teaching ability which descended to her daughter, Miss Martha Beach", according to Mrs. Fannie M. Miller in her address to the women's society called the Hytheham Club on January 19, 1910.

In 1856 Odd Fellows Academy was located in the current Paw-Paw Museum lot. The Odd Fellows movement began in Baltimore as a trade and social organization that provided local schools as a charitable service. In 1868, the Municipal Building in town held classes on the 2nd floor, and for a time there was also a district school where the iron foundry would be built. A total of two private and three public schools were listed in 1878, and the Bard's 1881 ballad also included an infants' school, a school taught by Professor Foulke and Reverend Hanna, and a Sunday School with John McClenahan as superintendent! This somewhat patchwork evolution of schools in the area would be coming to an end with the opening of Jacob and Evalyn Tome's schools.

Tome School

Tome School and Mansion House, Port Deposit, Md.

17. Tome School and Mansion House on South Main Street.
Building number 1 at the free Jacob Tome Institute for town children (left) was the red-brick Washington Hall opened in September 1894. This was also used for a time by boys from the private school on the hill, Tome School for Boys. The Tomes' Mansion House, on the right, was built in 1850, and initially had the Cecil Bank on the ground floor. A postcard published by Del Mar News Agency, Wilmington, Del.

Port Deposit was historically a place of mixed fortune, and, indeed, remains so today. It was, for a time, however, blessed with a philanthropist for whom every small town would desire. Jacob Tome became the county's first millionaire, amassing his first million dollars by the age of forty, an incredible sum at the time. Born in Hanover, Pennsylvania, in 1810 to Swiss Lutheran parents, Tome's family suffered misfortune when his father died prematurely, necessitating that he, just sixteen, and his older brother withdraw from school to become the family's bread winners.

Perhaps because of his own personal blend of misfortune and blessings, Jacob would go on to help the people of Port Deposit in untold ways. In 1872, he built the aforementioned Methodist Church and contributed to others. Although he did not have any surviving children with either his first or second wife, he was said to be dissatisfied with the quality and accessibility of education for the town's children.

In 1877, Tome deeded land for a schoolhouse in Port Deposit for African-American children.[5] The 1871 map lists "Colored School No 1" on Foundry Hollow Road, and School No 2 near Rock Run. The actions of Jacob Tome and other town and county officials clearly indicate that their intention was to progress to "equal, though separate" education, and this may have been achieved for a time, but, "separate and inferior" became the reality of many businesses and organizations, until the Civil Rights Acts of 1957 and 1964 and the successful defense of these laws in court began to lead to a more perfect equality in the late-twentieth century.

Tome is best known locally for founding "a six form" day school, that is, a school covering six grades for pupils from grades 6 to 11. This was free of charge to Cecil and Harford County residents. This school, which opened in September 1894, was Jacob Tome Institute (J.T.I.); in 1899, Evalyn Nesbitt Tome opened another part of Tome School for children under 10 in Jefferson Hall (the enlarged Banking House).

Before he died in 1898, Jacob Tome left $2.5 to 3 M (equivalent to $63 million to 3 billion today) for the continual upkeep of the school. With half of this, the trustees built a boarding school on some hundred acres on the bluff above J.T.I., completed in 1902. The Tome School for Boys was built on an entirely different scale than the "town school". No expense was spared, it seemed, and facilities included boarding houses, laboratories and cottages for staff members. Tome School was said to rival any private school on the East Coast. The prospectus boasted an indoor swimming pool and batting cages. Also a primitive air-conditioning ventilation system was installed, and wonderful cultural, social and academic opportunities were provided, along with the sporting facilities. The "Handbook of American Private Schools", published in 1916 stated that "the trustees of [Tome] School created what is from every point of view probably the finest secondary school equipment in the world, expending a million and a half in carrying out their plans." The tuition, room and board that year was $700 per year (equivalent to $16,000 today), or $150 per year for non-boarding day students. Boys from the town, for a time, attended the "hill school".

———— (I) ————

Second, third and fourth generation Murrays would directly benefit from Tome School education and employment. The infirmary's nurse when Tome Institute opened was Sarah Murray of the Downtown Murrays. The infirmary had a doctor's office and an X-ray room. Her nephew, Jerome Patrick Murray, as other nephews, attended the school on the hill, when town pupils were allowed to attend there.

18. Sarah and Ellen Murray at The Infirmary at Tome School on the hill.
Sarah (left) was the infirmary's nurse. The infirmary was built on the north-east part of the Tome School for Boys on the hill. This photograph was taken shortly after its opening in 1901. Courtesy of Patricia Ellen Murray.

Jerome told this story about the "hill school":

I attended Tome School on the hill as a day student [from the "town school"]. Many boys boarded there while they attended high school. The boarders were mostly from the eastern states.

In one history class, the teacher, Pap Havlin, was quite an admirer of Abraham Lincoln. A boarding student from the South evidently did not share Professor Havlin's opinion as he chanted the following:

Abraham Lincoln
Dead and 'stinkin'
Turkey buzzards are
'Pickin' on his bones.

This was too much for Professor Havlin. He picked up a bamboo pole that was used in those days to hold newspapers in the library, and whacked that student on the head.

Then he handed the pole to a boy to return to the library. He was to tell Mrs. Campbell, the librarian, that he would pay for the pole later!

Jerome did not graduate from Tome, opting to leave school after 12 years, without a diploma, rather than having to pass German. According to his daughter, Patricia Ellen Murray, there may have been a connection between Jerome's "inability" to continue to learn German language and his brothers' service in World War I, during the time Jerome was a Tome student. His older brother, Joseph Murray, son of Mary Ellen Murray, was listed as a WWI veteran in the 1930 census. Both he and his younger brother, Paul, were drafted in 1917. Joe was sent to fight in the trenches along the western front. Jerome would have been sensitive to all things Germanic. To complicate the matter, Tome School brought a native German speaker over from Europe. On May 8, 1912, a *Sun* headline read "High Honor for Tome, German Government to send a Master in that Language! Prussian government to assist in the German Department." This may have been an honor for then Director, Thomas Stockham Baker, Ph.D. (1909-1918) who studied in Germany and started a strong program in the Languages at the Tome School, but it must have been a nightmare for Jerome.

19. Jerome Patrick Murray, 1920.
Murray Family Album.

The Manual Training Department at Tome was a place where Jerome learned the basis for many of the skills he would apply in life. There were machine shops and mechanical drawing rooms, electric saws, a lathe, and a forge for metal working. This was more like it. The basement of his home above Foundry Hollow would be jam-packed with machines, saws, sanders and tools.

Jerome did distinguish himself on the sporting fields, and was honored on the evening of June 6th in 1915 by being capped with Tome's Pythian-Olympian Society cap (2nd Team) for his sportsmanship and sporting abilities on the Base Ball team. At the celebration, his coach, George B. Taylor, made a speech.[6] A photograph of the Tome baseball team c.1915 shows Jerome pictured in the back row. He is wearing a distinctive navy blue pullover sweater with a raised laurel wreath motif around the neck, likely the Tome or Pythian-Olympian Society insignia. One of the coaches in the team photograph is also proudly sporting the striped cap of Rising Sun's Base Ball team, the champion semi-pro team in 1904.[7]

Jerome was often called out of classes from the "town school" to play for the "hill team". Although his prowess on the field may have adversely affected his studies, he would have played out the sheer pride and joy of playing baseball for the hill school. He also later played on the Port Deposit semi-pro team.

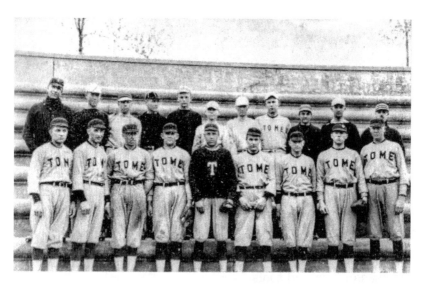

20. The Tome School Baseball Team around 1915.
Jerome Murray in the back row, fifth from the left, played for the "hill school" team. Courtesy of Port Deposit Heritage Corporation.

Although Jerome preferred baseball to German class and did not graduate, a number of the 2nd and 3rd generation Murray girls successfully graduated from J.T.I. Of the 2nd generation were Bertha Foran from the Class of 1904; Mary Ellen "Nellie" Murray in the Class of 1906; and Elizabeth

Murray, Class of 1908.

The school had three streams at this time: academic, commercial and scientific. Bertha followed the commercial stream and showed great versatility in the financial-based office jobs she later held. Not much is known about Nellie, but that she went to New York, and died shortly thereafter of consumption (as tuberculosis was called) in her early 20s. Elizabeth Murray attended the two-year teacher training college, called The Normal School, (later Towson State Teacher's College, and now Towson University). She taught for 49 ½ years, first in Port Deposit, and then in Baltimore, living north of Fell's Point and taking a trolley to teach at her school. After initially boarding with various families, she found a home of her own. It was not just her students she was devoted to: great-nieces and great-nephews, far and wide, were remembered at their birthday times with generously-sized parcels arriving at their side doors packed with treats such as Animal Crackers, Cracker Jacks and Poppy Cock, as well as American children's classic hard-backed books, such as *The Ted and Nina Storybook* by Marguerite de Angelis (1935), *Make Way for Ducklings* (1941), and *Blueberries for Sal* (1948) by Robert McCloskey, and *Goodnight Moon* by Margaret Wise Brown (1947).

Amongst the next generation were Anne Murray, the youngest of the Rock Run Murrays, and Mabelle Thompson and her sister, Alma Thompson, all Class of 1920 graduates. The Thompson girls were from a farming family in Harford County. This story, *Boarding in Port Deposit,* told by Mabelle's daughter, Patricia, highlights the sacrifices which families made for the sake of educational opportunities.

Dublin School, a Harford County school, had only ten grades when Mom attended. She was a year older than Aunt Alma, so she went another year until Aunt Alma caught up, so they could go to Tome together. Then they both went to the 11th and 12th grades in Port Deposit. After two years, they graduated from the Tome School in 1920.

In order to do this, they had to board in Port Deposit. Their family knew Nathan and Emily Nelson. The Nelsons had lived in Harford Co. and then moved to Port Deposit. Miriam, their daughter, Mom, and Aunt Alma walked to school. They became friends with Daddy's sister, Anne Murray. She was in Mom's class. That is how Mother and Daddy met.

Mrs. Nelson was an "immaculate" housekeeper. Years later, Miriam visited Mom in our home. Miriam reached up and took a glass from Mom's cupboard saying, "This is clean, isn't it?" Mother laughed about it. When someone would complement Emily Nelson on making a good cake, she would say, "It ought to be good. It has 'so many eggs', 'so much sugar', etc." Mother often quoted that saying when she was complimented on something she had cooked.

Nathan Nelson was a tenant farmer and he and his wife, Emily, lived at 99 N. Main Street with their son, William, and daughter, Miriam. William Nelson was a couple of years older than the Thompson girls, and worked as a machinist in Perryville. His presence in the house would have made extracurricular life interesting. Alma was a talker, Mabelle more an observer.

I'm not sure how often they got to go home. When they did, they rode the train from Port Deposit to Conowingo, which was a village before the Susquehanna was dammed. Granddad Thompson would meet them there with his horse and buggy, driven from Scarborough. He must have taken them all the way to Port the first trip, as I know they furnished their own bed!"

Looking back, it was probably a financial sacrifice to Granddad Thompson. Tome School was a private school, but free to Cecil and Harford Counties. However, he would have had to pay for their board. Boarding in Port Deposit would not seem like much today, but in 1918, I imagine it was quite an adventure for two country girls.

Mabelle and Alma's parents, John Emory and Sarah Bailey Thompson, were proud of their daughters' accomplishments and Commencement Week exercises were very special for the Thompson family. These were very traditional occasions.

When Nellie graduated in 1906, the paper reported on the full three days' activities.[8] The chapel exercises and commencement sermon were held on the first evening. These were followed by separate girls' and boys' class-day exercises held the following day. Then there was the evening reception at the Director's Residence. The Director's residence on the hill was across the landscaped gardens from Memorial Hall, where the following day, the commencement itself was held, with the address usually given by a man of letters and honors. That evening, the prom would be held right there on the grand campus. It was a packed agenda. In 1917, during the war, the Assistant Secretary of the Navy, Mr. Franklin D. Roosevelt was the guest speaker, and urged the boys "to stick to their school boy ideal as their guide through life and to consider national service a privilege and not a duty." Roosevelt stayed in Van Buren House right on the campus.[9]

When it was Mabelle and her classmate's turn in 1920, the usual pattern held, but this year, the address at the girls' commencement on June 10th was delivered by non-other than the educational reformer, Miss, later Professor, Florence Bamberger, A.M. of Columbia and Johns Hopkins universities.[10] No wonder Alma Thompson chose a career in teaching. A summer photograph of the three wistful friends, Anne Murray, and Alma and Mabelle Thompson in the Italianate Gardens was probably taken that week. White dresses with cinched waists and flounces had been carefully made by the girls in the sewing room especially for this week's ceremonies.

A sturdy envelope marked "THE JACOB TOME INSTITUTE

MONTHLY REPORT - PLEASE RETURN IN THIS ENVELOPE" was mailed to Mabelle, just two days later, addressed "Street, Maryland", with two 1¢ stamps hastily applied. It contained grades for each month, January and June exams, and had semester and final grades. Each month was signed "Mrs. Emory Thompson" in her copperplate handwriting, except for this last report in June. Mabelle received grades of 100 for Conduct; 92, English; 98, Mathematics; 93, History; 95, Civics/Art; 85, Physical Training; 91, Shorthand; 91, Typewriting; and, 92, Bookkeeping. A mark was not given for her penmanship, but exquisitely executed pictures of a fan, and a log cabin, made with literally hundreds of delicately-shaped *O*s, showed her fine hand. Mabelle was following Tome School's "commercial stream", and she returned to Tome with her classmate Anne Murray to obtain additional secretarial training. She got a position in Bel Air, but only for a time because her mother died only months after she graduated. Then she was needed on the farm to cook and care for her father, and her Uncle Oscar and family. Both Alma and Mabelle married, Mabelle actually returning to Port Deposit in 1926, by car this time, to marry her classmate's brother, Jerome Patrick Murray! It would not be too long before she herself would be signing report cards.

21. Anne Murray and Mabelle and Alma Thompson, and child in the Italianate Gardens during Commencement Week in June 1920. *Murray Family Album.*

The Wall Street Crash of October 24, 1929 and the onset of the Great Depression in the early Thirties led to a loss of applications to the "hill school", and a poor return on their investments. It was financially crippled, in any case, due to excessive spending. Although looking back, some might arguably feel that Tome's bequest was mismanaged, who could have predicted the impact of the stock market crash? The "hill school" clung on, but then closed on June 1, 1941. The "town school" would continue though, and another generation of Murrays in Port Deposit would benefit from this unique school.

Change of Fortunes

For people all over the United States, the financial downturn pushed even the wealthy into relative poverty. With the loss of the upstream trade that resulted from the damming of the River, the lucrative lumber supply dried up. The decreasing demand for granite from the depression led to the closure of the quarry. Altogether, these losses led to a dramatic downturn for the town and its people.

Jerome was fortunate to be able to find employment on new hydroelectric dam projects in the Tennessee Valley under the T.V.A. program enacted in 1933 by Franklin Delano Roosevelt. This involved stints away from his family, and ten years of moving his wife, Mabelle, and three older girls from place to place in the southern states of North Carolina, Kentucky and Tennessee. They had not been living long in their own home up the hill from Center Street on Port Deposit Road, and their oldest daughter, Mary Mabelle, had only just started school at Tome. Later on, in 1944, the Jerome Murrays were able to move back into their own home in Port Deposit, bringing Ann Carolyn, born in the Hiwassee Dam village, N.C., who was more than ready to begin at Tome.

While they were living in the south, the Second World War began in Europe, and when America entered the war in 1941, the U.S. Navy, with the recommendation of F. Roosevelt bought the site of the Tome Hill School and adjoining 1,000 acres at Bainbridge on March 28, 1942,[1] so well suited because of its location near major waterways. The United States Naval Training Center (U.S.N.T.C.) Bainbridge was built for the training of tens of thousands of recruits, and opened in 1942. Economically, "Bainbridge" was a stabilizing force for the town. It certainly made life interesting for the Murray girls who lived across the road and could see the sailors marching, hear them singing, and even calling out to them from across the road! When the last evening Taps were played and the Navy left in 1976, hundreds of buildings were left, eventually becoming derelict until the Department of Labor's Job Corps took over. Wiley's Manufacturing Co. was another major industry, located at the river side, where Creswell's Ferry once operated. For forty four years, it built boats and heavy equipment for construction firms, the Army Corps of Engineers and others, until closing in 1983.

Through the 1950s and 1960s, Port Deposit, and indeed Cecil County, experienced civil rights as well as economic struggles. However, the celebration of the town's history during the County Tercentennial (1974) and American Bicentennial (1976) brought a revival of interest and pride in the history of the town. Efforts were made to preserve its buildings. Like-minded townspeople joined together and formed the Port Deposit Heritage Society, eventually "Corporation". Considerable effort was put into the restoration of the Paw-Paw Building, only ever called "Paw-Paw Hall" by the Murray family. Under the leadership of Grace Humphries, the town was recognized as a historic district in May 1978, and was listed on the National Register of Historic Places.

Over time regeneration of the town's waterfront properties have led to the establishment of Tome's Landing Marina and Riverfront areas. There have also been initiatives for restoring the old Tome School area on the hill, and a continuum of new restoration projects, businesses and organizations becoming established in the town.

The extraordinary changes in Port Deposit throughout the 1800s and 1900s affected the lives of many of its families, including my own. The town was host and home to some very unique periods and people. Throughout its formative period and beyond, it has been a place which has welcomed people on a short or long-term basis. Its evolution will continue, as many who have visited or experienced Port Deposit, continue to feel its pull. The enduring beauty of its river and stone, which were formed millions of years ago, has forged a link through the ages, and will continue to do so for a very long time to come.

Part II.

Tour of Murray Port Deposit

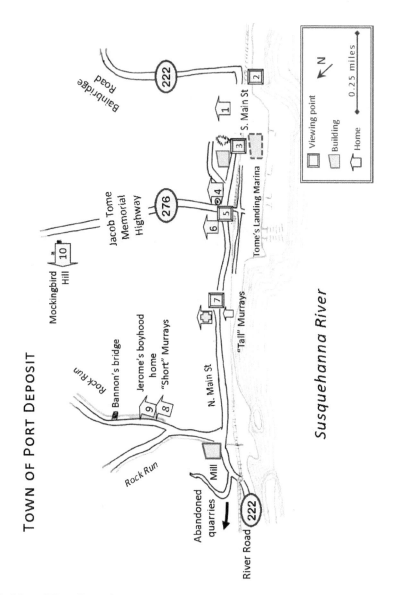

22. Map of Port Deposit.
The buildings and locations described as tour stops in Part II are designated as numbers 1 to 10.

23. Murray Family Tree.

The main characters of the Port Deposit Murray family are listed with the first generations on the lowest limbs.

Before the Tour

Well before the turn of the twenty-first century, a revival of historic interest in the town led to town tours, notably the Candlelight Tours of the grander houses and historic buildings in downtown Port. Long recognized for its beautiful granite buildings and homes by the now-calmer river, a new realization of the extraordinary lives that were played out here, generated renewed curiosity.

Hidden are stories of the *ordinary* people and families who were part of the town's glorious, and maybe even its inglorious past. Those who witnessed the granite quarry's work, the winter floods' destruction, and even the pre- and post-Civil War migrations would have much to tell.

From my own family, my grandfather, Jerome Patrick Murray, a grandson of Irish immigrants, was an irrepressible story teller, a teller of tall tales, and funny personal anecdotes. Even in his older years, if you could slow down and sit by him, you would usually be rewarded with a story. My aunts and my mother, through what they heard from him, and witnessed themselves, also passed these narratives on, through the oral tradition and written word.

On July 24, 2004, my aunt, Patricia Ellen Murray, then aged seventy-one, took my sons and me on a car tour of Port Deposit. She showed us the locations, homes and buildings that were pertinent to the Murray family, and we heard again the stories reflecting the lives of four generations of the family who lived in Port Deposit. Patricia's stories are included in this part of the book as unattributed quotations.

A map of the locations of the tour stops might help in orientation (see 22), although the journey is a relatively simple one. Our sightseeing starts on South Main Street at the old McClenahan Mansion. We will start the tour at the homes of the industrialists, and will proceed down the steps of the social hierarchy, to their employees, my relatives.

Stop One

McClenahan Mansion – 90 S. Main Street

24. McClenahan Mansion.
The original wooden house was built c. 1840-50, by previous owners before it came into the McClenahan Family, who rebuilt the house with the granite addition. Photograph courtesy of Dorothea Henrich.

Daughters of Irish quarry laborers found employment as personal servants to the McClenahan family itself. The teenage daughter of John and Bridget Bannon Murray, Mary

Ellen, and her cousin, Hannah, worked for the McClenahan family in the late 1800s and early 1900s. Mary Ellen walked to the house on North Main Street from Rock Run every day to cook for them, while Hannah lived and worked in one of the other households as a nurse-maid. Mary Ellen spent most of her days in the kitchen and cellar, but would also have been required to help serve the meals upstairs in the dining room with the mahogany woodwork and crystal chandelier.

The McClenahans were a large family. Margaretta J. Megredy and Ebenezer Dickey McClenahan had four sons and four daughters and lived on N. Main Street before moving to a wooden clapboard house here. Two of their sons, John Megredy McClenahan (born in 1833) and Robert Emory McClenahan (born in 1843) took over the quarry in 1868, just after their father turned 61. John and his wife Laura, a Marylander, had five of their 9 children by that time. His brother Robert and his wife, Mary Perry, from Syracuse, were to renovate this house into a mansion.

When my great-grandmother was working here in 1880 as a servant, there were four McClenahan residences in town. All featured granite. In the 1880s the wooden house at 90 S. Main Street was "turned around and placed against the granite cliff in the back, and a new-cut granite addition was added onto the front," with two foot granite walls and a surrounding wall.[1] Another residence was the McClenahan-Nesbitt double home at 60 – 62 S. Main Street, which was built by John McClenahan, the north half for his son, John, and the south half for his daughter, Virginia McClenahan Nesbitt. The fourth residence was across the road at 57 S. Main Street, the Hayden-McClenahan House, where John's third son, William McClenahan lived. The McClenahan dynasty was large and growing at both ends, you could say. Besides the families upstairs, there were below-the-stair servants coming and going daily, as Mary Ellen did. Each household had live-in servants, too.

My aunt began her stories, after stopping in front of this house.

This house was where Mary Ellen Murray Murray, my grandmother, was a cook for the McClenahans from the age of about 14. She was given a "cats' eyes" bracelet made of abalone shells set in silver from Japan, by the brother of Mrs. McClenahan, Captain Perry, who was a sea captain and sailed to the Far East. He brought all the servants something. Mr. McClenahan was the owner of the Quarry.

One of Mary Ellen's stories was about cooking a turtle. It seems as if they put a diamondback terrapin in the oven to bake it. It was alive. They couldn't keep the wood stove oven door closed, because it kept escaping. They finally had to prop a block of firewood against the door to keep the turtle inside as it cooked.

Another story was about a big white Persian cat the sea captain had brought back. Three days in a row, the cat brought a gift to the back door steps.[2] The cat's idea of a gift was a copperhead snake. Snakes are found in the cliffs at the back of the house.

Mary Ellen used The Appledore Cookbook: containing practical receipts [recipes] for plain and rich cooking *by Maria Parloa (1884). The front half of the cookbook was for plain cooking, and the back half for richer food. There were no recipes for Maryland terrapin, only for mock turtle soup. In the back of the book, in her very pretty, flowing, cursive script, Mary Ellen had included recipes almost exclusively for baked goods, including for marble, cream sponge, sugar, fruit, cream chocolate and spice cakes, as well as sand balls, cream puffs, mince meat, soft ginger bread and fig pudding with hard sauce. Cooks then needed to be versatile, and there were simple instructions for home remedies like Oil of Winter Green Lineament, Hand Lotion, Alpurient (Epsom Salts) and Laxative, as well as furniture polish and carpet cleaner!*

Miss Hannah Bannon, Mary Ellen's first cousin, was a

housemaid and nursemaid for the William McClenahan family who lived at 57 S. Main Street in 1900, when she was twenty. Above-the-stairs, there were indeed two babies to nurse, and more on the way. In addition to William's offspring, there were the extended families of the other three households, so there was plenty of work to be done.

As was often the pattern of the day, widowed mothers moved in with their married sons or daughters. Mrs. Sarah E. Everist moved in with her daughter, Mary R. and son-in-law, William McClenahan, who was the mayor, and ran a stationery and news dealership. For decades, Mrs. Everist was listed (probably listed herself) on the census reports as "Head of Household".[3] When she died, a simple obituary listing was submitted to the local paper.

Mrs. Elizabeth Perry, mother of Mary E., wife of Robert Emory McClenahan, moved from Syracuse to live with her daughter and son-in-law. He was the youngest son, a granite dealer. One bonus to Mrs. Perry was that her own son often visited. He was none other than Thomas Perry, a decorated naval officer who had graduated from the Naval Academy in Newport R.I. on September 21, 1861 and was duly promoted to the rank of Acting-Midshipman. He moved up the ranks through postings in the South Pacific and North Atlantic. He was even on a Special Service mission in 1870.[4] By 1880, when Lieutenant Commander Perry was thirty-seven, Mary Ellen was cooking for him. Because Port Deposit was his official home base, he spent time here at Christmas and on leave, and the servants became like a family to him. His gift to Mary Ellen of the bracelet was a great honor to her.

When Mrs. Perry died, she received the greatest posthumous compliment a woman in her seventies could expect. Her obituary in the *Sun* on July 29, 1885 read, "Mrs. Elizabeth A. Perry, a highly esteemed lady, died at the residence of her son-in-law, Mr. R.E. McClenahan, which she had made her home for some years, at an early hour this morning. Mrs. Perry has been in feeble health for some time. She was about *55 years of age*."

Thomas Perry continued to favor Port Deposit as a home, and the *Baltimore American* reported on December 22, 1907, "Admiral Thomas Perry (retired) has returned from a several weeks' gunning expedition in North Carolina, and will probably remain for the winter with his brother-in-law, R. Emory McClenahan."

On the 12th of May of 1910, the census enumerator for Port Deposit recorded that Thomas Perry was residing just outside of Port Deposit "on the farm-camping", with his married servants from Japan, S. and Ren Watanabe and their one-year old daughter, Shizue. Using the ice from the river, the Watanabes began making ice-cream, no doubt for little Shizue and Thomas, and they also offered some to Mary Ellen to try. Although Mary Ellen left the service of the McClenahans upon marriage at age 25 in 1884, they remained friends.

Mary Ellen had three hand-written recipes for Chow-Chow and chili sauce to suit Captain Perry's taste for Japanese cuisine, and these required large volumes of vegetables, fresh and pickled and three-and-a-half days of preparation. The cellar of the McClenahan Mansion still "retains its original water trough for keeping vegetables cool before refrigeration",[5] and this was also an ideal location for the ice box for freezing the Watanabes' ice cream.

Mary Ellen's Chow-Chow

1/2 pk. (peck) green tomatoes
2 heads of cauliflower or cabbage
1 dozen large onions cut fine or two quarts small onions
30 cucumbers cut fine or two hundred small pickles
Two red carrots sliced
1/2 pt. grated horseradish

Cut the tomatoes and cauliflower, onions and cucumbers and pack in salt overnight, then draw and put to soak in vinegar and water equal parts, two days; draw and mix spices (1/2 pt. white mustard seed, 1/2 cup ground pepper, 1/4 cup of cinnamon, 2 oz. celery seeds). Boil with 1/2 gal. vinegar, 3 lbs. sugar, pour over three mornings in succession, add the last morning 2 boxes of ground mustard, 1 oz. turmeric, Oil to suit the taste, 1/2 doz. red peppers chopped fine, and three heads of celery chopped fine.

My trail ran cold for Robert Emory and Mary McClenahan, but *Stone* magazine in 1899 ran a news item in its "Quarries" column reporting that Robert E. McClenahan of McClenahan & Bro. Granite Co. was in charge of a quarry near Woodberry Station in Baltimore County. Woodberry Quarry became a sizeable enterprise for ballast stone for large construction projects.

The Bannon and Murray girls were never to return to "service". Mary Ellen found herself firmly ensconced in her own kitchen in Rock Run with a growing brood of her own, and Hannah too escaped by setting up a dressmaking business with her younger sister, Alice Bannon, first on the outskirts of Harlem during the Harlem Renaissance, and later on, in Morningside Heights, right in the shadow of Columbia University.

As we next head to the most southern point in town, we will pass by the site of the old Tome Mansion at 70 S. Main Street, and Tome's Carriage House at 80 S. Main Street, which has been beautifully conserved for special catered events and occasions.

Stop Two

Susquehanna River

25. Susquehanna River looking south from the northeastern shore.
The Interstate - 95 bridge is in view. Courtesy of Rev. John J. Abrahams III.

We marvel at the revolution in travel that occurred in the twentieth century, when those whose lives spanned the period from the end of the 19th century to the 1960s witnessed the transformation from horse-power to rocket power. Residents in a riverside town may have been equally impressed with the advances in modes of transportation in the 1800s. Port Deposit was regarded as a major port, because of its extensive wharfing and warehousing industry at the mouth of the Susquehanna. It became the second largest port in Maryland, after Baltimore, and the largest town on the Susquehanna between Havre de Grace where the river meets the bay, and Columbia, Pennsylvania. The lumber, granite, metals and cast-iron stoves and machinery being produced here, not to mention grains, whole and milled, and all the upstream commodities, helped to drive these advances, and the new links joining waterway, road and rail were vital for its continuing wealth.

In the river, arks, rafts, ferries and fishing boats were joined in the 1820s by tow boats, tall Chesapeake Bay schooners and passenger steamboats. Between fifty and 100 vessels might have been anchored off the town at any given time. In 1826, one thousand five hundred arks arrived in Port Deposit, averaging 300 per week, but of course there were fallow and full periods.[1] The river could freeze over for weeks, if not months, and a low, summer river would also curtail the passage of the arks and rafts. There was a high concentration during spring's high waters. The *Cecil Whig* regularly reported on the state of the river at Port Deposit and commented on how this would affect its trade – folks living further away in the county were dependent on the import-export markets in the town, and would not saddle up the horse for a long journey if the paper warned otherwise.

When we four Murrays next pulled off the road to view the river and bridges near the town's southern end, my aunt told the boys and I about the importance of the river for her father:

Growing up along the Susquehanna River, it is only natural that my daddy loved the river. He liked to boat, building many of his own. He also enjoyed swimming, ducking [duck hunting], and fishing.

Daddy told about ducks being so thick on the river that another one could not land. You were allowed to use live ducks for decoys, which he did. Once he returned home with four Canvasback ducks. His brother Bill couldn't believe that he had gotten them so quickly and accused him of shooting his live decoys. Jerome proudly produced his two live decoys as well.

Granddaddy used to row his duck hunting boat, a bushwhack boat that he made, down past these bridges to duck hunt on the "Susquehanna Flats". The first bridge in view now is I-95 [from Perryville to Havre de Grace], the next is Route 40. He could see ducks, mostly Canvasback, all the way across the water. But this is not so today because the area was over-hunted. He would row his boat down the river from Port Deposit to the flats at Perry Point and would row back. At least 8 miles each way, rowing, without a motor and carrying all those decoys. If you ever went on the river with him, it was in this type-boat, with three seater boards, coming up in a point at the front.

Throughout its whole period of human habitation, the river has been used for its natural resources. Of course, there would be peaks and troughs, especially after the devastating floods. The whole area around the mouth of the river where it meets the Upper Chesapeake Bay was known for its duck hunting by the European settlers as well. It was common in that area to use decoys in duck hunting. Jerome, an avid duck hunter, started at a young age:

Craig Russell and I decided that it would be more fun to go duck hunting than to go to class. We were up there at Rock Run in the rowboat. The guns and decoys were ready. We looked up, and there on the bank was our professor. There was nothing to do, but pretend we hadn't seen him and proceed.

The next day we were expecting to be "bawled out". The professor asked us how many ducks we had shot. After we told him, he had his say. We had to run "laps" of the track for several days.

These wooden decoys Jerome used as a schoolboy were an important part of his gear. In the early 1920s, after finishing, or rather finishing *with* school, he bought one hundred carved decoys for $125 in total from a man called Henry Jackson in Aikin, Perryville, near where he hunted on the Flats. These decoys were of the Susquehanna Flats School, unbranded, but very similar to John "Daddy" Holly (1818-1892) carvings. The decoys were thought to have been hand carved by Henry Jackson's son, Harry Jackson, but this has remained a mystery. Some of these had the leather thong-type of line attachment and were typical of those made up to the 1920s. Other ones had a staple and ring-type of line-tie point. Jerome branded these with the letter 'M' for Murray using a special hammer. Only much later did he acquire some made by Daddy Holly, Bob McGaw and R. Madison Mitchell, famous carvers whose creations can be seen in the Havre de Grace museums.

The duck decoys Jerome owned were primarily shaped and painted as Canvasbacks, but there were Redheads and broadbills[2], and a few Black Ducks, as well. Drakes outnumbered hens at least three-to-one. Jerome cast his own lead ballast weights, using a cone-shaped mold, and they were scratched with an "M" with a nail as the metal hardened. So keen and creative was Jerome that he even made four lead decoys like those used to weigh down the flat-bottomed boats used further down the Bay. For these, he would push a wooden decoy in the wet sand, and then fill in the hole with molten lead. When lighter-weight folding decoys came into fashion, Jerome also made some of these.

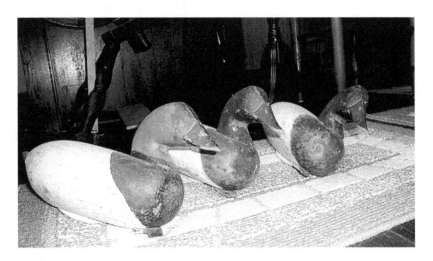

26. Jerome Murray's working decoys.
These are three Canvasback of the hundred Jackson decoys, which were made before 1920.

For his working decoys, Jerome would have been in favor of taking out ducks with slightly different features, so he could figure out which worked best under the various conditions of the mudflats and river, to ensure that the wind brought in ducks he was anticipating that season. The ducks typically flew northwards up the bay in the spring, and down in the autumn, and with luck, would turn up towards his side of the river.

Jerome kept his bushwhack boat in different locations: either anchored somewhere near the Rock Run pier, or off Steele's Island, when he was in fishing mode, or, up near the south end of town to be closer to Perryville for duck hunting, near where we had stopped. Then, according to his daughter, Mary, who was sometimes recruited, they would load twenty to 30 of these decoys and lead weights, as many as his boat could hold, and he would row the boat, decoys, gear and gun down to the Flats using his favorite wooden oars. Each decoy and weight weighed four pounds, so the decoys themselves added about a hundred pounds. The flow of the river would have helped on the way downstream. A brace of ducks would have made the tougher journey home worth the effort, though.

How many would he set out? "Well, this would really depend on the site, the number of ducks in the air and how much time you had", said my brother, who has inherited and honed the skill of carving.   "You would also factor in whether you were going to leave them out overnight, and if the weather was closing in. And you needed to leave some room on the water for the ducks."

Reports of the day say that duck populations were already decreasing by the late 1800s. Waterfowl hunting was banned in the spring season, and greater restrictions began to be made in the 1910s to limit the numbers of migratory waterfowl a person could shoot. Before they were outlawed, big punt guns used to line up along River Road on the bank off Steele's Island, and would blast 20 to 30 ducks at a time to feed the diners of Baltimore restaurants.

Canvasbacks are regarded as the fastest flyers. The thrill of hearing the high-powered beat of their wings flying at speeds of up to seventy miles per hour, spotting the birds, and wondering if the decoys had been spotted at that speed was part of the sport. My father, Charlie Bolgiano, used to visit his fiancée, Betty Murray, around 1950, and Jerome would take him out.   Charlie recalls that Canvasbacks were a great challenge and that it helped to shoot into a crowded sky to maximize the chance of dropping one. "I missed plenty of them", he remembered, over sixty-five years later. "The Chesapeake Bay was an important part of my life." Having lived on Kent Island in the Bay, and being used to hunting ducks from a blind, the river would have provided a different challenge. Jerome's boat had an optional 18-inch wide piece of canvas around the top edge to provide some camouflage, and Charlie would have admired the ingenuity and sportsmanship of Betty's father.

Like his field hunting and freshwater fishing, Jerome was serious about his ducking, which was as much of a part of his way of providing for his family, as it was for enjoying an outdoor sport. The opportunities of meeting other boaters and hunters, and taking family with him also formed part of his enjoyment. Whenever reporting back to his family, he spoke of seeing Canvasbacks or Redheads, but invariably when Mabelle, brought it out of the oven, it was just plain "duck"!

One summer, Jerome paid his daughter, Betty, to repaint the decoys, which had badly faded with use, in order to keep their value. Trespassers poached some, but there were plenty left, and he used some of these in making lamps for his family. Later he manufactured some duck and goose decoys, and carved and painted fine miniatures on wooden bases.

Fishing, too, was a major industry for Port Deposit and the region, and in the 19th and early 20th century, tons of fish were harvested from the river every day.[3] In the spring, herring, perch and shad were fished, with the migratory shad running up the Susquehanna from the Atlantic.[4] Towards the summer, rockfish and bass might be caught. In May 1886, a fishing report in the Baltimore *Sun* gave the price of herring as 20 cents/hundred, and shad as 13 dollars/hundred. The paper recorded that "rainy conditions prevented rock fish or striped bass from biting."

Commercial fishing for migratory herring and shad in the lower Susquehanna was done on an entirely different scale. Off Port Deposit, the fishing season lasted for 22 days and the seasonal fishermen slept on bunks in cabins erected on long wooden floats anchored in the river. Up to half a million herring and shad were dropped on the floats when the nets were raised. Photographs of the fresh catches often show hazy areas from the dazzling reflections of the scales. The fish were sorted, cleaned and packed in barrels there on the floats.[5] Winter ice was used for this purpose.

The riverside was a place of excursions, too. "The shores at Port Deposit, where the rafts were halted and reassignments were made, were points of rendezvous for people of the town and the surrounding country, and Port Deposit attained its palmiest days of commercial activity."[6] Steamboats from Baltimore brought passengers up the Chesapeake for day excursions to Port Deposit as well, for a time.

The Rail Road

27. Railroad looking north from the Marina Park crossing.

The coming of the steam railroad train through Cecil County was both a driver of progress and perhaps unwanted change for Port Deposit and other riverside ports. The railroad connected the town and beyond to the canal and quarries at Canal Station (near McClenahan's Quarry) and Quarry Station (near Keystone Quarry at Mt. Ararat) for freight. Goods like coal, lumber and stone could be transported in hours rather than days to major destinations in the northeast. The *Baltimore Gazette and Daily Advertiser* of May

12, 1835 reported that "the Rail Road between Baltimore to Port Deposit on the Susquehanna river [would be] the last link in the chain of direct intercourse by Rail Ways between Washington and New-York."

As one novel form of transportation became available, investors changed tack, backing the most rapid transport of goods over long distances. The railroad along the river put the canal out of business. Different companies coordinated the construction of the beds, rails, switches and turntables. John Keaveny was a contractor for the railroad as well as for the McClenahans. He kept the law offices busy with conveyancing, or property law, as he bought up land (owning 101 ½ acres by 1877), sold it to the State, bought and sold more, and negotiated new deals for all of his ventures.

The railroads provided a great number of skilled jobs and the opportunity to commute to other towns, principally Perryville and Rising Sun, as well as points beyond, as there were well developed branch lines throughout the county. There were also passenger stations at Rock Run, Port Deposit (Town Station) and across from Tome Steps (built by Jacob Tome for the pupils). At these stations, there were separate waiting rooms for men and women. In 1866, Ellen Garrison Jackson, an early civil rights activist, was waiting in the ladies waiting room in Port Deposit with another teacher, when they were "thrown out" for not being white. True to herself and her family, she complained and the stationmaster was arrested.

A later steam train commuter was Miss Bertha Foran who was dating Jerome's Uncle Jim Murray, from Rock Run. She took the Octoraro branch line, and was mentioned in the poem, *The Gilligan Brigade*, set in 1918, when she was about thirty-five. Bertha took the train to the Perryville office where she worked for a financial company, preparing people's income tax forms. Because she was also caring for her parents who were in their early seventies at the time, she would have been anxious to arrive home on time. This poem, distributed on Onion Skin typing paper, expressed the frustrations of all the commuters. *Gilligan* was the name of the steam train on the Octoraro Branch line of the Philadelphia and Baltimore Central Rail Road, as well as its conductor.

THE GILLIGAN BRIGADE

They rise up in the morning promptly on the stroke of five,
And stagger in their sleepiness, though more dead than alive,
To the station, and beneath a star-lit sky or in the rain,
They yawn and rub their half-closed eyes, while waiting for the train.

Now "Brother" Holden's first aboard, he comes from Rising Sun,
Miss Reynolds and Miss Taylor from Colora's suburbs run,
And at the station platform pant, and wait, and wait, and wait,
The "blooming" train, it happens, is just one half hour late.

At last it comes: Through Rowlandville and Octoraro "Junc,"[7]
The darn thing keeps on moving but it's running pretty punk,
It crawls through Canal Station 'neath the faint rays of the sun,
And blows off steam while waiting for *Miss Foran at Rock Run.*

It stops at Port Deposit, also at Tome Institute,
It pauses at the Quarry8 and its whistle gives a toot,
It crawls along through Frenchtown and it coughs and snorts until
The crowd is safely landed at the town of Perryville.

Be patient, fellow sufferer, the worst is yet to come,
The day's work now is ended and they start the journey home.
They trail out from the office through the mud and through the slime,
For fear by some mischance, perhaps old Gilligan's on time.

But Look! They clench their fists and grind their teeth and storm aroun'
And cuss the Railroad inside out, both up the scale and down,
For gathered in the waiting room at just five thirty-eight,
The old report is given them, "she's thirty minutes late."

They talk the matter o'er while waiting for that train to come,
"Old McAdoo should be kicked out – His Roads are on the bum."[9]
"The train crew wants that overtime!" They argue and debate,
And then, in consternation learn, she's now an hour late.

But suddenly the crowd moves out: They push and jam and swarm,
Then, gathered on the platform, find it's a false alarm,
The train that's coming 'cross the bridge is but a heavy freight,
And Gilligan is now one hour and thirty minutes late.

But now at length it does appear. The gang is soon aboard,
They settle down into their seats and humbly thank the Lord,
The "Skipper's hand's upon the rope, He gives a gentle pull,
She moves and "Billy" Rittenhouse starts in to "throw the bull."

She jogs along to Frenchtown though she acts as if she's fagged,
She pulls up to the signal tower and there she's promptly flagged,
She backs onto the siding there and there they let her lie,
While wreck-trains, work-trains, coaches, freights and hand-cars all
pass by.

She starts and lets some on at Quarry, others off at Tome
She stops at Port Deposit where a weary bunch goes home.
Then onward up the river shore, she chugs her weary way,
And lets her last commuter off some time near break of day.

A curse upon you, Gilligan!! My anger towards you's rife,
Alone we can depend on you to take the joy from life,
But when this Plant shuts down and we have quit or lost our job,[10]
We vow we'll never on you ride – We swear, so help us Bob.

We learned about the modern use of the railroad, while
viewing the tracks running parallel to the river:

> *This was the Pennsylvania Railroad, and now it is used by the CSX*
> *freight train. Back in Daddy's time, they rode to Perryville, and other*
> *places. This track went right in back of the school and when trains*
> *came, the class had to stop as it was* right *in back of the school!*
>
> *I'm sure before me it would have been the way that Mother and her*
> *sister, Alma, came from Conowingo to Port Deposit to go to school, but*

in "my time" the steam engine was gone.

Progress in the use of new modes of transportation may, on the surface, have signalled advancement, but most change brings some disadvantage, over and above the loss of a certain way of life. A factor contributing to Port Deposit's prosperity was the annual float trade from Pennsylvania, down the river in the spring. Much of Pennsylvania's enormous timber output came this way. The viability of the saw mills and the lumber trade, not to mention the warehousing and redistribution at the "port of deposit" were affected when the rails replaced the river traffic. The "railroad strangled Port Deposit's economy"[11] by sealing off the townspeople's trade, when goods could be more directly and swiftly transported to their market places. The Conowingo dam, too, so necessary to secure the businesses and homes from the ravishing floods and ice gorges, was also a factor in the decline of the port. It is true that the canal could have been used to bypass the dam, just as it had been used to circumvent the rocks, but there were other factors, too.

Pennsylvania's forests were becoming depleted by the early 1900s and the source of wood for the wooden arks and rafts was threatened. The river was not as bountiful as it once was, and the production of 100,000 barrels of fish every year could not be sustained. As Jack Brubaker in *Down the Susquehanna to the Chesapeake* wrote, "The Susquehannocks' Susquehanna is not ours."

Adaptability may be the key perhaps to our communities' prosperity and survival. The conservation efforts of the river, fish and waterfowl commissions in identifying the sources of loss and pollution, for example, and identifying solutions for sustainability and repopulation will preserve the river's recreational use. Some of the factors that led to changes in Port

Deposit's loss of a local economy to the extent that it occurred are also applicable to other Susquehanna riverside towns lining the north and west branches of the Susquehanna, and its main stem flowing south from Central Pennsylvania. One certainty in the lower Susquehanna is that the river-bay ecosystem will continue to evolve. Governments, organizations, industries and citizens of these towns can work together to safeguard this precious resource. The transformation of Tome's 1850s Gas House just south of Tome's Landing marina into a special center for the Northern Map Turtle is an excellent example of such a step; a collaboration of the state of Maryland, Towson University, the local marina, town officials, architects and builders, it has been hailed as an important preservation and ecotourism effort.

———

Being driven down past 84 S. Main Street reminded me of Mrs. Maggie Fox, a friend of our family. Maggie had already passed away, and we could not help remembering her pride in her baking and flower boxes. It had been the same when she was a girl in "Dirt Bank", the cherished daughter of the Perugino family of one boy and three girls. Maria "Mary" Ciarlo and Giovanni "John" Perugino, emigrated from Italy just after the turn of the century, Maria, with her family, and Giovanni, aged 16, with his. John worked his way up in the quarries from water boy and tool carrier, to blaster, and eventually to skilled stone cutter. Maggie married a crane operator at the quarry, Tommy Fox, had a son, Tommy, Jr., and spent her life working her way up, and into the hearts of townspeople.

Very nearby, we will stop again. The town's superb educational institutions for the young people of Port Deposit and its surrounding areas are a must!

Stop Three

Jacob Tome's "Town School"

28. The Tome Steps.
These granite steps were built by the Jacob Tome Institute for the pupils arriving by train at the Tome Station, so they could ascend the cliff terrace to the school on the hill. The seventy five granite steps were built in the early 1900s. Courtesy of Dorothea Henrich.

Reminders of the Tome School built for the "town's children" required that my aunt turn off the engine of her red car. Patricia, or Patsy, as she was widely known, always bought Impalas and they were always red. It had something to do with being identifiable, she maintained. As a career schoolteacher, being identifiable was important; as a career aunt, it was even more important. Tome School was a vital part of the town, and made a lasting impact for second, third and fourth generation Murrays. My aunt wanted to make sure that we knew about these buildings and what happened inside them.

The great Washington Hall at 57—59 S. Main Street was where the classroom-based learning started for the upper school and it contained the well-equipped science laboratories. It was referred to as Building #1 by the "hill school", and it was shared by both schools, the Tome School for Boys (the private boys school on the hill) and Jacob Tome Institute (the free school for boys and girls). Bordering this building were the train turntable, the train tracks; wharf and river; the brand-new sports fields, and Main Street. It opened on September 14, 1894 during the period of steam trains. When the train pulled in back of the school, lessons had to pause such was the noise and vibration. What was left today of Washington Hall was simply a very delicate archway, with Jacob and Evalyn Tomes' facades carved in the red sandstone masonry.

In its day, the Washington Hall sports fields were lively enough during Physical Education classes, but when J.T.I. were playing football, or the town softball and baseball teams had evening games, this corner of town came to life. The Port Deposit Black Sox also played here on the wharf. Betty recalls that when playing softball, they never used gloves. Few had gloves. To make sure her hands were hard enough, her father, Jerome, and later her fiancé, Charlie, played games of "Burn" and "Hot" with her, to ensure that her throwing was fast, long and accurate. Charlie had a mitt. He willed her to burn his hands, while he threw the ball back as hard as was bearable. Betty was 3rd baseman, so this training was important. Patsy Murray played on 1st base and Mary on 2nd and they could get in plenty of practice on their front yard, even with the sailors watching. The girls on the town's softball team did not have uniforms – blouses and jeans were the order of the day.

The games were played on the wharf behind the school. It was common in big games for a fly ball to be hit into the river, so fielding needed to be sharp. When Betty came back to teach at Tome after college, she was back out on Washington Hall fields, and Charlie became her assistant at the weekends, carrying buckets of water over the gridiron for the boys' football team!

The Tome School Steps located to the right of Adams Hall at 64. S. Main Street are forever identifiable with Tome School in Port Deposit. Solid looking and with a beauty from their symmetrical design, these seventy five steps of stone built in the early 1900s represent much more than a simple stairway. As Patsy tells in her story, the granite stone that was used for these steps was quarried by the Irish and other immigrants, and the steps made on this stone, were those of their children and grandchildren. The chance for an education, the foundation of knowledge, skills, experience and enlightenment, these were the steps that lifted so many families out of poverty and towards potentially fulfilling and contributing lives.

Tome School steps connected the "lower school" to the Tome School on the hill. The path goes up trees to an old Navy fence. Most of boys in town went to the "hill school" in Daddy's time. Mom and Aunt Alma, being girls went to the "lower [town] school" for grades 11 and 12. Daddy's sisters Aunt Anne (Honey Carney's mother was in their Class of 1920) and Aunt Elizabeth also went there. That is how Daddy and Mother met. Mom graduated in 1920. Anne and Elizabeth also graduated from Tome School. Both the boys' and the girls' commencement exercises [graduation ceremonies] were held up on the hill in Memorial Hall.

Notice the stones on the School Steps are all Port Deposit granite from the local quarry. A good many of our relatives worked there. That's how they "got here". Poor Irish laborers. I am sure that the potato famine caused our relatives to emigrate – those English! I'm glad they did, though.

Daddy went 12 years to Tome on the hill but did not graduate. I think because he dropped a course in German. Then he was probably ready to quit.

Mary, Betty, Ann and I all graduated from the Jacob Tome Institute. Our exercises were held in the large Tome Methodist Church.

Although Mary Mabelle, the eldest of Jerome and Mabelle's girls, started school at Tome in 1933, going to first and second grades in town, the family's move to the south in 1935 meant that Mary, Betty and Patsy, attended schools in the villages and towns all around the Tennessee Valley, following Jerome in his jobs on various dam projects for the T.V.A. They lived in some workers' villages and attended the government village schools. They made friends in some places, and adopted the accents, but it was always intended to be temporary.

Despite the fact that the girls were more-or-less thriving in the south, while visiting their home on Port Deposit Road (now Jacob Tome Memorial Highway) in the summer of 1943, ten years after moving south, Jerome and Mabelle made the decision to return to Port Deposit. This was prompted in part by their desire for the girls to return to Tome School as much as it was due to another reason you shall hear about later.

So as soon as Jerome had obtained a civilian job at Bainbridge U.S.N.T.C., which they would see from their front yard, they moved back north. It was just in time for Mary to start her Senior Year at J.T.I. in September 1944. Patsy and Betty were going to be 6th and 10th graders, respectively, and it would be their first time as Tome girls.

Despite Mary's years attending *nine* different schools in the South, she excelled in her senior year at Tome, and became the Class of 1947 Valedictorian. At the opposite end of the school in terms of years, Ann, who was born in the south, was also more than capable of holding her own when she started first grade at Tome Junior School in September 1945, then in Jefferson Hall, the old Banking House. WWII had just ended.

Betty relished her days at Tome, enjoying basketball, photography and softball. The *Jactominian* yearbook of her senior year (1945) was small, thin and austere, in marked contrast to earlier luxury editions. This was due to low class numbers and little chance to collect sponsorship due to WWII, and difficulty in selling ads, from the time's austerity, and hence it was produced on a shoestring budget. All the same, it contained all the essential features so seniors could remember their last year in school. Betty was listed as President, Honor Society (2 years), and being on the *Jactominian* Staff. Also, she was in the Glee Club. Her yearbook "epitaph" reads "We cheer with and for her. Good example of brains and an outdoor gal. Friendly word for everybody. Genuine sweetness and sincerity. Three cheers for our gal Betty."

Early on into J.T.I., Patsy was identified as being on her way to becoming one of the outstanding members of her class. Ann, too, was promoted two grades in one year, although that made her mad. One legendary story about Ann happened in her first year. Outside at recess one day, a bird flew over and splattered her arm. Ever the pragmatist, Ann wiped her arm on the fence, and to her and her family's amazement, a wart there disappeared.

Two photographs of Betty from her senior year are telling. One snapshot shows her proudly wearing a large navy blue felt "T" sewn on her sweater, over a plaid skirt and loafers. This must have been her sought-after School Letter for sporting achievements that she had sewn on her basketball sweater. She and the other senior girls were hanging out at the bottom of the School Steps. The "Hill School" had closed by that time, but the location was obviously the place to be for seniors. A very shy Francis Sice, the only boy in the class, had been forced into a camera frame after that. Francis would have enlisted in the military if he could have, but he had a serious lung condition, and would not have been physically able to serve. This was all to his sisters' and the school girls' benefit, especially as he was three years older. Betty said, "It gave the class a "single boy". He was enrolled on the "Commercial Course" along with his sister, Ann, and six other girls. Betty and Barbara Murray from Bainbridge were on the "Academic Course".

A formal enlargement was made from a school negative taken at the June Prom held in Adams Hall on June 6, 1947. The class of '48 gave the dance for the class of '47. Betty was the "Queen", elected, or rather appointed, she says, because her mother could sew. Indeed, Mabelle made a beautiful jade green taffeta gown covered with organza and sequins, with translucent sandals, thereafter called "glass slippers." The teachers had arranged for Joe Ward to ask Betty to the dance, as they knew his family had a car and he could drive.

The Senior class attendants were Betty Anne Craig and

Shirley McCardell. The young Heralds, who held mega-phones, were Harold "Bing" Caldwell and Arthur "Spanky" Benjamin, whose sister Evelyn, was the crown bearer, holding a cushion. Ruth Ann Pitt, the class of '48 president, had the honor of crowning the queen. Ruth Ann's older sister was Peggy Pitt, Senior Class advisor, who had written in Betty's yearbook, "May success and happiness be your constant companions." Other beauties were from the class of '48, Jackie Coolridge, and Janet Walker; class of '49, Mirandah McElkeny, and from the class of '50, Mary Anne Bitner.

The Commencement that June was a special occasion, as it was the school's Fiftieth Commencement. Betty was to be Valedictorian, as her sister had been. It was held from June 8 to 10, 1947. Even after fifty years, the pattern still held true. The first event was the Commencement Sermon, held on the Sunday evening in the Tome Memorial United Methodist Church. It had military overtones, perhaps carried over from wartime. The Senior Chaplain of the Veterans Hospital at Perry Point gave the sermon, and the School Hymn was "Fight the Good Fight". The Anthem sung by the Girls Glee Club, was the "Evening Prayer from Hänsel and Gretel", the beautiful and haunting composition by Engelbert Humperdink.

When at night I go to sleep
    Fourteen angels watch do keep
    Two my head are guarding
    Two my feet are guiding
    Two are on my right hand
    Two are on my left hand
    Two who warmly cover
    Two who o'er me hover
    Two to whom 'tis given
    To guide my steps to heaven.

Class Night was held the following evening and class-mates, including Grace Burlin, Helen Love, the McCardell sisters and Barbara Murray, took turns leading the various addresses, the Class History, Will and even Prophecy. Betty composed a poem for her graduation. One change from the old traditions was the dropping of an invitation to the Director's Residence afterwards. Cecil Ewing, the Director of J.T.I.'s "Town School", a Pennsylvanian, had lived locally as a schoolteacher for many years. Anyway things had changed for Tome directors, too.

A little book called "Graduation Memories" found in my mother's old department store shirt box had information about her Tome friends and her graduation. She listed her favorite sport as basketball, and her favorite class as Physics.

On the last page of the book were listed in careful detail all the gifts and prizes she received for her graduation. First she listed her awards - $5 from the Lion's Club, Director's Prize, Book for the Edward's Prize, Honorary Science Award and Certificate, the Valedictorians prize was a Reader's Digest, Gold Honor Pin, Glee Club Pin, Basketball sweater and a gold 'T' pin, with a basketball dangling from a chain. Gifts were carefully listed. If she received a monetary gift, Mom thought-fully wrote the amount and then in parenthesis what she purchased with the money...pearls from Patsy, Silver Lizard pin and Hand Lotion from Ann Carolyn, $5 each from 'Granddad' and Aunt Bertha, Gold Leaf Pin from Aunt Sarah and Aunt Ellen, a pocketbook, 3 hankies and $1.11 from Uncle Bill, material from the Carney's, an umbrella from Aunt Elizabeth, $20 (jacket) from Uncle Paul, Toilet water and card from

Jane, a Slip and bra from the "Thompson's Kemp, Hazel and etc.". "Daddy" gave Mom the money he earned from selling one of his thoroughbred puppies – $25 in addition to "$50 for clothes, etc." There were nylons from Ben and Mae Ressler, a cosmetic bag from Betty Burton, $10 (alarm clock) from Aunt Ice, an Evening in Paris set from Anna and Mary Ann Bitner, and a suit, blouse, evening gown, and evening slippers made by Mother.[1]

It seems as though the good fortune that was smiling on Betty, also touched her two sisters, and confirmed Jerome and Mabelle's wisdom in returning to Port Deposit. Patsy's 8th grade report card for that same year, listed straight A's for her subjects, Arithmetic, English, History, Literature, Science and Spelling, with 0 tardies and 0 absences. The only comments were "Class leader. Alpha honors for the year." The Director, Cecil A. Ewing signed it and stated that Patsy was duly "promoted to grade 9" and the report card was signed at home by "Mrs. J. P. Murray".

Patsy and Ann would now be leading the Murray academic cause and did not let the good name down. When they became Valedictorians of the classes of 1951 and 1956, the complementary Readers' Digest subscription was still being awarded. With Patsy's five $5 prize awards, she looked through the catalogs at home, and when she saw a cuckoo clock for $25 in the back of *Good Housekeeping*, she was sold. "After being so serious about my studies for such a long time", she said, "I wanted to try something a little cuckoo." Her wind-up clock was put in pride of place on the living room wall facing the door, so everyone coming in the house could, if they were of a certain age and mindset be treated to the sight and sound of the cuckoo!"

29. Adams (Town) Hall.
This granite building at 64 South Main Street was built in 1905 as the gymnasium of Jacob Tome Institute. Courtesy of Dorothea Henrich.

The 3rd and last Tome School building was Adam's Hall which was built in 1905.

Adams Hall is now the Town Hall. The upstairs of Adams Hall was used for a library for several years until it moved into the old post office. The downstairs had a pool and it was covered over for the purpose of town hall activities today like Board Room meetings.

But this was the gymnasium to the Tome School in our day. Betty, Mary, Ann and I played basketball here on the second floor. It had a very small court compared to today's standard. I used to play "kick the can" around the building at lunch in sixth and seventh grades. I think Ann did, too."

In September 1951, Betty was to return to Tome as a teacher, with her diploma in Education from the University of Maryland, and Certificate from the Maryland Department of Education to teach a Special Subject (P.E.) in an Approved

Non-Public School. "For some reason, they thought they wanted me to teach at Tome", she said. With a fresh contract signed by Walter E. Buck, President of the Board of Trustees, and Cecil A. Ewing, Director, to teach Science, Physical Education, and Algebra, Betty, would be teaching 9th grade. Ann, her sister, was going to be in the 7th grade, so that was a close call for both!

When Betty announced at home that she would also be coaching basketball, Jerome got in on the act. He was working as a construction foreman at Bainbridge, and came home one day with some chewing gum in a paper bag. It was still wrapped in its paper, but it was rotten. If you tried to unwrap it, it fell apart. "For some reason", she said, "I put the gum near the sinks for the other team. I remember listening in to them getting into it, and hearing them say, "Ewh! Ewh!"

Betty like her father was a hard worker. Although she may not have met quite all of her contractual obligations, "efficiency of teaching, willing cooperation with the Director, or *ability to maintain discipline*", she gave it her best. When her 1952 income tax return 1040A was filed, it listed her income as $2,965.40 (Jacob Tome Institute, $1,320; Cecil National Bank, $332.32; along with other sources of income from the boards of education from Montgomery and Prince George's counties). It was clear that Betty entered married life as a bread winner. Her husband, Charles, was a laboratory instructor of Chemistry at the University of Maryland. That is how she met Charlie, or "Chuck", as her Instructor. For a brief time, she had the responsibility of financially supporting her husband so he could complete his dissertation in Organic Chemistry.

Many married women of that generation eventually gave up work and their careers, taking on new opportunities for teaching in their own homes. Many of my great-aunts and great-great aunts were able to attain a higher level of education than their brothers. This was possibly because they were not required to work in the quarry as teenagers. They did not necessarily start families, and some remained as career women, living rich and fulfilling lives. Many Murray girls have also become teachers. The following famous quotation is so true. *If you educate a girl, you educate a woman. If you educate a woman, you educate a family. If you educate a family, you educate a nation.*[2]

Although Tome's "town school" on Port Deposit's Main Street carried on until 1974, around when J.T.I. opened in Northeast, Maryland, the Steps remain here in Town, an enduring symbol of Evalyn and Jacob Tome's generosity and commitment to education for all. Despite the enactment of civil rights laws, schools were not fully "integrated", that is open to black, mixed race and white students at the same time until 1964, incredible as that may seem.

The Tome Mansion, built in 1850, complete with a bank, made way for an outdoor swimming pool, which was built by the Lions Club. The Tomes believed in giving opportunity to all. Patsy through her own school teaching at Bainbridge School would also do her share to make sure that all received equal chances in her classroom and on her playground, as all of her nieces and nephews witnessed first-hand. Children naturally strive for togetherness, and Miss Murray fostered this.

Stop Four

Gerry "Lafayette" House – 16 S. Main Street

30. Marquis de Lafayette.
Samuel F.B. Morse was commissioned by the City of New York to paint this portrait of Lafayette during his tour of the United States as Guest of the Nation. It was completed in 1826. Photograph by Glenn Castellano, Collection of the Public Design Commission of the City of New York.

Another defender of liberty and equality was Gilbert du Motier, who lived from 1757 to 1834. He was ahead of most American reformers in the realm of human rights. Born into nobility, the marquis de La Fayette (according to the French spelling, or Lafayette as we call him) recognized the dignity and humanity of every person, and risked life, limb and liberty to win the same for others. Cecil County was an important base for General Lafayette during the American War for Independence. He spent time in this area scouting the lay of the land and acquiring provisions for men and animals. The town of Elkton (then called the Head of Elk) was a meeting place for both the Colonists and the British.[1]

By this time, Lafayette had proven his loyalty to the colonists' cause. His leadership and personal bravery at the Battle of Brandywine in Chester, Pennsylvania were without question, and his financial and political clout in France assured much needed support for the colonial cause. He earned Washington's recommendation to Benjamin Harrison, who was leading the Continental War Committee, that he receive command of 1,200 enlisted troops.

The year 1781 was a dramatic one. "On March 2, 1781, three days ahead of schedule after a very fast march south through mud and freezing rain, Lafayette's troops reached Head of Elk. Washington's orders were to stay there"[2] until the signal to move south near the coast to meet French transports, with the goal of capturing the traitor, Benedict Arnold.

"On March 8 …, Lafayette violated Washington's order and began to embark to Annapolis." Lafayette went on to Virginia, but the expected French transports had been beaten back, and he had to explain himself to Washington. "Lafayette and his army began to march back to Head of Elk." Washington then ordered him to march back north to the New Jersey area, but the day after, told him to take his men south after all! Lafayette's trooped promptly mutinied.

> When Lafayette's men left camp they had been told
> not to bring much gear since they would be gone only
> a short time. They had now been on the march for six
> weeks. Their clothes were in tatters, and many had
> worn out their shoes. He [Lafayette] told his men that

*they were free to go. Ahead of them, he said, lay a hard
road, great danger, and a superior army determined
on their destruction. He for one meant to face them
[the enemy], but anyone who did not wish to fight
could avoid the crime of desertion by simply applying
for leave to return to camp in Morristown [NJ].* [3]

Furthermore,"Lafayette rewarded his men for their loyalty by spending £2,000 [French livres] on his own credit to buy desperately needed clothing, shorts, shoes, hats and blankets; but it was his appeal to their pride that stopped the desertions." There were a number of such moments during the Revolutionary War when patriot success seemingly dangled by a thread, to be saved by the bravery and steadfastness of a few.

In Head of Elk, Lafayette received a note from Washington instructing him to head south by land rather than waterway, as they had previously planned. On or around the 11th April, some of Lafayette's army stayed the night in the woods at Brick Meeting House, and others ten miles further on in Harrisville,[4] and the next morning they crossed the river just above Conowingo at Bald Friar's Ferry, in flat-bottomed scows.

When Lafayette and his army crossed the Susquehanna, they were heading for Virginia to head off the Redcoats under command of British General Cornwallis who were moving into Richmond. (Richmond had recently been appointed the capital of the Colony of Virginia. Previously Williamsburg was the capital.) Cornwallis had been ordered to construct a port on the Chesapeake and Lafayette followed him to Yorktown. Lafayette excelled in military strategy, and his troops helped to contain the British in Yorktown, Virginia until the French fleet arrived in the Chesapeake Bay, defeated the British fleet and prevented a British escape by sea.

The French General Rochambeau and Washington passed through the Head of Elk on September 6 to 7, and joined Lafayette a few weeks later. Once the large French and Continental armies arrived they overwhelmed the British by siege, surrounding Cornwallis at Yorktown and forcing his surrender on the nineteenth of October, 1781. This was to end the American War for Independence. That all of this was able to come together depended upon many pieces fortuitously falling into place.

Lafayette wrote to his wife, Marie Adrienne, in France,

> The end of this campaign is truly brilliant for the allied troops. There was a rare coordination in our movements, and I would be finicky indeed if I were not pleased with the end of my campaign in Virginia. You must have been informed of all the toil the superiority and talents of Lord Cornwallis gave me and of the advantage that we then gained in recovering lost ground, until at length we had Lord Cornwallis in the position we needed in order to capture him. It was then that everyone pounced on him.[5]

Lafayette became a personal friend of George Washington, and entrusted his young son, Georges Washington de La Fayette, to Washington's care at Mount Vernon during the French Revolution. Lafayette proposed buying a farm with Washington near Mount Vernon, but rejected the system of slavery that came with it, and the deal did not come to fruition. They remained friends until Washington's death.[6]

In 1789, just after Maryland became a state, Lafayette became a naturalized citizen of America in the statehouse in Annapolis, Maryland, a status that would pass to his male heirs. This was at the start of the French Revolution. In January 1824 Colonel George Edward Mitchell of Fair Hill, Cecil County, petitioned Congress to have President James Monroe invite Lafayette to celebrate the country's fiftieth anniversary as Guest of the Nation.[7] Naturally, Lafayette planned to come back to his home state.

It was during his tour of the United States that lasted from August 1824 to September 1825 that he twice visited Cecil County. Again on this occasion, he was accompanied by his son, Georges Washington de La Fayette, aged forty-four, and, his secretary, Auguste Levasseur, who kept a journal. Extensive and detailed planning included federal, state and local government officials, representatives of the military and old friends. The telegraph inventor, Samuel Morse, painted his portrait for the City of New York during the tour,[8] the educational reformer, Mrs. Emma Willard, a promoter of education for young women, met him at the boat, and the author, James Fenimore Cooper, of *The Last of the Mohican* fame, helped to chronicle his travels. Meetings with each of the former Presidents also topped the itinerary. He met John Adams in New England. On his way to Virginia and Washington D.C. (to meet the aging Thomas Jefferson at Monticello, Washington's family at Mount Vernon, and Monroe), Lafayette came to Cecil County.

On or around the 8th October 1824, he travelled from Philadelphia to Baltimore, via Frenchtown (on the Elk River) to take the overnight steamboat down the Chesapeake Bay to Fort McHenry. From the journal, published and translated in 1829:

> The night was far advanced when we arrived at Frenchtown, where the steam-boat United States had waited for us a long time. At a short distance from Frenchtown, general Lafayette was met by a numerous deputation, and the aids of the governor of Maryland, who informed him that they were charged to convey him to Fort McHenry, where the governor had established his head quarters to receive him. Among this deputation, Lafayette recognized with pleasure many of his old friends, especially two Frenchman... At the moment of our embarkation we learned that Mr. John [Quincy] Adams, secretary of state, had arrived at Frenchtown, on his way to Washington, and that he had accepted with pleasure the invitation given him to join the company of general Lafayette, to

whom this was an especial satisfaction, as Mr. Adams was also an old and kind acquaintance.[9]

According to Alice Miller, old Squire Abrahams recalled Lafayette's visit to Port Deposit during this trip. Mr. Joseph W. Abrahams, Esq., Justice of the Peace was one of the town's oldest citizens when he died in January 1889, and no doubt, his memory was sharp, as he was still very active late in life.

After his official visit to Washington D.C., he continued to travel south to New Orleans, then headed up the Mississippi and Ohio Rivers, and toured up and down the whole country, visiting every state. During this journey, more than three dozen entries were made in the journal about slavery. Cotton was not a cash crop in Europe, and the abolition of slavery was further advanced there. Off the battlefield, Lafayette was a listener and an observer, a quiet campaigner, rather than a rabble-rouser, and he noted his concerns.

Just before his arrival in the lower Susquehanna Valley nine months later, he visited the site of the Brandywine battlefield at Chadds Ford, Penna. where he had an emotional meeting with old soldiers from the battle in September of 1777. It was on that 11th of September, just after turning twenty, that he took a bullet in his thigh, necessitating a period of recuperation near Plymouth Meeting.

Following his meeting with old comrades, Lafayette stayed in Chester, Penna. and then travelled due west, on the old road to Lancaster, where he met clergymen from all the various denominations. The diary entry read:

> I have already, I believe, mentioned the remarkable fact, that at the south, as at the north, and from the east to the west of the United States, we had met with men of different manners and languages, submitting for the general good, to the same democratic government; living in harmony, in the enjoyment of domestic happiness and of public prosperity under the shield of the same institutions. Having made this observation, we naturally concluded that

neither great wealth nor diverse habits of the people of this country, are obstacles to the establishment and the administration of the republican government, which is founded on an equal appreciation of the interest and rights of all. Nothing perhaps more strongly confirmed General Lafayette in this opinion, than a view of the city and county of Lancaster, where are found men from all parts of America and Europe, and of almost every diversity of religious faith, yet all attached to the wise and excellent institutions by which they are governed.

This was around July 30, 1825 and his secretary also recorded:

On quitting Lancaster, we travelled to Port Deposit, on the shore of the Susquehanna, where we were met by a deputation from Baltimore, with whom we embarked, destined for this later city. On our way we visited Havre de Grace, a small town on the Susquehanna, and its entrance into the Chesapeake.[10]

Lafayette's route from Lancaster likely passed along the river road, passing the burnt remains of the Port Deposit (Rock Run) Bridge, the gristmill at Rock Run, and the Old Sorrel tavern. The one-story Paw-Paw church was also on this path. No doubt, the carriage or coach stopped at the square, near the stone Creswell Home, for the meeting of the deputation from Baltimore. The young John G. and Rebecca Webb Creswell were living there at the time.[11] A neighbor, Joseph W. Abrahams, who later recounted the event, was then a young man. Lafayette was entertained at the large Washington Hotel on the southeast corner of that square, and dined in Port Deposit.

Based on the journal recordings and etchings of Lafayette's visits to other towns and cities, the road through town would have been lined with well-wishers and, the main buildings and hotels, like the Commercial and Farmer's Hotel and Red Brick Row, would have been decked out with red-white-and-blue bunting for the occasion. Lafayette would have been cheered by crowds while being escorted by the militia to the

Gerry House, or rather to Magredy's home,[12] as it was at that time. Built only a decade before, it did not yet have its decorative porches. The home's very scenic setting on the shores of the Susquehanna overlooked the docks and wharves. Steamboats were enormous for their day, but not all were reliable, as Lafayette found out when his Ohio River steamboat sank.

For the Murray family, the wrought-iron railings added to the Gerry House in 1850 when it was the home of Mr. Cornelius Smith are of special interest, not least because of the skill displayed by the blacksmiths during their intricate crafting. These delicate rails embellished with the sheaves of wheat and harps were made in Baltimore, rather than in the local workshops of the industrial blacksmiths. That was a city with a market for grand gates and railings. Many modern descriptions of the Gerry House elaborate on its unique architecture and titleship, and these physical and legal details are indeed fascinating and impressive. Added to these honors are those it received when it hosted such a extraordinary man as Gilbert de Lafayette.

31. Gerry "Lafayette" House, Port Deposit, Maryland.
Lafayette and his entourage visited this home during his Guest of the Nation tour in 1824-25. Courtesy of Dorothea Henrich.

Stop Five

Downtown Port Deposit

32. Main Street Looking South, Port Deposit.
*This 1940s view of Port Deposit from the Town Square shows the busier,
commercial buildings (Sunoco Gas station and Atlantic Marker) around the
historic buildings of town on the east (left side), the Town Fountain, the Cecil
National Bank Building, Carson's Pharmacy Building, Oldham Building and
the Gerry House, and on the west (right side), the Winchester Hotel and the
Rappaport Building. This is the route the Murray girls travelled on their way to
Tome's "town school". A sailor from Bainbridge is depicted heading towards
Winchester's. Published by Del Mar News Agency, Wilmington, Del.*

The beauty of many small towns is due to their simplicity.
Civic buildings for all of the town's people lie amongst homes,
shops and businesses. The heart of Port Deposit still exists
at the center of the town. Only the interiors of the buildings
have changed.

Looking north as we left Gerry House,

The building on the left by the telephone pole was the post office– now it's the public library. To the right of the Post Office is where the road goes down and across the train tracks to new condominiums called Tome's Landing. They're along the river. Across from there, going up the hill is Tome Highway (Route 276). I remember the gas station when we walked to school. Now there's a small café – ice cream shop there.

Post Offices

The United States established a post office in Port Deposit in 1816. In the last century and a half, the post office has been located in at leastthree different places in Port Deposit: 15 N. Main (the oldest of the three, in the current fire station), 13 S. Main, and 11 S. Main. Street (its current location). The humorous story behind its move from Abrahams Building was reported in *The Cecil Whig* in June 1873.

> *The Post Office has been moved from Abraham's building to the room formerly occupied by Rambo's hardware store. This is certainly a very wise move, as peaceable persons can have some room for keeping out of the way of those pugilistic gentlemen who infest the Post Office, when the mail is being opened.*

At the time, Captain Alonzo Snow, veteran hero of the Civil War, was the Post Master, earning $1,300/yr.[1] He had been the commanding officer of Battery B formed in August 1861 in Port Deposit, which went on to distinguish itself for its bravery.[2] If Snow could not keep the peace in the post office, no one could. His command was clear, "MOVE!"

One daily duty for Ann Carolyn Murray on her way home from Tome school was picking up the family's mail at the Post Office (13 S. Main). This called to mind some personal memories by her sister, Betty:

> *When I was working at Tome, we didn't have a mail box in front of the house. We had a post box at the post office, Box 82. Ann Carolyn would pick up the mail after school and bring it up the long hill. Sometimes Charlie would send me a letter from College Park. He would print my name in big letters, rather than writing it. I remember a time Ann said, "Can't he write?!"*

Another time, he sent a collection of little seashells, sea horses and little treasures that he found at the beach. By the time they arrived, the package was reeking. Other personal letters came from Jerome. Betty explained why Jerome was away again.

> *My dad didn't enjoy working at Bainbridge [as much as] he enjoyed working on the dams. I remember going down south with him and visiting his friend, Jim Lewis, and seeing about a job. He moved back down south, while we stayed in Port Deposit. He took the car with him.*
>
> *Jerome would write to Mabelle and each of the girls from Tennessee, the years he was back there. Being a phonetic speller, we got some funny spellings, but we smiled knowing who'd written it. Once, he began a letter, "Dear Sweetie Ann", but instead "Sweaty Ann" came out from his pencil. Sweaty Ann and Sweaty Betty and the other girls really laughed.*

Ann carried a special letter in a small envelope up the hill in June of 1951. It was addressed to Mr. and Mrs. Jerome P. Murray's Box 82 in Port Deposit and in the corner was a 3-cent stamp, and there was a postmark from Stevensville, Md. The letter was written in the hand of Chloe Bolgiano, Charlie's mother.

Long Point Farm, Stevensville, Md.

Dear Mr. and Mrs. Murray,

May we write to tell you how happy we are to know that Charlie has selected Betty to be our daughter-in-law. We feel that Charles has been blessed, and we think Betty is such a sweet and lovely girl. We have grown quite fond of her. We could say many nice things about Charles too, but will only say to you now, is that, in all his life, he has never given us one moment of heartache or worry. Walt and I want to come see you as soon as Charlie's school is over. He will no doubt, be driving up to see his Betty, and we will ask him to include us on one of his first visits. In the meantime, if you are down this way, do stop in to see us.

With best regards to you both and looking forward with pleasure to meeting you.

Sincerely,

Walton and Chloe Bolgiano

Mabelle found a calling card printed with *Nicholas Charles Bolgiano, Second Lieutenant, United States Marine Corps Reserves* in the envelope. One can imagine the excitement received with that letter. Jerome was back in Port Deposit. He was always one for a wedding and besides the peonies required his attention.

The current Post Office at 11 South Main Street was decorated with a mural of the War of 1812 during the bicentennial observance of that war. With battles up and down the Chesapeake Bay, and the attacks and burning of nearby Havre de Grace and Principio Iron Works in May 1813, Port Deposit expected the same. Within sight of the river, the town built a blockhouse holding weapons and ammunition, which was in the current square.[3] Because of its level access from the river, Port Deposit could easily have been invaded. In a letter, my aunt, told this story:

When I was in the 7th grade, there was an iron cannon ball in the window of Einswaller's photo shop at the bottom of the hill. According to my teacher at the time, Miss Marion Touchstone, the British came up the Susquehanna and all the locals got in a little block house and fired on the boats. The British thought __many__ people lived there, because of all the firing and went back down the river.

This strategy thwarted an invasion of Port Deposit, it was thought. In Havre-de-Grace, though "one of the gun batteries fired a shot of defiance at them when they initially passed by" and it was said to provoke their attack. Many theories abound, including a warning from a citizen of Lapidum about Port Deposit's strong defences.

The cannon ball was found by Navy employees who were digging a culvert under the road. They were putting in a big pipe to lead the creek under the road to the river. Miss Touchstone said they thought it was a British cannon ball. I believed it. I don't know what came of it but it was put on display there for some time.

According to county historians, the British, under Rear Admiral George Cockburn, did indeed visit the Susquehanna River in May 1813. They brought nineteen barges to Havre de Grace, and started firing shot, shells and rockets.

"Ferryboats and fishing craft were destroyed and farmhouses plundered and burned. A detachment went to Bell's Ferry [now Lapidum near Rock Run on the Harford County side of the river] where a vessel and warehouse [filled with flour] were destroyed by fire, but Port Deposit ... was not visited."[4]

Is it possible to reconcile the local school-teacher's version with that of the town's historian? Maybe it was actually an American cannon ball made in Principio that was found,[5] or perhaps the schoolteacher knew best how to bring alive the War of 1812 for junior historians in this waterside town.

Town Fountain

33. Town Fountain.
Made in 1903, the Beach Fountain was received as a gift in May 1904. It stands in the Town Square in front of the Cecil National Bank Building at 6 South Main Street (now the Bainbridge Museum). Photograph taken in 2004.

Of all of the town's landmarks, the Town Fountain (1903) is the one that signals our arrival when visiting Port Deposit. "The town fountain was donated by the teacher, Miss Martha Beach, in honor of her mother, Mrs. Miranda Beach, who was also a teacher", said my aunt, always appreciative of a teacher's effort. "It is very old. There is something for everyone – a place at the bottom for cats and dogs, a place for horses on the back, a place for people, and on top, for birds."

Bank and Drugstore

The Murray girls worked in two of the businesses in the center of Port Deposit just beyond the fountain. "Aunt Mary worked in the bank some." Since that time, this distinguished building has been converted into the Bainbridge U.S. Naval Training Center Museum at 6 S. Main Street.

"The building to the right was Drennan's drug store.[6] Betty worked there in the summer—Tuesday was her day off. She got in trouble once for giving a black person a drink from the indoor fountain." An advertisement for Drennan's Pharmacy in the 1946 *Jactominian* read, "Congratulations Graduates – Our policy is to serve you to the best of our ability for a Healthier and Happier Future." To this, Betty countered:

> I know the pharmacist didn't want to serve black people with white people. A man asked for Coke and I gave it to him in a glass. We were supposed to give them water in a paper cup. Only whites got glasses. I guess I did get in some kind of trouble."

To this, Betty added:

> The pharmacist was upstairs. If men wanted confidential help, I was supposed to knock on the pipe with something so the pharmacist would come down.

The ad also read, "Prescriptions a Speciality"!

Other establishments

Standing anywhere near the town square, one wonders how the east side could have accommodated the sizeable Washington's (later Reynolds) Hotel, or the Edith Chick House, that became The American Store. In the old Murray days, there was Mr. Alonzo Barry's Picture Place and Katz's gentleman's outfitters and jewellery store. Katz's moved to Baltimore, making way for the Cecil National Bank. The Murray girls working here got to know some of the other businesses in their day like Jackson's Five and Ten, near the Post Office, Knauss's Hardware store, and Rappaport's Department Store, where they bought their socks, under-wear, and, fabric, to make the rest of their clothes.

Places they passed daily, and heard about were the Royal Restaurant, owned by Fred S. Brown, and Winchester's Hotel, Bar and Restaurant where Mary Anne Bitner's mother, Anna, and her aunts worked. In the late 1940's they advertised, "Beer and Wine and Whiskey, telephone Port Deposit 2891". Sailors, when off-duty used to go to "The Winnie" for soda and sandwiches.[7] Dorothy Bittner Luglio and Mary Agnes Bittner became partners in Winchester's Restaurant in 1946, after Dorothy took over her sister Gertrude's share. Two decades later Dot's husband, Ed Luglio, bought the whole building, bar, restaurant and hotel, and they raised their daughter, JoAnne, there. JoAnne Luglio Bierly, now Secretary to the Board of Director of the Port Deposit Heritage Corporation (operators of the Paw-Paw Museum), remembers being part of a family-run business. "I grew up in the restaurant, washing glasses and bussing tables. But there would also be perks", she said. "I had plenty of slumber parties in the hotel room atop the bar and restaurant, too!" Now Winchester's bar and restaurant has been converted into a pizza parlor, with a good view of the Gerry House.

Other establishments in the center of Port were Robert Leslie's Ford dealership, a gas station and a garage. These were replacements for the livery, carriage maker, grain deal-ers, and Express Agent, all necessary when "horse-drawn" was the order of the day. From the late 1800s, Falls Hotel and

Restaurant was operating. It grew out of the Farmers and Commercial Hotel. It had a livery for the care and stabling of horses. Members of the Falls family operated the livery, cooked, bar tended and ran the hotel. A picture of Jack Falls sitting on bench down near the livery shows the long leather straps used to tie up the horses.

The Underground Railroad and The Iron Foundry

34. Remains of Howard M.E. Chapel, former Underground Railroad Station.
Only ruined walls remain of the Howard Methodist Episcopal Church building built in 1853, which served as a stop on the Underground Railroad. This photograph was taken at the site, at the southwestern end of Jacob Tome Highway behind the Bainbridge Museum. Photograph taken in 2016.

Tales may be told someday about how the Howard Methodist Episcopal Church building provided safety and security for hundreds of people fleeing slavery. However, this is unlikely. Silence is the hallmark of a successful safe house. Members of the African-American community built the church in 1853, and being one of the northern-most stops on the Underground Railroad in Cecil County, it was one of the nearest stations to the Pennsylvania border. Guyas Cutas in January 1876 in his Letter No. 1, mentioned an Old Factory Building that stood for many years behind the Washington Hotel in Foundry Hollow. "I never knew what was manufactured there. In later years, the colored people held religious meetings in both the "Factory" and "Still House".[8]

Port Deposit was on the Havre de Grace-to-Columbia route of the Underground Railroad, with options to continue by river or road on the journey north towards the Mason-Dixon Line. Recorded William Still:

> *It was customary for the agent at Havre de Grace, bringing a fugitive to the river, to kindle a fire (as it was generally in the night), to give notice to a person living on the opposite side of the river. This person well understood the signal, and would come across in his boat and receive the fugitive.[9]*

Abandoned mills near Perryville and on the route to Port Deposit may have been used for hiding places.[10] The Havre de Grace to Perryville crossing (on ice) was used by Frederick Douglass in 1838 when he escaped bondage in Baltimore using the railroad to New York. The Susquehanna on the Penna. side was regarded as a border crossing into free territory.[11] Columbia, Penna. was a safe place, where fugitive slaves could not be caught,[12] and the river route could be taken all the way to Cooperstown, New York. Harriet Ross Tubman Davis, the famous great-escaper from Dorchester County, Maryland, avoided the Susquehanna crossing by travelling northeast through Delaware during her own and untold other escapes that she led.

The residential area near the stove foundry, at the base of Foundry Hollow Road in Port Deposit was a busy place. The census taker listed twelve households in 1870, the first census after the state prohibited slavery. Most men were employed as laborers or servants, a couple worked in the quarry. Although little has been published, given the strength of the African-American community in Port Deposit (including the north and south ends of town, at Rock Run Hollow and Still House Hollow), it is certain that residents of Foundry Hollow helped to feed, clothe and shelter those who passed through, just as members of the church did. The "unsung women" who cooked, nursed, dried clothing and sewed were the unsung heroes of the movement. The 1870 census lists the names of sixteen women living here, mostly black, some mulatto[13], "keeping house" or "working out"[14], who could not read and/ or write. Some households were comprised of families with no common last name.

There was another dimension to the silence, according to Eric Mease, who interviewed elderly people about the Colored Civil War Troops from the county.

> *When their elders spoke of the past, the children were hustled out of the room, never to hear the stories. None of the interviewees had a definitive reason for their black elders not relating stories to the younger generation. They could only theorize that the stories were too embarrassing or they just didn't want the children to hear and remember the hard times of the past. In other words, it was time to move on.*[15]

The 250th anniversary of the establishment of the line of demarcation between Maryland and Pennsylvania, which came to be the coveted finish line for many seeking freedom occurred in 2017, and this Underground Railroad site, like many along the border, passed an important milestone, as their histories are inextricably linked.

The Armstrong brothers founded their stove foundry just north of the Creswell House in June 1854, although an iron foundry was present since 1828, operating "with motive power by water."[16] Armstrong and Co. Stove Foundry (later J.C. Bibb, Jr.) employed 38 people in 1880, but this is probably an underestimate of workers in this industry. It was a demanding place to work, as all foundries were from the physical stresses of pouring hot iron into molds to make parts for the cast-iron stoves, and cookware. In England, foundry workers developed health problems and had shorter life spans. Some of the workers in the foundries in Port Deposit became disgruntled, and resentful from poor management practices.

From *Port Deposit In Verse*, published in 1881:

> *The foundry owned by Bibb & Son,*
> *Who make their home in Baltimore,*
> *Is yet by Billy Armstrong run,*
> *Who was interested there before.*
>
> *He and brothers business started,*
> *And he continues foreman still;*
> *His brother suddenly departed;*
> *Not having time to make a will.*
>
> *The property of course was sold,*
> *And Bibb & Son came here to buy;*
> *Offered the position him to hold*
> *And he concluded for to try.*

But lately there has been a change,
Which does not give the men much joy;
Another foreman now does manage,
Mr. N. Pramer, late of Troy.

They cannot now do as they please,
But will have to work more steady,
If to do so they should refuse,
He'll have other workmen ready.

The Baltimore *Sun* covered the tragic death of James Armstrong, one of the owners, on July 5, 1878. James ran a branch of the firm at 60 Light Street, Baltimore until pistol shots killed him in the foundry's showroom near the post office in Port Deposit. Under the headline "A Triple Tragedy. Shocking Affray at Port Deposit", the article described the serious casualty on the Fourth of July. This was the story of a worker, William Magill, a cousin of the Armstrongs who had lost some legal battles against the firm. "He turned to violence, it was thought because he was never compensated for his inventions, because he then lost his job after the lawsuits failed, and because he was humiliated with the pawning of the belongings of his Port Deposit home of two decades."

Thomas Armstrong, another brother was shot in the leg and later Magill turned a gun on himself, to become the last of the three tragedies. The bleeding bodies were taken into Frazer's drugstore, and then later Thomas was carried to his home across the street, where his leg was amputated by attending local and city physicians.

A jury hastened for the inquest the same day consisted of notable townsmen and office-holders, including William A.

Long, H.C. Nesbitt, John W. Malone, William J. Stebbings, Joseph E. Reynolds, Adam Peeples, George A. Vannort, Joseph R. Miller, John McClenahan and Joseph W. Abrahams, Justice of the Peace. By then, it was all over. This was another sad case where the need for reconciliation was neither recognized nor acted upon. In any event, the iron foundry workers of Port Deposit became unionized, with 75 members of the Iron-Moulders' Union of Port Deposit, No. 211, marching in that first Labor Day parade in 1890.

A son of Thomas Armstrong was a teenager when his father was shot. He was a clerk for the firm and worked his way up to become vice-president. David R. Armstrong became a popular mayor for Port Deposit for many years.

Stop Six

Old Creswell House– 1 Center Street

35. Creswell House and Richards' Hospital.
The stone house on the left was the birthplace of Honorable John A.J. Creswell. Doctors who later owned the house built a hospital extending to the right. Photograph taken in 2017. Courtesy of Dorothea Henrich.

The walls of this most beautiful stone dwelling at 1 Center Street have witnessed the childhood of one of the most important men in the history of the abolition of slavery. The old, stone part of the house itself sits high up on the north-west corner of Center and Main Streets, and pre-dates Lafayette's visit to Port Deposit. Colonel John Creswell, who served in the Revolutionary War (1775-1783), lived further up the hill, on the Hope and Anchor Farm estate. His son,

John G. Creswell, married Rebecca E. Webb from a Quaker family in Southern Lancaster County, and they had three girls, Lizzie, Sidney and Caroline, and then a boy, John A. J. Creswell, who was born in this home on November 18, 1828. This son, the third John Creswell to live here, became the most famous. Dickinson College in Carlisle, Penna. knows him as "The Forgotten Abolitionist".[1] Some noteworthy facts about his life are included in the *Founding Fathers* section.

The town walking tour guide lists this house as "Mrs. Murphy's Hotel". Rebecca Webb Creswell became Mrs. Murphy, when she remarried, long after John G. Creswell passed away. Her husband, Dr. Thomas L. Murphy, a highly educated doctor, was a sought-after public speaker, and they ran a tavern in this large home.

Three more doctors would have their home and clinic in this building. Dr. Clarence I. Benson originally saw patients in the brick building to the right of Gerry "Lafayette" House. Later he moved to the Old Creswell House, building a hospital section at the back. Later this became the domain of Doctors G. Hampton Richards, Senior and Junior. Senior was a surgeon, and he enhanced the hospital wing off the back, which was converted into apartments.

Here is where the Murrays went to see the doctor. Jerome Murray once brought his dog to Dr. Benson's. Neither Jerome – nor his dog, were familiar patients of Dr. Benson's.

I think the reason Daddy was healthy all his life, was because he worked and walked. He liked to hunt and most of his life had hunting dogs. They would walk many miles out in the country.

On one hunting trip he had his Irish setter with him. They were on the hills north west of Port Deposit. If you walked towards the river, you would be over the granite quarry.

Before he could be stopped, the setter ran forward and over the top of the quarry, which was a 200 ft. cliff. He plunged down the slope of the quarry and landed on a ledge. Daddy climbed down and got his dog. The dog's leg was broken.

He took his dog to Dr. Benson. Dr. Benson set his leg. Now the interesting thing about this is, that later Dr. Benson would be the one to deliver three of his daughters — Mary, Betty and Patsy. Can you imagine a general practitioner today setting a dog's leg?

The next time Jerome went to the doctor's it was to take his wife, Mabelle. In June 1927, she gave birth to their first child, Mary Mabelle, in the hospital addition in the back.

Founding Fathers

36. Portraits of John A.J. Creswell and Jacob Tome.
Courtesy of the Library of Congress and the Port Deposit Heritage Corporation.

John A.J. Creswell (1828-1891)

An incisive lawyer, persuasive orator and efficient businessman, John A.J. Creswell was born in 1 Center Street, Port Deposit. He was educated just eight miles away, at West Nottingham Academy near Colora, which is the oldest boarding school in America. He became extremely important to President Abraham Lincoln and the Pennsylvanian

Representative Thaddeus Stevens in the 1860s. Some said that politically, he blew with the wind and that his support of the Radical Republican wing of the party that pushed for unconditional emancipation was the most convenient course of action at the time. A thorough study of his formative years at college, his early years at the county seat in Elkton as a lawyer, and his actions later as U.S. Senator and then Postmaster General under President Ulysses S. Grant, are proof of his principled and unwavering stance for abolition of slavery and equality for blacks, even when the state swung towards the Democratic-leaning South in 1867.

Since John A.J. Creswell's father died when he was only a toddler, his mother raised him; many credit her with influencing the development of his character. Rebecca herself was a property owner, owning 340 acres in 1877 and claiming an estate value of $60,000. While land was the embodiment of the Creswells' great wealth (the ferry being the source), it brought them many protracted legal entanglements. Ultimately, Rebecca Creswell Webb's lasting legacy would not be through her property, but through her son.

John A.J. Creswell's election to Congress as a Representative in the pivotal poll of November 1863, the alliances he formed, and his keynote speeches in the House before the vote for the Thirteenth Amendment in January 1865 (for the abolition of slavery) and in the Senate before the Fourteenth Amendment in June 1866 (giving citizen's the right to vote and equal protection under the law) have been chronicled by Osborne and Bombaro of Dickinson College,

The choice of John A.J. Creswell to help set the process in motion was an excellent one. Who better than an influential Border State southerner to explain the need for abolition within the Union? Few had done more to maintain Maryland for the Union than Congressman Creswell. And few had played

a more central role in fashioning Maryland's new state constitution, which the voters had just approved, banning slavery within their borders. Creswell is not well-remembered today, but was a powerful symbol of the nation's dramatic movement toward abolitionism in the 1860s.

Lincoln's Emancipation Proclamation of January 1, 1863, brought great consternation to the Maryland state legislators, but also great power. Lincoln would continually make appeals to those who could help to bring about both the abolition of slavery, and the preservation of the Union. President Lincoln wrote to John A. J. Creswell in March 1864, *"I am very anxious for emancipation to be effected in Maryland"* and immediately again, *"It needs not be a secret, that I wish success to emancipation in Maryland"*, just in case there was any confusion.[2]

Mirroring action in Washington D.C., a major move of the Radical Republicans of Maryland was to enshrine in state legislation the freedom of any enslaved man who enrolled to serve in the Union Army, and to support the "bounty", a monetary payment that would eventually be paid to them or their former owners. The (white male) voters of Maryland ratified the new constitution, which outlawed slavery, in the autumn of 1864, with the soldiers' votes making the difference.[3]

Later, when state legislators swung in the opposite direction and Creswell had lost much of his influence, he could rely on the Amendments of the U.S. Constitution, to shore up the progressive efforts towards reconstruction. These were a guarantee of freedom and equality. Creswell, in the face of considerable hostility, upheld his principles, and was indeed the keynote invited speaker to the celebrations of leading African-Americans in Baltimore in May 1870 after the passing of the Fifteenth Amendment (upholding the citizen's right to vote).

It is fitting that the community of Foundry Hollow came together to aid the building of the Howard M.E. Church and the northern migration of African-Americans, in the shadow of Creswell House.

Jacob Tome (1810-1898)

Jacob Tome, the town's philanthropist, became a relative of the Creswell family through marriage. His first wife was Caroline Webb, and she was a niece of Rebecca Webb Creswell.[4] Mr. Creswell and Mr. Tome's lives were very different, but you might say they shared a philosophy. The philosophy was to help those less fortunate than themselves.

Jacob Tome was a financier of projects and said "Save your pennies and they'll turn into dollars." His pennies turned into a million dollars by 1870. Initially attracted to settle in Port Deposit by the prospects of lumber trading, he took a job as a clerk around 1833 with a timber firm of Downey and Montgomery, and then learned the tricks of the trade under the guidance of Mr. David Rinehart, a timber merchant with considerable wharfing along the river. The young Jacob waited until late spring or early summer when the river was glutted with timber, before buying the arks as a source of wood.[4] He also bought sawmills, and learned about bookkeeping and banking through night school in Philadelphia. After work, he rode horseback to Perryville, took a train to Philadelphia and attended night school there, only arriving back in the morning.

Through his local businesses, his land and transportation investments, Tome eventually made a fortune, and with his success, he brought banking to this boomtown, setting up the first bank in his own home, and later becoming the President of Cecil National Bank. There was an interesting caveat. After he left $1,000 on the railroad train to Philadelphia in the early 1870s, some would say that Jacob Tome not only specialized in making money, he also specialized in losing it. Tome was a generous, yet modest philanthropist, and his biographer, a contemporary at Jacob Tome Institute wrote,

Few men have been characterized by such modest estimates of themselves as was Mr. Tome, and any attempt to place him on a pedestal, would provoke a smile. He was absolutely free from insincerity in any form; and yet no man was more truly cordial and sympathetic. There was a vitality in the grasp of his hand, and a warmth in the expression of his face which indexed his feelings.[5]

When his $2,500,000 endowment to the Port Deposit school was announced in January 1889, literally hundreds of newspapers across the country from the *Kalamazoo* (Mich.) *Gazette* to the *St. Albans* (Vt.) *Daily Messenger* ran notices of it. On January 25, he told the *Baltimore American*, "I have lived for fifty-six years in Port Deposit and made all my money there, and I think it is only right that I should spend some of it there for the good of the people who have helped me along. ... I know what it is to fight your own way in life, and, if I can, I want to make the road a little smoother for others." He elaborated further when to the *Philadelphia Inquirer* published on January 28, Mr. Tome said, "I want to give poor boys and girls a chance. I know what it is to fight your own way in life, and if I can I want to try and make the road a little smoother for others. My purpose is to erect the necessary schools and workhouses for five hundred children. It is not to be a boarding school or a charity house. What the Johns Hopkins University is to the mind the Jacob I. Tome [Institute] shall be to the hand."

Tome had in mind that sound and practical vocational training, even beyond the normal school years would be of great benefit, and the papers talked of his "Industrial Schools", "Business Schools" and "Seminaries". At his funeral at the Tome Memorial M.E. Church in March 1898, Bishop Hurst reflected, "Every child in Port Deposit ought to carry in his memory for the rest of his days, how much a boy can do; how much a young man can do by getting himself into proper relations to attain a noble and pure business career."

Politically, Jacob Tome held elected and appointed positions in the Maryland state assembly and legislature between 1861 and 1867, during a very critical period spanning the American Civil War (1861-1865) and the post-war Reconstruction. The crucial revisions of the Maryland state constitution to abolish slavery happened during this period.

Tome belonged to a faction of the Union Party called "Unconditional Unionists" who wanted immediate emancipation of Maryland's slaves without compensation of their owners. In 1860, 4.5% of Cecil County residents were slaves, although there were far fewer than this in Port Deposit and areas bordering Pennsylvania. By that time, in word and deed, Jacob Tome was against slavery, but back in 1850, he, in fact, registered his ownership of two slaves, a 25-year-old man and a 21-year-old woman. One or two other wealthy businessmen in Port Deposit also owned slaves. It is likely that his association with John A.J. Creswell, and his support of the growing Republican Party of the north, led to his total conversion in the freeing of his slaves and his conscience. Like Creswell, Tome could then afford to be unyielding in his public and political stance.

An interesting personal fact about Jacob Tome is that after his first wife died, he tied the knot with a much younger woman (Evalyn Nesbitt was 45 years his junior)! In his photographs, he appears to be a very serious person, but one cannot help wonder if Evalyn teased him a little bit about being the "older man". Although neither Jacob Tome nor John A.J. Creswell had any surviving children,[6] through their commitment to duty and sacrifice, they gave birth to freedom for the otherwise enslaved, and wisdom to the otherwise uneducated.

The Town Clock

37. Port Deposit Town Clock and Water Witch Fire Station.
The fire station occupies Abrahams Building across the road from the clock. Photograph taken in 2004.

Within a stone's throw of Creswell's House, my aunt asked, "Have you ever seen the town clock?" The town clock is a practical reminder of the town's effort to commemorate key anniversaries. The grandchildren of Jerome and Mabelle Murray will never forget the nation's Bicentennial in 1976. Five granddaughters and one grandson from the 5th generation of Murrays were the last act in Port's Bicentennial Parade during the weekend of September 10-12, 1976.

It all started a year before, when "prairie" was in style. Mabelle and Patsy purchased yards of red gingham fabric, plenty of each sized check: 1/8″, 1/4″, 1/2″ and 1″. From this, my younger cousins, and my little sisters and I, received dresses uniquely suited to each of us, in size, style and red-and-white check combination, the bodice, skirt and belt all made with different sized gingham. Mabelle was an expert and she knew how to flatter a body shape or personality with each piece of clothing she made. Some girls even got bonnets.

We had no inkling of what our aunt was dreaming up. She always bought us "cousin shirts", but we had already received our red, white and blue tank tops for the bicentennial summer. Somehow or other, Aunt Patsy orchestrated her sisters to bring the grandchildren from Harford, Prince George's and Lancaster counties for Port's celebration of the bicentennial. We were to bring our dresses, which was a worry for those who had grown, but that did not matter. We had so much fun with the Murrays, that we would do practically anything for them.

Mabelle also made Davey a blue gingham shirt and this together with a straw hat, and a yet unidentified prop, made up his costume. We started at the quarry, after the penultimate act, ambling down Main Street, the girls initially unsure if they should be doing anything special. The younger four girls set off, and I, being the self-conscious "granny", complete with granny glasses, walked behind. We were nothing without Davey, though, who stole the show. People watching would have seen the red gingham dresses bobbing along, but then came a little boy, aged eight-going-on-forty eight, in his blue shirt and jeans, smiling and strolling with a long blade of straw grass sticking out of his mouth, working tooth and jaw! This is what drew the chuckles that day, as Main Street, Port Deposit became an appreciative stage for this budding Hollywood actor-director and set builder!

Besides the dresses in my mother's closet, only two

mementos survive. One is a Polaroid picture of Maggie "Micheline Perugino" Fox in her colonial – prairie-style mob-cap and breeches, standing in town. Maggie, game for anything, a daughter of Italian immigrants, born in Dirt Bank and living on South Main St., was proof of the American dream at its very best.

The other souvenir is a wooden nickel commissioned by the Heritage Corporation for the occasion. Stamped on one side was a jumping rockfish, and there was careful hand lettering, "Elizabeth Elaine Murray Bolgiano", a testament to Patricia Ellen's regard for her sister, the town and the special occasion.

The Water Witch Fire House – Abrahams Building – 15 N. Main

"In front of the fire station is an old fire bell", my aunt continued. "The Fire Company is called Water Witch because *many* years ago they bought an old engine from New Jersey and it had "Water Witch" on it. To spare expense of changing the engine's name, they became the Water Witch Fire Company." In June of 1873, "The Port Deposit News" column of *The Cecil Whig* reported that the town "was treating itself to a new fire engine after an impressive demonstration of the Water Witch engines."

My aunt told us that the building was Abrahams Hall and it was the first place in town where Catholics held services. According to Fr. John J. Abrahams, this was a home of the Joseph W. Abrahams family, and Catholics worshipped here in the middle of the nineteenth century.[7] Given reports in the paper, one wonders if they could really restore the decorum of Alonzo Snow's post office.

A train of twelve [railroad] cars literally packed with passengers, arrived from Baltimore on the 4th of July to attend the St. Teresa picnic, near Port Deposit. It is represented to have been the most drunken crowd ever here. Several fights were had, and blood flowed freely.[8]

Abrahams Building was also the polling place in Port Deposit for many years. The Murray girls remembered the presidential elections of 1948 and 1964, the first elections following the deaths of Presidents Franklin D. Roosevelt (April 1945), and John F. Kennedy (November 1963).

Betty was a nineteen-year-old sophomore at the University of Maryland when she first voted in November 1948. Voters had to travel to their home polling station, so she took a Greyhound bus from College Park to Perryville. Uncle Paul Murray, then 50 years old, drove down to meet her and take her to the polling station. She remembered going in the booth, and marking an X on the ballot paper next to the name of Harry S. Truman, Democrat. He was running to be elected president in his own right, following his swearing in as president, after FDR died of a cerebral hemorrhage. *"People didn't want to change horses in the middle of a stream"*, she said. Give'm-Hell-Harry's surprise upset of Republican, Thomas A. Dewey, famously led to the embarrassment of the newspapers who announced that Dewey had won, and it made Betty happy about her mid-semester trip home, too.

Patsy used to take Great-Aunt Bertha Foran Murray to vote in the Abrahams Building. The day, November 3, 1964, would be the last time Bertha would vote in a presidential election. "Aunt Bertha always voted Democrat but was suspicious of Lyndon B. Johnson (Dem.) getting into office so soon after JFK was assassinated. *I just couldn't go against my father*, she said later, though he had been dead a long while." Her father, the blacksmith, Thomas Foran, was a typical die-hard Irishman and Democrat and it was certain that Aunt Bertha had voted for LBJ, who became President in the greatest landslide victory-to-date in the history of the United States.

Our tour continued down Main Street and as we passed by the Old Banking House at 20 N. Main Street, we were reminded that Ann Carolyn and Mary Mabelle Murray went to Junior School there when it was Jefferson Hall. Tragically, it burned in a fire that raged and raged in 1969. It has since become a stylish apartment building, and as it was a hot day, residents were sitting on the steps, so we did not stop.

We also passed by the distinctive granite based "Swiss Chalet" at 68 N. Main Street, which was built by the McClenahan Quarry Company as their headquarters in 1894. Just three years after the historic strike, they constructed a vault with thirty-inch granite walls! Their office at the time of the strike when James Duncan was the negotiator was located in the redbrick municipal building at 53 N. Main Street.

At Paw-Paw Hall at 98 N. Main Street, we paused. Its unique history and part in the preservation of the town, and vice versa, was well known. The separate worship stall for African-Americans and the role that enslaved people played in its construction were perhaps unknown to my children, but there were other Murray places to see, so we pressed on, pledging to return.

38. Paw-Paw Museum.
Built as the first church in Port Deposit in 1821, the building later served as Odd Fellow's Hall, which burned. Its replacement also became derelict, and was restored by the townspeople and the Port Deposit Heritage Corporation. Photograph taken in 2012. Courtesy of the Port Deposit Heritage Corporation.

Stop Seven

Middle Town

St. Teresa's Roman Catholic Church – 162 N. Main Street

39. St. Teresa of Avila Catholic Church.
Built in 1866, this photograph was taken in 1980. Courtesy of Rev. John J. Abrahams III.

My aunt pulled up into the parking lot next to St. Teresa of Avila Catholic Church at 162 N. Main Street and turned off the engine. There was no question this place was important to the Murrays. She would have been preaching to the converted. Instead, we heard some stories from the older days.

Six generations of Murrays have attended since it was completed a year after the Civil War finished. Mary Jane and I are still sitting in the "Murray pew", third from the front on the right. Parishioners used to pay "pew rent". I always joke that I want to use any "left over". Betty can tell a story about when the priest would read out the yearly collection returns and the Murray family would be the only one with $ and ¢s.

In the old days, families were supposed to pay pew rent monthly in advance, and that pew effectively belonged to your family. If it was unpaid, due to death or arrears, the pew could be taken away and given to a paying customer. Jerome objected to the pew rent, and so paid in dollars and cents. The claiming of the "left over" pew rent was a topic of conversation. Maggie Fox's grandparents from the Ciarlo side paid pew rent, allowing a granddaughter to sit in their pew.

Many family members were married in St. Teresa's. When Jerome wanted to marry Mabelle Thompson in 1925, they were married in the rectory because Mabelle was Protestant. Thankfully, times changed. Three of Jerome and Mabelle's daughters were married in the church itself; Betty and Charlie in September of 1952; Mary Mabelle and Pierce in September of 1955, and Ann Carolyn and Dennis in August of 1962, in what seemed like a fairy-tale wedding. Even my marriage received an American blessing in the summer of 1989, after getting married in Lancashire, England.

On each occasion, the Murrays held the receptions at their family home out on Tome Highway, with Mabelle making sandwiches. The exception was when something fancier was ordered for Ann's wedding. Auntie Ann and Uncle Dennis were probably the first to involve all their little nieces and nephews, one way or another. My mother reminds me that I (aged 2) spent the reception stepping on the bride's dress, but it was nothing to her.

Sacraments, like the sacrament of Baptism have always

been special events in the life of Catholic families. Jerome, Mary, Betty and Patsy were baptized here, Jerome's parents and siblings also. Before they went down south, Mary received her First Communion and Confession at St. Teresa's. However, because Catholic churches were scarce in the south in the 1930s and 1940s, the younger sisters missed their "staging posts", their chances to receive their sacraments as they grew up. One Sunday, when out driving, the family passed by a Catholic church. Jerome suddenly stopped and got Ann baptized. The housekeeper acted as her godparent.

The Murrays could not find a southern church with CCD, or catechism classes, and Patsy and Betty had to wait until they were ten and 14 to receive First Communion. They stayed with a family in the countryside of Harriman, Tennessee for two weeks, "played with people we didn't know, slept in a bed in their living room with their daughter doing the same thing, and rode in the rumble seat of a jalopy!" Finally, after all this, they received the three C's – Confession, Communion and Confirmation, all at the same time.

Daughters of the "Tall Irish" Murray family, Aunts Sarah and Ellen Murray, lived directly across from the church at 159 N. Main Street in Port Deposit. Sarah and Ella came as a package, you might say, and like sometimes happens with twins, their names merged into one. They were literally called Aunt Sara'n'Ella by nieces and great-nieces for their whole lives. Church life would feature very strongly in Sara'n'Ellas' lives. The Murray family album contains a formal portrait of Father Arnd, at the time of his ordination in April 1893, so they probably became like family to him, as he had lost his own mother. Father Arnd lived in the rectory across from them at 164 N. Main Street from between 1893 and 1901.

40. Rev Peter Paul Arnd.
Father Arnd, from Baltimore, was ordained in April 1893, and came to Port Deposit later in the year.

Before Aunt Sarah died in 1952, she and Ellen arranged for a black-painted, wrought iron fence to be placed around the Murray family plot at Mount Erin Cemetery in Havre de Grace. Later the caretakers had to take down the fencing so they could cut the grass, but left the posts in place. After Ellen died in 1955, the priest, Father William Couming, said, "We won't hear such rosary beads clicking again!"

But Ellen would not be the last Murray to say the rosary. Still waters ran deep in Jerome. In February of 1950, after her twenty-first birthday, Betty received an envelope at her dormitory in College Park, Maryland. It had a return address of 435 Watson Street, Camden, Tennessee. It was from her father.

Dear Lovely Liz,

Happy Birthday to you. Happy Birthday to you my dear. All twenty-one of them. And to help you celebrate I went to early mass and to communion. I also said some prayers for you and hope you have many more happy birthdays. On the way back from Mass I stopped in Waverly and mailed a letter to your Maw and thanked her for the long lean lanky piece of crying female that she presented to me 21 years ago today, and who far beyond my expectations turned out to be our now Lovely Liz. I mean every word of this – No Irish Blarney. For as you know – I never got to kiss the stone, but may have inherited some natural <u>instink</u>. If I was not home to help you eat your cake was there spiritually. Guess Jane and Ice were there, Ice was there as your nurse 21 years ago too. Betty, you don't know how lucky Mabelle and I have been to have four daughters and all healthy. Of course I would liked to have had a boy. But I always said if they were well and no deformities that was all I could ask for. So I still see we were blessed in many ways.

Breakfast was late this A.M. almost 11. I had to leave at 10 of 7 am and did not get out of church till after 9:30. So it was after 10:30 before I got back. About 12:30 I went down to Swensons and we worked on his boat frame. He is going to build a boat like the one we built in Watts Bar. We have the frames made and center board put up to use as a frame. They brought John Henry's supper up to him and stayed and talked. Paul and Bobbie had dirty feet and now I will have to clean the floors again. Kids don't care a hoop.

My stove sure is a dandy large size.

Glad to hear you are not going to worry about lessons. Did you eat your peanuts at U of MD or take to Port? Don't know why that check should worry you. This is the only time you will ever be 21 and maybe only time I may be so generous that is have the cash. Keep it all. I do not have or take time to be lonesome. .. Betty, I am even saying the rosary daily. (Ain't I good?) Sara and Ellen must of put the finger on me.

Nite Lovely Liz,

Jerome

Roman Catholic readers may recognize Jerome's long fasting before receiving Holy Communion – three hours was the minimum requirement in those days, according to the rulebook. Jerome would have fasted from mid-night or more likely suppertime, until his breakfast at eleven. So, a breakfast for a Catholic on a Sunday back then really was just that. One positive benefit was that the late breakfast often became a brunch.

True to form, the town and parishioners celebrated the 150th anniversary of the founding of St. Teresa's Church, on July 17, 2016. Patricia Ellen Murray, had high hopes of joining in, and she did in a way, everyone thought. Father John J. Abrahams and Father Jay R. McKee, the pastor, were to lay their rosary beads on her coffin only a few days later. Fr. Abrahams in tribute said that "the passage of Patricia was a sign of God's Grace given to the church by the Murray Family of many years."

The "Tall Irish" Murray Home

159 N. Main Street

41. The "Tall Irish" Murray Family Home.
The Joseph and Mary Ellen Donnelly Murray family lived here from the 1860s-1870s until 1955. The house was given to the Murrays by Mr. John Keaveny. Photograph taken in 2010.

Across from the church at 159 N. Main Street is the home of my great-great-grandparents, the "Tall Irish". Joseph Murray from County Galway and Mary Ellen Donnelly Murray from County Mayo, lived here.

Joseph and Mary Ellen had eight children in thirteen years, including Aunts Sarah and Ellen, and William Joseph Murray, who was the father of Daddy. One baby died in infancy.

Joseph and Mary Ellen started a family in Port Deposit with Baby James Edward, who was one in 1860. They had been married in St. Patrick's Church in Baltimore in December 1857. Families of this size and spacing were just as common among the rich, as they were the poor, among the black as among the white, and among the immigrant and native alike.

Daddy's father was William Joseph Murray. His father, Joseph, worked with a Mr. Keaveny. Mr. Keaveny's horse kicked Joseph Murray in the head, in a stable, I think, and killed him. Joseph was in his late thirties when he died. Mr. Keaveny gave this house to Joseph's widow, Mary Ellen.

The story of John Keaveny (sometimes written Keaveney) is remarkable in its own right. He also was an Irish Catholic. Full of vigor and ambition, he married Ellen Young from Delaware, and they came to Port Deposit before 1860, initially raising their first child, Mary born in 1857. Their children were of similar ages to those of the "Tall Murrays", and they owned multiple homes in that area of North Main Street, probably living on the cliff side of the street on property that would become the land for the M.E. church.

Mr. John Keaveny was an innkeeper in 1860, aged 34, but then he began amassing property—some homes, but mainly acreage. The land, his energy and his business acumen were the key to his success. The land became necessary for the construction of the Port Deposit to Columbia Rail Road. In 1870, his personal estate was reported to be $10,000, and in 1880, he owned more than 100 acres, probably continually selling and buying more. In the early 1870s, the *Whig* reported weekly on the progress of Messrs. John Keaveny and J.J. Buck, his business partner and a granite dealer.

Mr. Keaveny started out as a contractor for the railroad and once the railroad was completed, he became a contractor for McClenahans' quarry.

Mr. Keaveny, along with a Mr. Michael Brady, also manufactured nitroglycerine and Vulcan powder, a kind of dynamite composed of nitroglycerine, sodium nitrate, charcoal and sulphur, at their works near Port Deposit, until around 1876, possibly when the railroad was completed. These chemical compounds, together with the availability of rip-rap stone from Buck's Quarry up in Rock Run, and Keaveny's land would have allowed Keaveny and Buck to avoid the middlemen. They constructed the roadbed themselves, leaving the laying of the rails to the railroad companies. In early 1872, the *Whig* reported that Keaveny and Buck "were making progress down Conowingo creek to intersect the bridge". In August they "were finishing their contract to Peach Bottom. They appear to know how to work Susquehanna Stone." This left Keaveny reliant on the workers, the wagons and the horses, and these, it turned out, were not entirely under his control.

A horse plague struck North America in the autumn of 1872 and was to affect up to 7 million horses in the United States alone. In late November, it was reported, "the disease is spreading rapidly in this vicinity. All horses disabled and contractors could not move anything. Almost all businesses were affected."

This pandemic was due to an equine influenza virus, which caused profound weakness and coughing. All travel and business stopped, not only in Cecil County, but also across North America. Nearly all horses recovered, but the disease did not peter out until the spring. In Port Deposit, this was a winter they did not forget. The river was frozen from early December until the end of February 1873.

For the Murrays, the fatal blow of the horse's hoof that killed Joseph would not be forgotten either. Although there are no records, it was thought to happen around 1873. Records do not exist of his death or burial, and the family may not have had the money to announce it in the *Whig*. Accidental deaths were frequent. People of all ages drowned in the river, a child even fell out of a tree and died, and fatal carriage accidents occurred on a regular basis in town. Railroad and quarry workers were also particularly susceptible to life-changing accidents or instant-death. Mr. Keaveny's generosity to the Murrays in giving them the house across from the church was appreciated. Mary Ellen had eight children to raise, and the church community would rally around her, too. Her baby girl, Ann Elizabeth, died within just a year or two of Joseph's death. Who would know what was to lie just around the corner for the Keaveny family either.

For a time, John Keaveny seemed to be unstoppable. In 1871, this Irish immigrant was elected as a town commissioner, like the other successful and wealthy businessmen of the town, and by 1878, he became the President of Commissioners. On March 18, 1875, during the winter flood and ice gorge that rose so quickly, the *Sun* reported, "Mr. John Keaveny of our town was in great danger of being overtaken by the flood, but his good horse saved him." Sadly, he was not as robust as he thought. In 1880, he still owned more than 100 acres, but in March 1883, in only his 57th year, he suffered from a debilitating stroke. His funeral was at St. Teresa's Church at 9 o'clock on Saturday, the 31st, and his funeral cortege travelled to Mount Erin on the 10.55 train from Port Deposit. It "was attended by all the best people of Port Deposit and vicinity".

Mary Ellen Murray was one of the best people. She would have known how Ellen Keaveny felt faced with five children to raise, from Kate, aged 18, to the new baby Blanche, who was only a few months old. The Keavenys had a niece from Ireland to help so that at least was something. Ellen would move back to her home and family in Wilmington. Their luck ran out with John, you might say. Ellen, her parents, her niece and most of their children would only come back to Cecil County to be laid to rest next to John and the babies who did not survive.

The Murray family story resumed. *William was about twelve when his father was killed. He then became an apprentice to a blacksmith, and at 16 years became a "fully-fledged" blacksmith. I have his forge and anvil on my porch. Some tools are in the cellar and garage. He worked at the quarry. He made and sharpened tools.*

William also found a bride. On December 6, 1884, William Joseph Murray, aged 23, the second son of the "Tall Irish" Murrays from 159 N. Main, married Mary Ellen Murray, aged 25, the second daughter of the "Short Irish" Murray family from Rock Run. The wedding took place at St. Teresa's and Father J.L. Barry was the priest. The bride's parents, John and Bridget Bannon Murray, and Bartholomew Kelly, a stone cutter friend from Rock Run, officially witnessed their marriage. William J. and Mary Ellen were planning to set up their own house in Rock Run, and William would soon start buying land.

In addition to the mother of the bride, Mary Ellen Donnelly Murray, who was 46, the Main Street Murray household consisted of James Edward, 25, who was a moulder at the stove foundry; William J., the groom; Sarah Jane, 21; Jack, 19; Mary Ellen "Ella", 17; Thomas Jerome, 15; and Patrick Henry, who was 13.

From the bride's family who were living in Rock Run Hollow, were Bridget, and John, both aged around 50, and sons

Thomas, 24, and John Patrick, 17, who worked in the quarry with him. There were also their eldest daughter, Margaret, 22, a seamstress; Elizabeth, 17; Jim, 15, who would marry Bertha; Catherine, 12; and Joseph 7. Mary Ellen, John, and Bridget became grandparents a year later.

Things were not rose-colored for all of the Murrays on Main Street, though. Pressures on the family were publically revealed less than two years later. Jack, the middle son, got into big trouble. When Jack was about twenty-one, he stole a watch from a Mr. James Farr, who was an Irish farmer, later a fisherman. The story hit the *Sun* the next day, on September 25, 1886:

> *Port Deposit, MD – Sept 24. - Last night Jack Murray went up to James Farr, who was standing in a store, and it is charged, grabbed his watch from his pocket. On Farr attempting to regain possession of his watch Murray knocked him down. Constable White [clerk in the circuit court] arrested Murray, but before he could get him to the lockup he broke away and escaped. In the melee the watch was dropped and recovered by the owner.*

This is where a "stiff upper lip" learned from the old country may have come into play, that handy way of ignoring another's embarrassment or shame. No doubt, there were cold shoulders from some, though. Jack disappeared off the radar for some years, but within fourteen years he was living back home on North Main Street. Aged 43 in 1910, he worked as a linesman with the telephone company. Later, he became an electric company linesman, and then worked for a telegraph company, during which time he boarded on S. Main Street. Perhaps Jack lived closer to the edge than some. As for Mr. Farr, he must have seen the misdemeanor for what it probably really was, a cry for attention. The Farrs' beautiful daughter, Nellie, became a Murray herself, marrying the youngest Murray, Joseph, from Rock Run!

When Jack died, Aunts Sarah and Ella "didn't know what to do with him". Somehow, they hadn't planned on Jack coming back home. They had become a little distant, but family was family, and being family, they laid him out in their living room, and prayed the rosary.

Sarah and Ella worked hard to keep the family name going. "When I was young", Patsy told us, "Great-Aunts Sarah and Ella were thought to be career women. Aunt Sarah was a nurse at Tome School on the Hill. Aunt Ella washed people's hair and did hot oil treatments in her own shop. And sewed." They both sewed, but Ella was regarded as the real seamstress.[1]

With their income, they built a refined and interesting home. They bought a San José Mission wall clock from the Company Store just before it closed, and made Irish lace. Sarah crocheted her monogram "S" in a "filet crochet" lace pattern in a damask linen towel. Irish crocheting techniques were used to make doilies, too. Two tools of Ella's hairdressing trade survived: her old metal curling irons, the kind you warmed over a stove or hot coals, and a 1920's ivory-colored celluloid hair receiver, that she used for her hairpins. Her old Davis sewing machine with a treadle base and spare needles was also salvaged.

The deed proving their ownership of their home, promised since their father's death in the early 1870s, was finally granted to Ella and Sarah Murray by the Keaveny family in December 1929, after Ellen Keaveny died. Sara and Ella, perhaps relieved of this insecurity, bought lot 19 on N. Main Street that had Odd Fellow's Academy (now Paw-Paw Museum) in April 1945 from the Jacob Tome Institute, almost 24 years after the purchase was instigated. What a proud acquisition! It was property that had passed through the Creswells, and Tome, and his Institute – all of the two generations of Creswells appearing in person for the transfers of this property from 1829 onwards – and their deeds measured the size of the trees, as much as the generations of their family, but relied mainly on the positions of the immovable stone: "Beginning at a stone contiguous with a sycamore about one perch above high water mark on the North East shore of the Susquehanna River and running thence North forty two degrees and a half West six feet to a stone ...."

Books passed down from this Murray family house may be revealing. Mrs. Charlotte Newell, an English teacher at Tome, gave the poetry book *Links of Memory* to Mrs. Mary Murray in December 1912.[2] This is intriguing because Mrs. Murray's children would have finished school by then. Mrs. Newell was actually a young widow herself, and she boarded in town with her children and other teachers, possibly in Jefferson Hall. Perhaps it was an exchange of kindnesses or help with children that led to the gift. Another book *How to Write Letters* (1880) probably belonged to Jerome's Uncle Thomas Jerome (1869-1942), who moved to Elkton and became a store keeper and politician.

A fascinating book, just 6.5 x 9 cm^2, bound in calf-skin and wrapped with floral end papers was embossed simply *Don't*. Appleton & Company, New York, published this tiny gem in 1887. It was given to Patsy as a teenager in the 1940s, by Aunt Sara'n'Ella with a note, *When you learn all your "don'ts", you'll know all your "do's"*. It was an etiquette book for "avoiding improprieties in conduct and common errors in speech" and it contained frank advice for every room and social situation.

In the Drawing Room:

> DON'T always make yourself the hero of your own stories.

> DON'T be sulky because you imagine yourself neglected.

For Womankind:

> DON'T forget to thank the man who surrenders his seat in the omnibus.

> DON'T, young lady giggle or affect merriment when you feel none. If you reward a bonmot with a smile, it is sufficient. There are young women who every time they laugh cover their faces with their hands, or indulge in some other violent demonstration to whom we say, don't.

And perhaps a favorite reminder for the gentlemen:

> DON'T Expectorate … One should not ever spit upon the sidewalk, but go to the gutter for the purpose.

Finishings and furnishings such as these of the Second Generation Murray girls might have tipped them over into the category of being "lace curtain Irish" a slightly derogatory label for some in the Irish-American diaspora. (The Kennedys also rose from being "shanty Irish" to being "lace curtain Irish".) However, the Murrays were not snobs, and neither did they put on airs. "Sara'n'Ella" had their own humor and genuine grace. After Jerome's association with all the dams, they got a joke going that Mary, Betty, Patsy and Ann were their "dam nieces". As a sign of the times, they would say to those visiting, "We've had a hold-up", to which was explained, "There's the hold-ups!" and pointed to the wash line in the back yard with trousers hanging to dry. Recipes also exist for their dandelion, beet and parsnip wine.

The aunts often gave Daddy some homemade shaving lotion at Christmas. Perhaps their homemade peppermints and candied citrus rind. Mary was invited to come and learn how to make peppermints. They wanted to show her, saying "It is the devil to make."

Aunt Ella's Peppermints

2 c. sugar
2/3 c. water (preferably hot)
1/4 tsp. cream of tartar
1 egg white
5 drops oil of mint (no more than that)

Directions: Stir sugar, cream of tartar; add water until dissolved. Keep stirring until it starts to boil and cook until it forms a soft ball (more towards hard ball rather than soft). Do not stir after it starts to boil. Beat egg white in rather large bowl, not too much stirring or it would make the candy meringue like. When candy makes a soft ball, remove it from the stove, add oil of mint, and let it stop bubbling. Then gradually pour it into the beaten egg white, beating it first with an egg beater until well mixed. Tint with green food coloring, if desired. Then, with a large wooden spoon, slowly stir until thick and creamy (loses shiny luster and holds shape). Drop on waxed paper. Makes 2 ½ dozen.

The Murray family connection with the Keavenys continued for some time after the latter left Port. Perhaps the table of misfortune had tilted somewhat. Ella collected rent for Mr. Keaveny's daughter, Blanche, from Keaveny-owned homes near them on North Main Street. Blanche was a student nurse, age nineteen, living at St. Joseph's Orthopedic Hospital in Philadelphia in 1920. Then she moved back to Wilmington, eventually nursing her mother. At the time Ellen Keaveny died, aged ninety-one, she and Blanche, 38, were renting a home. Ellen Murray's letters and the checks from the rents of Mr. Keaveny's properties in Port Deposit probably provided the Keavenys with their last real connection with the town.

Aunt Ella was the last one at 159 N. Main and died there in 1955. Daddy and his brother Joe settled up the estate. I have a number of the items Daddy bought or received. They had written in their instructions that Patricia was to get the candelabras. Later Blanche Keaveny, Mrs. Keaveny's daughter, wrote me that she was to get them. I still have them!!

Whenever I drive through Port Deposit, I always feel torn. I have to first locate St. Teresa's church on one side of the road, and then quickly move my glance to the Murray house on the other. I have never been inside, but through the stories and mementos, I know who lived there.

The Old Sorrel Inn

158 – 160 N. Main Street

42. The Old Sorrel Inn.

This photograph of the coaching inn was taken in 2014.

The distinctive building to the right of St. Teresa's at 158 – 160 N. Main Street "was a stage-coach stop years ago", we were told. The mail coach had a scheduled stop here by 1803. This inn, "The Old Sorrel", was probably originally called "The Sorrel Horse" based on a document listing the route and schedule.[3] The regular route from Lancaster to Port Deposit stopped here, the same route that Lafayette would have taken on the Lancaster to Port leg of his journey in 1825.

The Old Sorrel may also have been English; a Sorrel Horse Inn & Public House, dating from the fifteenth century, is still operating in Suffolk County, on the southeastern coast of England. A "sorrel horse" is a red-copper brown-colored chestnut horse, usually ridden western-style, as the old Pony-Express mail horses were. This inn had different purposes over the years.

"Great-Grandmother Mary Donnelly Murray sold things such as shaving lotion, baked goods and peppermints in a little store here. I do not have proof", said my aunt, "but I always thought that it was in the basement of this house, which was right across from her front door." One of the town's documents states that a bakeshop operated on the south side, with an oven built into the wall. The Port Deposit Historical Society's application to the U.S. Department of Interior, also describes this house with its granite basement that opens onto the sidewalk. The Irish were used to doing a small amount of shopping for their Sunday Lunch on their way home from church, as portrayed in the movie, *Brooklyn*. Besides, Father Arnd might have paved the way for Mary Ellen to sell her baked goods after Mass, provided he would receive some samples.

By 1789, established mail routes in Cecil County replaced express mail, carried by fast riders on horseback. For the "Pony Express" rider, carrying money at predictable times was a guaranteed recipe for robberies though. The stagecoach riders and their guards carried arms as a necessary deterrent. Payday robberies would not end when the stagecoach was phased out. Just up the road, Black Bottom was a notorious local place for a payday holdup.

Black Bottom is a three-mile stretch along the Susquehanna River between the Conowingo Dam and Port Deposit. When the Dam was being built, during the middle-to-late twenties, Black Bottom was at its peak. People of questionable character were living in the wooded area along the road. I suppose some were working at the dam. The others --- who knows?

The word was out that there had been holdups along the road. The day was pay day, and my daddy and Uncle Paul had been paid, and they were carrying others' pay. They were on the way back home in Uncle Paul's car, travelling through Black Bottom.

Suddenly, several men were standing across the road with the notion of committing a holdup. Uncle Paul gunned the motor while Jerome hollered, "GET OUT OF THE WAY, WE'RE COMIN' THROUGH." Uncle Paul headed toward them. They scattered, and that was the end of the holdup.

I don't suppose any of the young children in Port Deposit would even know the location of Black Bottom. A few of the old-timers would. My Aunt Icelene would hurry home from a visit to my mother, not wanting to be near Black Bottom at dark.

The Union Hotel is located in Black Bottom and during the construction of the dam, it was in fact a brothel, according to the Doolings, who restored and reopened this famous restaurant. Its notoriety now extends to its food and drink, and a visit to this 18th century log cabin tavern is well rewarded.

The Sice and Foran Family Homes

202 & 200 N. Main Street

43. The Foran family and home in the aftermath of the 1910 ice gorge.
Mary V. Foran is on the front porch , and Bertha is by the tree. John, Annie and Thomas Foran are being photographed in the vacant lot on the river side of the road. The porches and sidewalks are full of people talking or strolling on a Sunday. Foran Family Album.

People have a homing instinct for the quiet of a church, the warmth of a community, or even a cathedral of trees. For immigrants especially, church communities also provide family. Dozens of Catholic families came to Port Deposit from post-Famine Ireland. Two of these were the Sice and Foran families. Their eventual location near St. Teresa's was probably deliberate.

Joe Sice and Jerome Murray knew each other from the

quarry and as neighbors in Rock Run. Old Joe Sice, a stone cutter at the quarry, and his son, Young Joe, both registered for WWI, like Paul Murray, and his older brother, Joe. Young Joe Sice and Paul were just eighteen then.

Young Joe Sice married Alice Bittner[4], born in 1903, who was the second oldest of eleven siblings. They had four boys and three girls, including Francis, Peggy, Ann and Henry, names heard in the Murray household as classmates of the girls.

Young Joe Sice's grandparents, John and Mary Elizabeth, emigrated from Ireland (Mary as a little girl from Mayo), just as did Jerome's (and Bertha Foran's next door). Like Jerome, Joe also did not graduate from Tome. Two years were enough for Joe. Jerome possibly got Joe into working on the dams with the Murray boys. They were employed by the Rundel Corporation, and carpooled with Norman Bannon, a young cousin of the Murrays. Patsy recorded this story of one commute.

> In the middle twenties, Daddy, Uncle Paul, and some other fellows from Port Deposit worked at Safe Harbor, Pa. They took turns driving their cars. One morning after a storm, Norman Bannon took his turn to drive. In the car with him were Daddy, Uncle Paul, and Joe Sice. Up River Road they went. The storm had caused some trees to fall into the road.
>
> Norman Bannon said, "Watch this Studebaker take this tree." It did, going through the branches. On a repeat performance, however, things did not go so well.
>
> As my daddy said, "We hit the business end of the tree." I don't know how the others reacted, but according to the story, Joe Sice was squealing in the back seat!

I do know that the car's radiator was damaged, and they had to return to Port Deposit to get Uncle Paul's car. Off they went again. However on the road to Quarryville, Pa., trouble struck again. The car was going around a sharp curve. To their surprise, a rear tire came off the car and rolled across the field. I don't know how the others reacted, but according to the story "Joe Sice was squealing in the back seat!"

Upon recovering the wheel, they fastened it on by taking a lug nut from each of the other wheels. When they finally got to work, they found out that there had been tire thefts the evening before. This led them to believe that someone had been interrupted in the process of removing the lugs from Paul's rear wheel.

There were many more trips to Safe Harbor, but none so exciting as the day they hit the "business end" of that tree.

The Forans were next-door neighbors of the Sice family.

The house on the right of the Sice's belonged to Bertha Foran Murray. She married Daddy's Uncle Jim, the youngest boy in his family. He worked in the quarry as a blacksmith. Bertha went to Tome School and graduated in 1902. I wear her class ring. We always visited her as teenagers, and she gave us $2 for Christmas. In later years I took her to the grocery store. She and Jim dated about twenty years. They couldn't marry straight away as they were caring for her father and his mother.

The Foran family lived in a number of different houses in Port Deposit, but possibly their favorite home was in what was a large, wooden, clapboard house at 200 North Main St. Here, the Forans experienced the devastating 1910 ice gorge. One photograph from its aftermath is of three generations of Forans, the two blacksmiths, Thomas and his son John, and little granddaughter, Annie Foran, dressed in their Sunday best. They were standing on the riverside of the street, while women had gathered to talk on and around their porch. Bertha, then in her late twenties, was in an apron busily to-ing and fro-ing. Other photographs from the Foran family album show the layers of ice piled up high like an ice wall, lining the way to the Company Store. Their neighbor, John Carson, was pictured there.

Dr. William C. Carson, a 77-year-old widower that year, was a druggist in Port Deposit. He was responsible for the Carson Pharmacy Building in the Square. Dr. Carson and his three sons, William, John and James all practiced pharmacy in town in 1910.

Bertha, the youngest of the third generation of Forans in Port Deposit, was born in 1883. She was the main caregiver at home. A naturally shy and serious girl, she was also kind and affectionate. Bertha took commercial courses at Tome; later, she became an office cashier in the Company Store, a bookkeeper in the department store, an office worker in Perryville and a stenographer in the lumberyard. It was during the time she commuted to Perryville on the steam train that the poem *Gilligan* commemorated.

Jim Murray loved Bertha, and bought her an exquisite diamond engagement ring and a gold armband. Bertha was fifteen years younger than Jim was, and although time was moving on for them, they could not get married. Jim was occupied caring for his mother Bridget, his real estate and political concerns and his own blacksmith shop at the quarry as well. After years of poor health, Bridget Bannon Murray died in 1918, and Thomas Foran in 1921. However sad that was, it gave Bertha and Jim a chance to be married.

Bertha turned thirty-nine and Jim was fifty-four when they were married on February 27, 1922. Amongst other family, friends and parishioners at St. Teresa's Church that Monday were his nephew, Joseph Murray, aged 38, and her niece, Annie Foran, aged 27, who was working in a Philadelphia department store by then. They were the official witnesses, and Rev. Miles J. McManus was the officiating priest.

Jim and Bertha moved further out to a farm on the northeast side of Rock Run for a while, installing her sister, Mary Virginia, next to them. They had a radio, and other luxuries, and life was good. They became godparents to little Betty Murray, Jerome's second daughter.

Jim continued blacksmithing, as he turned the corner into his sixties but time would not be on their side. Jim and Bertha spent longer being engaged than as a married couple. Jim died in 1932 when he was sixty-four. Bertha and her sister moved back to Main Street.

Bertha became a devoted aunt to Jim's great-nieces, just as she had been with her brother's daughter, Annie. Annie, 15, then living in Baltimore, stayed with Bertha during Port Deposit's Centennial celebrations on the July 4th weekend in 1913, when "every building in town [was] a mass of colors", and three days of athletics, baseball, historical talks and a parade were capped off by evenings of carnival and fireworks.[5]

<hr />

I visited Aunt Bertha at her home at 200 N. Main Street as a four year old. My sister and I recall walking into a very dark street-level basement of a house. Bertha was in a dark color, but we were not scared. A friendly hand reached out and took mine, and I found a dime in it. Later on, my aunt gave me Bertha's small, wooden crucifix and black-beaded rosary, hand-held gifts, surely precious to her.

Bertha moved away from town after marriage and lived on the Murray farm up Rock Run Hollow. She always wanted to get back in her town house. She finally did, in a sense, by renting an apartment in the downstairs level of 200 N. Main from Alice Bittner Sice, Francis and Henry's mother. Bertha died in that house. Francis, from next door, found her lying on the floor.

It was June 1965, and Bertha was 82. She didn't have far to go to the church. The gravestone she shares in the Catholic cemetery in Havre de Grace, bears the simple inscription, Jesu Merci.

<hr>

We could see chrysanthemums in bloom on the hill terrace behind the church and cliff-side homes that Sunday in late summer. Sometime before, my son, Ben, spotted a sign at a church in Lancaster. "Mums for Sale! There's Mum's for sale!" he shouted. In England, "Mum" is the most common nickname for "Mother". My mother laughed and laughed at Ben's excitement that mothers could be bought or sold.

Finally, we left this area of old "Middle Town", and as we were driving to Rock Run, we spoke about a very special person whose home was on the cliffside. It was Hannah Taylor whose vocation was to take clothes from anyone to provide to anybody else. Hannah would carry on a tradition of giving that the town was known for, and she was one of many who closed the gap between the races. When my own home fills with clothes to sort, I think of Hannah for inspiration.

Stop Eight

Rock Run!

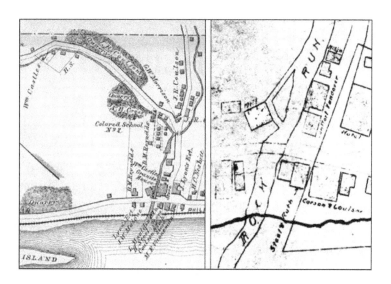

44. Maps of Rock Run from 1877 and 1856.
Left: Map from An Illustrated Atlas of Cecil County, Maryland, 1877 from The Sheridan Libraries of The Johns Hopkins University; Right: T.A. Solomon's 1856 Map from Port Deposit Heritage Corporation. The proximity of three (shaded) quarries to Rock Run can be seen left, while the diversion of the water supply to the mill is illustrated right. Artwork by Robert Longuehaye.

Even today, Rock Run Hollow has a touch of mystery about it. The water-carved valley follows the course of the water's flow as it descends, again and again, until it descends to the river. *A Gazetteer of Maryland and Delaware* in 1904 recognized these two inseparable features. There was a listing for

Rock Run "the village in Cecil County on the Philadelphia, Baltimore & Washington Rail Road", and Rock Run, "the small tributary of the Susquehanna River at the mouth of Rock Run Village". The village became a fixture of cartography, when in 1821 commissioners appropriated funds to lay a road "from Elkton to the Susquehannah Bridge at Rock run, and a road from said Susquehannah Bridge up the river, to intersect the Great Road from Rock run towards Lancaster, near Evan's Orchard."[1] Five or six homes in Rock Run, as well as the businesses and gristmill completed the Rock Run village in 1856. This was to change drastically as the neighboring quarry expanded its operations.

The lumberyards, quarries, foundries, mill and farms at Rock Run Hollow all provided work, and later people found jobs at the railroad, the hotels, boarding houses and stores that sprouted uniquely around each other. A veritable medley of families found a home in the village, close to work and each other. Those who were able to buy their home usually stayed for generations.

Rock Run is most easily located by the stone gristmill standing at the corner of Granite Avenue and US 222. The mill was built circa 1725 and operated under water, then steam power. A 32.5 to 50 foot fall of water could drive the four-foot paddle wheel at 18 horsepower, revolving 5 times per minute. The internal machinery of the mill consisted of four pairs of burrs to grind the grain, and an elevator, conveyors and a hopper to produce 500 barrels of flour, 67.5 tons of cornmeal and 20 tons of feed per year.[2]

45. Rock Run Mill.
This gristmill was built circa 1725, and was operated by John Steel, as one of the first millers. It was originally powered by water from Rock Run. Photographed in 2017. Courtesy of Dorothea Henrich.

By 1877, the map of Election District Seven showed about thirty-five homes in Rock Run, distributed along both arms of a "Y". Going northwards away from the river on the left fork, was Race Avenue,[3] leading to Liberty Grove, and a sizeable quarry run by J.R. Coulson. On the right side of the fork, was drawn an extension of Granite Avenue, called Rock Run Road, which meandered northeast, right along the course of the creek.

Some of the earlier established inhabitants were J.C. Waters, R. Burns, and P. Grace, as well as P. McNulty, a dairy man, T. Kelly, a stone cutter, and Wm Burlin, a quarry foreman. Some men were Marylanders, like Wm Burlin, Messrs.

Harris and Shade, and, St. Clair, the miller. Others came from Delaware or Pennsylvania, Virginia or North Carolina. By the end of the 1800s, the majority would be migrant people who settled in Rock Run. There were the African-American families, the Griffin, Vance, Henry, Hopkins, Cooper and Lee households; the German families, Gerhauser and Smithson, who was the butcher; the Italian families, Gilardi and DeMaro; and the Irish, the Forans, Kellys, Duffys, Peoples, McNultys, the Bannons and the Murrays. The family of J.W. Abrahams, the Justice of the Peace, lived further out their fork of the road, and he would come to know this community intimately in his careful census recordings and legal dealings.

Roughly, half of the householders in Rock Run rented, and the majority of these families and workers were transient. Intermarriages between neighbors led to a more established neighborhood. Some Rock Run families took care of children from other families, even adopting them in one instance.

In 1900, nineteen African-American families lived in Rock Run out of 50 households, and during peak quarry years six of these households took in two or more boarders, with thirty boarders in all. The vast majority of boarders were working men. By 1910, the number of African-American families had grown to 34 out of 60 households. This expansion probably reflected the great migration northwards, as well as the industrial growth in the town. There were also at least three veterans of the Civil War living in Rock Run, the African-Americans, James Cooper, who farmed, and James Collins and William Cornish, who quarried. They served in the U.S. Colored Troops for the Union Army.[4]

First or second-generation European immigrants from Ireland, Italy and Germany comprised 65% of the white households in 1900 and 1910. Of these, three or four households took in two or more boarders. There were also fifty-five people living in Dirt Bank, with about equal numbers from different backgrounds.

Cross-generational, extended family members living in the same home was typical. This way of living was just as common with the McClenahans and Tomes as it was with the Griffins and the Murrays. It is clear that it was economically advantageous for this to happen and may have reflected a trend nationwide.

Male heads-of-households and older boys from about age sixteen invariably worked if able, regardless of ethnicity. Such was the work ethic that a number listed their occupation as doing "odd jobs", or even being "on the street". Listing an active job status was obviously important to their sense of pride and security. After all, many of the immigrants were not naturalized citizens, and the African-Americans, like the Irish, wanted to avoid scrutiny at all costs.

For the women, there was an odd dichotomy. Even in 1910, it was rare for white married women to list they were working outside their home, or to be holding any other occupation other than "keeping house", or even occasionally being "at home". William McClenahan's widowed mother-in-law however had her "own income", while his widowed mother, Laura McClenahan, was a "capitalist". Without exception, though, the black women, married, mothers, or not, were laundresses, washwomen, cooks or servants. It is quite possible that most white and black women were actually doing the same work.[5]

The wealthy of the town and country had live-in servants and nursemaids, such as Hannah Bannon of Rock Run. Nevertheless, many more cooks, laundresses, coachmen and other servants worked in "private homes", commuting to the homes of their employers, as did Mary Ellen Murray, before she became Mary Ellen Murray *Murray*, that second Murray being her ticket to independence.

The late 1800s was a period of great opportunity and growth, but with the terribly demanding and physically stressful work, and the growing numbers of mouths to feed at home, many men would drown their sorrows on a Friday evening in one of the three saloons in Rock Run, including Jerry Morris's bar and lodgings. For the Irish, alcoholism would be a problem. According to Jerome, his father and his father's father had a problem with liquor. They were not alone.

Coogan in *Wherever Green in Worn* discusses this most intractable of problems for the first generation Irish in English-speaking countries. They suffered more depression and mental health problems than others did, due in part, he concludes from the miserable situations that led to their emigration and the hardships they endured.[6] Jerome did not have funny stories to tell about his father squandering his hard-earned money in the Rock Run saloons on payday. Jerome, consequently never touched a drop of liquor in his life, nor did his offspring — at least not under his roof.

Bottled-up feelings would not die out with first-generation Irish Catholics. Individual priests working in the community did what they could to alleviate suffering and to help families. Maggie Fox told Nancy Roberts that Father Arnd helped families settle in Dirt Bank. In addition, "with the help of the local priest a scholarship was secured for Villanova College" for her older brother, Frank, a boy who entered school in America without speaking a word of English, but graduated from J.T.I. in 1929. Fr. Arnd also planted poplar trees throughout Port Deposit.

Opportunities for women to socialize outside of church or schoolyards might have been rare. Good neighbors and families were so important. One Harford County woman, Mira Thompson, an aunt of Mabelle's, used to teach Irish crochet.

The close-knit communities of Rock Run and Port Deposit had many advantages over more integrated urban areas, with families and work opportunities both close by. Those who were far from home would recreate "home" in their new location.

Isaac B. Rehert, who settled on a farm in Rock Run in the 1950s, quoted his Estonian-born mother-in-law, someone who found a home on his farm:

> "Everyone", she said, "keeps some memory alive that to him means home. To some it is the image of a mountain, or of the seashore. A friend of mine keeps an old children's book that she used in school. Some become patriots-in-exile, or join the church of their fathers." She stopped and faced me again, then continued. "I have these gooseberries. When I work here among these thorns, I forget the strangeness of the world around me and imagine that I am at home."[5]

Many could argue that this was really America at its best. Notwithstanding those freezing Susquehanna floods, residents were blessed with jobs, food and freedoms. Within the class system that existed, there were undoubtedly clear social and economic hierarchies, and separatism existed. Progress towards a more perfect equality for women, black, and foreign people could be measured in steps – steps to equal, if separate schooling, churches, stores, even baseball teams and musical bands. Though far more steps and some very painful ones were required, the period from 1870 to 1910 was a truly unique time in Port Deposit. The Rock Run Bard, who published *Port Deposit in Verse* (1881), captured this tone in his characterization of this hollow and the town.

The Rock Run Bard is believed to be the fifty-four year old merchant, William Alrich, from Wilmington, Delaware who may have kept the Granite Store in Rock Run. In 236 stanzas, he described the town, its businesses and people through the social hierarchy, starting with the McClenahan Brothers at the Quarry and ending with the grocer, Thomas Ringgold. Never critical, Alrich made astute observations, but sprinkled his praise liberally. He saved his highest praise for Thomas Ringgold.

Thomas Ringgold, the African,
Keeps grocery and provision store;
Is an accommodating man,
Should have been mentioned here before.

He sells alike to black and white,
To rich as well as to the poor;
His customers he all treats right,
And turns none away from his door.

He does not ask their former state,
Neither their present condition;
To sell his goods at a fair rate,
Is the extent of his ambition.

And then when he shall cease to sell,
And from business retire;
His Lord will say to him done well,
Thou faithful servant come up higher.

The words throughout this ballad, capture the essence of Port Deposit more than any other document, and bring the vibrancy of Rock Run itself to life.

"Short Irish" Murray Home

36 Granite Avenue

46. Home of the John and Bridget Bannon Murray Family in Rock Run. *Photographed in 2004.*

The square-shaped one-story wooden clapboard house at 36 Granite Avenue was a home that John Murray and his wife Bridget, and young family moved into Rock Run in the 1850s.

This was the home of John Murray and Bridget Bannon Murray. He was from Co. Monaghan and she from Cork. They were Daddy's maternal grandparents, the "short Irish". They had 8 children. Our connection is their daughter Mary Ellen Murray Murray, who also had 8 children. John was a laborer at the quarry, and his four sons and three son-in-laws were all quarrymen for awhile. The house was rented first. Bridget had a brother that lived in the neighborhood.

By the summer of 1860, when Bridget and John were in their early thirties, their children were Thomas, Margaret and Mary Ellen, aged 4, 3 and 1. John rented this house for $99 per year, with the option to buy it after so many years, which he did. The family grew – John, Lizzie, and James came along in the following decade. The next two, Catharine Theresa and Joseph Andrew, born in 1872 and 1874 did not survive to full adulthood. Only one more baby boy came, and they named him Joseph, too.

Catharine passed away in January 1895, aged 22 with the epithet, "A patient sufferer at rest". It was clear that Catharine would require long-term care because John's will provided specifically for her and Bridget. Their middle son, John Patrick, was also not well. Many quarrymen developed silicosis, especially the blasters and stone cutters, and the silica particles caused breathing problems and lung pathology, which could take a life, as it had some of the other fellows at the quarry, like John Perugino around age 53. John's lungs were in bad shape, too. He overheard a doctor saying, "He won't live to be twenty". Just seventeen at the time, he "decided to run away and live a little", according to his great-grandson. Moving up river to Pennsylvania, John Patrick secured a different kind of work and lived for sixty-two more years. He worked for decades as an iron moulder for Keeley Stove Co. in Columbia, and married Mamie from Safe Harbor. They raised a family and put out many extensions in York and Lancaster Counties.

All three of John and Bridget's daughters opted to stay nearer to home. After marriage, two stayed in Rock Run: Maggie who married Jim Grace, the quarry's hostler; and Mary Ellen, who married William Joseph Murray, the blacksmith. Lizzie moved just around the corner to N. Main Street, after marrying a stone cutter, Aloysius Wentz. Lizzie and her husband lived in one of Jim Murray's houses next to the Carsons. She, from the "Short Irish" and Uncle Pat from the "Tall Irish" became Jerome's Confirmation sponsors.

Uncle Jim Murray was the second youngest son of John and Bridget, and a brother of Mary Ellen. He continued to stay in this home to care for his mother as Patsy elaborated further:

Later Daddy's Uncle Jim inherited it and married Bertha Foran. They moved to a farm further out on Rock Run Road. (Uncle Joe & Aunt Ione lived there later.) Uncle Jim rented this house [at 36 Granite Avenue] to his nephew Jerome and his new wife, Mabelle, so Mother and Daddy started there. Mary was a baby there.

Another Uncle Jim, Uncle Jim Grace to Jerome, was the head horseman at McClenahan's quarry at the time he married Maggie Murray. He had stories to tell his family and neighbors in Rock Run. At times, he was in charge of three hundred horses at the quarry. Heavy brewery horses as well as fire-horses were brought back from horse-buying trips to Baltimore. One tale from Jerome has it that "when former fire-horses were in the lot, the workmen had to make sure the horses were back in the stables, eating and quieted down before the quitting time whistle blew or they would run off and scatter stones and wagons everywhere. They'd really have wrecks there", he said.[8]

After the ice gorge of 1910, the town's newly formed Ice Gorge Committee thought of ways to warn the townspeople much earlier in advance of impending flooding. They devised a plan. It involved rigging up a steam siren at the quarry coupled to 115 pounds of steam. Watchmen would patrol the river shores nearby. "When the ice reaches the quarry", the plan went, "five blasts of the whistle will be given as a warning to the residents to flee to the hills."[9] Now can you imagine the panic this gave to the horses?

Cyrus Ferguson, who lived down low in the hollow near the mill, was a blacksmith, and his boarder Patrick Smith was a farrier, attending to the hooves and shoeing the horses. Patrick Smith knew about temperament, and the temper of a kicking horse was a bad as his landlord's, which you will hear about shortly.

Maggie Murray, Jim Grace's wife, was a seamstress and raised a family of three children, Mary B., who was a steam laundress, before marriage, Catherine J., who was a cashier in the general store, and John Murray Grace, who would join the ranks of the other Murrays amongst the forges and anvils.

Bridget also had her brother, John Bannon, and his wife Sara nearby. John and Sara were gentle people and good society for Bridget. After John passed away in 1911, and Hannah and Alice went to N.Y.C. as dressmakers, Sara lived at what was then 104 Granite Avenue with her son John, a Penna. R.R. conductor, and daughter Elizabeth. Andrew, her other son, was living next door at number 103, and he and his son, 17 year old Norman John, in 1920, were engineers: of a stationery engine (a fixed steam engine, usually for manufacturing purposes, such as at the Rock Run Mill) and a R.R. locomotive. Dolly Bannon, the wife of Andrew, also raised daughters, Sarah May and Helen Louisa.

Their cousin, Thomas H. Murray, the eldest son of John and Bridget, would have solicited votes from old John and young Andy Bannon when he ran for town commissioner in February 1905. He ran in a "heavily contested" election (when William McClenahan was the candidate for Mayor), and was elected with 189 votes. Bartholomew F. Kelly, the Murrays' friend from Rock Run, got 251 votes. These two young Irish quarrymen in their forties represented an important constituency. The local options laws governing the prohibition of sale of alcohol were beginning to bite and together with the downturn in river trade, some hotel and tavern owners from Rock Run were pulling out.[10] These issues, the impact of motorized vehicles and the perennial issues of flood prevention and aid were also of concern to residents.

In 1910, fifty-nine male workers from Rock Run were working at the quarries. They comprised 74% of all working men and boys from Rock Run and included eight stone cutters, three blasters, two-wheel cart drivers, a fireman, an engineer for a hoisting engine, the farrier, hostler and teamsters, general laborers, and of course the blacksmiths and their waterboys! To accommodate all of these, there were the boarding houses, either built for the purpose, or provided by families who housed local workers. In 1900, when 91% of the workers from Rock Run were at the quarry (99 out of 109 total working men), there were thirteen boarding houses in Rock Run. Today this seems incredible. Farther up Race Avenue, some of the large homes slowly disintegrating into the gorge seem to be clinging to their glorious past.

Before John Murray died on February 16, 1894 at the age of 62, he and Bridget went to the photographer. Individual portraits were made of this proud and hard-working couple. After decades of nest building, their house was nearly empty.

47. John Murray and Bridget Bannon Murray.
This photograph was taken by the Havre de Grace photographer Geo. W.C. Brown around 1890.

The Graces by then were in a predicament about their future, as motorized vehicles slowly replaced the horses and their hostler. A decision to bring the Grace family under the roof of 36 Granite Avenue would help both families. Bridget's health declined and in January 1916, Jim was granted Power of Attorney for her, as she was declared "feeble in body". There were eleven grandchildren then side-by-side at 36 and 38 Granite Avenue. The grandchildren were Bridget's mission, as Jerome discovered.

Stop Nine

Jerome Murray's Boyhood Home – 38 Granite Avenue

48. The William Joseph and Mary Ellen Murray Family Home.
Photogtaphed in 1990 by P.E. Murray.

When William Joseph Murray received the deed for this wooden paneled New England-style saltbox house and two lots from Walter J. and Martha Hall for one thousand dollars in May 1886, little did he know the lives or times that would be played out here, but it was something he wanted and needed, especially as little Nellie was already six months old. It was quite an achievement for William, who was robbed of his childhood to become a man of the family at the age of twelve.

This house at 38 Granite Avenue was the home of William Joseph Murray (from 159 N. Main Street) and Mary Ellen Murray Murray after they got married. They were born in Port Deposit and she grew up next door at number 36. They had eight children. Our connection is Jerome Patrick who grew up there. I can remember Grandmother Murray some. She died when I was seven. Uncle Paul lived there and continued to live there until death. This is where I remember visiting when we were young. At that time there was a picket fence with big boxwood bushes and sweet peas on the fence.

William Joseph, who bought this house, was born in 1861 and went by William. His nieces and nephews also referred to him as Uncle Will. His oldest son was also William, my Uncle Bill, who came to stay with me at Mockingbird Hill for some time when Uncle Paul died.

The grandchildren at 36 and 38 Granite Avenue would grow up under the watchful eyes of Grandmother Bridget Murray. There was a vacant lot between the two houses, and she would look out of her window at the children playing. From time-to-time when things were getting a little wild, she would come charging out to holler at them. Jerome would later say that "she was the meanest thing" and she called him "a hellion".

Explorers and Odd-jobbers

Jerome was not unruly, but like most boys, he craved outdoor adventures. He was a middle child, in a family of eight, which had its advantages. He and his brother Paul would roam far from Granite Avenue for their adventures.

When Daddy and Uncle Paul were young boys, they used to like to explore the nearby countryside. One day they found a dead skunk. They decided to find out what made a skunk stink.

Using their pen knives, they cut the skunk open. Inside they found a small sack of yellow liquid. They dropped it into the creek, and it floated on the water like butter. They found out why a skunk stinks!

When they got home, you can imagine how they smelled. Their mother made them bury their clothes in the back yard. I imagine there was no more skunk surgery.

In the springtime, the same pair would scout around looking for birds' nests. Once they got some baby crows. They intended to split their tongues. There was a myth at the time that this would allow them to talk. People recognized the crow's power of communication.

On what is now Dr. Jack Road, there are two old pine trees. Those trees were always good for pigeon's nests. This particular spring, they took home some young pigeons. It was their plan to train them.

One evening at supper, their older brother Joe, began to say, "Coo-Coo." They looked at their plates at what they had supposed to have been chicken, jumped up and ran to the back yard. Their suspicions were true. The pigeons were gone.

Their interest in animal training did not end with the pigeon dinner.

It is the nature of a cock rooster to fight. The more he is encouraged, the more he'll fight. When Jerome and Uncle Paul were boys they decided to train a cock rooster. They spent some time teasing him and getting him to charge them and fight.

During this time, their dad was working away from home on a job. One day on his return he was in the back yard preparing to feed the pigs. He bent over to get the pigs' food. The cock rooster was ready. He attacked their dad with his spurs. That was the end of the cock rooster and cock fighting.

Perhaps these experiences were the birth of Jerome's later sayings, "Don't count your chickens until they're hatched, catched and latched in the pen" or "Kill two birds with one stone". He also was often heard to say, "A bird in the hand is worth two in the bush!"

Life was not all about play. Even as a young boy, Jerome was an "odd jobber". One summer job as a child was being the delivery boy at the Company Store and another during the school year was carrying lunches. Two uncles on his father's side worked at the stove foundry. It was Jerome's job to pick up two baskets from his other Grandmother Murray (from Main Street) and carry them about three-quarters of a mile to Bibb's foundry located up Foundry Hollow Road (Jacob Tome Highway). Each basket was heavy, containing jars and plates with hot meals for the uncles. He got five cents per lunch and earned 15 cents per day. If his school lunch break was running short, he would stop into the store near the bank and invest in two cents worth of chipped beef and two cents worth of cinnamon buns. Sometimes he would go to the bakery on the way home and buy a cookie.

One of his worst jobs was a summer job as a "scratcher" at the foundry. This was a hot job, and it involved cleaning out the metal molds with a wire brush. Later on, he worked as a "bag-tie-er" at the bomb-cum-fertilizer plant at Perryville.

The burlap bags he tied up were "bone bags" full of stinking bone meal. Working as a water boy in the quarry was more enjoyable. At one stage, he and his brothers ran the Murray Garage down at the bottom of Rock Run.

Of course, the result of this work experience was that along with his in-built ingenuity and the skills that he earned in the mechanical workshops at Tome School, he could do practically anything – electrics, plumbing, painting and carpentry, laying bricks, stone or cement blocks. He paid for all of his bills, saving his parents from the cost of his dentistry. On the leisure side, he bought a hunting dog and decoys, built a boat and made his own nets.

A Riverside Way-of-Life

49. Andrew and Normon Bannon perch fishing on the Susquehanna River.
This photograph was taken around 1930. Courtesy of Brenda Tipton Knopp.

A boat came into its own during times of flood, as well as for river sport. From January 21 to 23, 1910, when Jerome was thirteen, Rock Run flooded.

"During the sleepless night of Saturday, January 22nd, the whistle of the quarry kept up its shrill warnings. At intervals of about an hour, it would wail out, warning of the arrival of another crest. All night long, men, women and children kept up the vigil. At last around 6:00 A.M. less than one and a half hours before day break, the gorge broke. Ice crashed into town and the water rushed down the street with a roar like the sound of the ocean."[1]

Before the Conowingo Dam was built, it was a sure thing that Port Deposit would have high water come Spring. Daddy recalled helping his tall grandmother move furniture up to the second floor more than once. Sometimes the situation was worse than high water. It was an actual flood. I believe that this story took place during the flood of 1910.

At the Rock Run end of town, the road was flooded, and many people needed to be rescued from their homes. The Fergusons were in such a state when my daddy and Craig Russell happened along in a row boat. They had been forced to move up to their second floor.

Now, Mrs. Ferguson and the two girls [probably Olive and Pearl] were quite upset and ready to be rescued. Not so, Mr. Ferguson. He had been drinking, and had decided that they would not leave.

Daddy stood in the rowboat with his offer of rescue. Mr. Ferguson stood at the window with his shotgun. Needless to say, there was no rescue, and Mr. Ferguson stood his ground until the water receded.

Although high waters and flooding can still occur, the river ice is a thing of the past.

You hear stories of winters years ago being worse than they are now. Well, this is true concerning the Susquehanna River in Port Deposit. The river would freeze over. The children of the town would then enjoy ice skating. I know my daddy and his brothers did, as I still have their strap-on ice skates. Some students who attended Tome School would skate across the river from Lapidum [on the Harford County side] instead of rowing across.

When my daddy was a young man, he and friends used to take a car out onto the ice. They would pick up speed and throw on the brakes, going into a tailspin. I always thought that would be great fun.

Ice racing also became a competitive town sport, and William McClenahan was a champion using his iceboat with 30-inch runners, and sails.[2]

But the ice was not always fun. My great Aunt Bertha told of a boy drowning. She was so upset at the time, that she took her ice skates and threw them into the river.

Of course, there was the profitable side of the ice. Ice was harvested using large saws, and seasonal fluctuations in the river height would determine the thickness of the ice (so a low summer river would be predictive of a poor ice harvest). Ice cream manufacture grew, and of course the possibility of icing fish and shellfish from the river and bay.

Growing up along the Susquehanna River, it is only natural that Jerome loved the river. Besides making boats, he also enjoyed swimming, ducking and fishing. The seeds of these life-long loves were sown in his childhood and cultivated later.

In the late twenties, my daddy worked on the Conowingo Dam. He operated one of the big cranes that you can still see along the roadway.

When you drive across Conowingo Dam, it is impressive to see the difference between the bottom of the spillway and the top, which is at road level. It is especially impressive when I think of my daddy climbing up and down the spillway. He would tie a long rope onto something at the top level. Then holding the rope, he would walk down the spillway.

The reason for this descent was that fish often became trapped at the bottom of the spillway. One could easily pick them up with one's hands. This is what my daddy did.

Upon filling a burlap bag with fish, he would get the rope and climb hand over hand up the side of the spillway.

It seems that taking fish from the spillway was frowned upon by the game wardens in the area. One evening a warden came to investigate. As the warden was standing along the roadway beneath the crane, my daddy and another worker were discussing the problem. Evidently, they managed to prove their ignorance of the situation, as the warden eventually went about his business.

I imagine my daddy gave a sigh of relief when the warden left. All the time they were talking, the warden was standing under a burlap bag full of fish tied to the leg of the crane.

Of course, my daddy knew how to fish the ordinary ways - - bank fishing, casting and trolling. For many years, he had perch nets along Steele's Island across from the quarry. He would bring them home in five gallon buckets. We'd eat fish and eat fish and become tired of them. Now, I have to pay twelve dollars at Owens Fish Market for one mess [of perch],³ and never get the chance to become "tired of them".

While the young boys were out ice skating on the frozen river, they often saw fish under the ice. This must have taken place in shallow water. When they spotted a fish, they would hit the ice on top of it. This would stun the fish. Then they broke the ice and got the fish.

But the most unusual method was the one I called "hitting the water". Daddy had told about doing this, and I didn't really doubt it, but I have to admit that seeing is believing.

One evening Daddy took my sister, Betty, along with Billy Brannon, our neighbor, and me out in his boat. It had rained, and the water was murky. He was rowing slowly along the shore of Steele's Island. He told us that bass hid in among the grass and rocks along the shore. He planned to find a likely spot and hit the water above with the flat of his oar. This was supposed to scare a bass. The bass would jump into the boat.

Splash! All at once he hit the water! A bass jumped out, missed Billy's back, and landed in the boat. I was a believer!

This happened in the late 1940s after Jerome and Mabelle moved the girls back north. His boat, a three-seater, was generally docked at Steele's Island near his nets. Jerome and the girls would swim the 400 feet (122 meters) out to Steele's Island to get the boat, check the nets and row over to the next island, Robert's, so they could swim some more, and perhaps look for arrowheads.

At that time, women recycled the material from the large sacks used to hold dry goods, like flour, meal and seeds, as well as animal feeds, in order to make clothing or household linens. More than thirty different textile companies were making this heavy and strong type of woven cotton. The cloth was printed with pretty, floral designs, and stamped with instructions.

For some reason, Mabelle thought she would make Patsy a swimming suit of feedbag material. Mabelle herself was a reluctant swimmer, and this was probably the reason for her naivety. The next time they went to the river, Patsy jumped into the Susquehanna. Instead of "Splash and Swim!" it was "Splash and Sink". The weight of the wet feedbag suit pulled her instantly under the water and she floundered in the river, the others oblivious to her danger. She said, "It was a wonder I didn't drown."

Patsy knew about the sink-or-swim school of thought when she told this tale,

Woody Duff, who managed the Acme Store, credited my daddy with teaching him to swim. It seems the thing to do was to throw someone overboard. They either sank and swam. I like to think my daddy was ready to jump in, if Mr. Duff had sunk.

Jerome, like many local children, was an early swimmer. At the age of four or five, Jerome fell though the outhouse at the back of 38 Granite Avenue, and into Rock Run creek. In later life, Jerome developed a naturally buoyant physique and loved floating on his back and watching the little fish biting at the skin tags on his belly. They would leave little red marks that he called "fish bites". Jerome's own nets would catch about 20-30 fish at a time, enough for the family and then some. He tried selling his fish when younger and giving them away when older, and was confounded when it was not always a success.

One spring he caught herring and salted them down in the barrels. He did not get a good price for them, so he never did that again. Told Betty,

> *Another time he netted a mess of perch from his nets. We ate fish and we ate fish, and we just could not eat another fish. He got the idea that he would offer some to Uncle Pat's widow, who was living in Woodstock. The fish were cleaned, scaled and iced, so we got in the car and drove and drove. You didn't call up people to say you were coming. You just went. Jerome thought he was taking a real treat from Port Deposit, from the Susquehanna. When we showed up with the fish, she didn't know what to feed us, so we had to sit down and eat the fish. We were so sick of fish... but you couldn't waste them.*

Jerome's act of intended charity may have had its roots in the Widows' Hauls in which the catch on the first Sunday of the shad season was donated to the region's widows and orphans. Fish was an important source of food for the residents, and the new herring season was marked by strings of fish in the back yards of Port Deposit.[4]

The Bannons living right over Rock Run creek were well-known for their fishing. In the late 1800s one June, the following ended up in the "Port Deposit Items" column of the *Whig*, "Some of our Isaak Waltons have been throwing the fly along the stream bordering the [Bannons], trying to deceive the trout while others take a south wind and bring in a good report from rock fish." Rock Run used to be much narrower and faster, when the water fed the working mill.

John Bannon's enthusiasm passed to the younger generation. Never one to dodge excitement, Andrew Bannon, had an interesting Sunday on December 15, 1912, prompting this story on the sports pages of the *Sun*, "Says He Saw a Mermaid. Susquehanna Fisherman Also Tells of Double-Ender Turtle:

> *Andrew Bannon, the watch dog of the Susquehanna floods,[5]*
> *took out of his "hoop-net" a terrapin which he declares was built*
> *like a ferryboat, a head on each end, both of them perfectly good*
> *heads and upon demonstration proved that either mouth had*
> *the appetite as well as aptitude for food. "Andy" says that at the*
> *same time he saw a fish that looked exactly like a small child.*
> *He struck it, but the hide was like leather.*

Down-to-earth pursuits in the village of Rock Run in the summer also included the organized "pic-nics," day excursions and week-long camp meetings. People came from churches, organizations and societies, some even coming from out of town. Some took place in Rock Run, but others took place further up the road in the woodlands of the Abrahams', as well as at the Woodlawn Camp Meeting House further north in the County.

Public Health in Rock Run

50. Mary Ellen Murray Murray with Betty and Mary Mabelle Murray.
In the summer of 1935, after Betty recovered from whooping cough, she and her sister, Mary, were taken to Rock Run to be "fattened up" by Grandmother Murray. Grandmother Mary Ellen was seventy-six in this photograph taken in 1935. Mary Ellen was a cook for the McClenahan family. Murray Family Album.

There was no limit to the fun found in those long leisurely summer days, but outdoor living was not a barrier to infectious disease. From the first half of the 19th century to the latter half, the average life expectancy increased from just 37 to 40 years of expected life, from birth. Pneumonia, grip (flu) and measles were common in the winter, and in the summer, there were also very serious problems with typhoid and cholera, due to poor sanitation and the contamination of the water.

In the back of Daddy's home in Rock Run, they had outhouses that hung over the stream. In the spring, higher waters meant they would get a continual flush. We knew where that water came out in the River.

In July 1872, a letter writer to *The Cecil Whig* offered up a plea for improved sanitation:

> Now that we are in the midst of hot weather, our citizens should take every precaution against sickness. The testing of the best physicians has demonstrated that one of the most prolific causes of typhoid fever is the effluvium arising from deposits of human excrement. Wherever the deposits are exposed to the intense heat of our July and August weather, may throw off minute particles, loading the air with the most disgusting odors, and carry disease into our houses. Elkton right now is very filthy, and there is no excuse for it. A few shovelfuls of dry earth will deodorize the filth, and carefully and constantly used no inconvenience will arise. A commode, well supplied with dry earth, may be kept in a chamber without annoyance. Can you not persuade our citizens to try this cheap and certain preventative? It may save a score of valuable lives this Summer and Fall, and will certainly make our town more habitable.

Six of Mary Ellen and Will's children survived to adulthood, but there were tragedies as well. Their middle boy, Thomas Harry, named after Will's uncle, died in October of 1895, just a few weeks old. Even sadder maybe, was the shocking death of beautiful, sweet Nellie, their first-born, who was one of Tome School's earliest graduates. She had gone to New York City to establish a career, but in February of 1907, aged just 22, she died of an infectious disease, and her body was brought back to Port Deposit in a coffin. She left behind a book she received for Christmas in 1898, *Abbé Constantin*, by the French author, Ludovic Halévy. This classic French novel told of losses affecting an abbot following a change in the ownership of the local chateau.

So many people perished from diseases that are either curable today with antibiotics or are preventable through sanitation, clean water, refrigeration and vaccination. Cholera, consumption (tuberculosis), typhoid fever, hepatitis, influenza, yellow fever, scarlatina, puerperal fever, pneumonia, bronchitis, diphtheria, tetanus, whooping cough, measles and smallpox, all preventable today, contributed to 2,652 deaths in the state of Maryland in the year ending June 1, 1860. Shots cost money though, not something everybody had. The following story tells of a special collaboration between Mary Ellen and an African-American mother in Rock Run:

> *Now-a-days children don't have to have a smallpox vaccination to enter school. When I was a child it was very important. Mothers often got their children vaccinated on the leg so an ugly scar wouldn't show. The scars from a smallpox vaccination in my daddy's generation did seem to be larger and uglier. Maybe it was because of the way the scabs were treated.*

> *When Daddy's mother had her children vaccinated, a colored lady in the Rock Run neighborhood had hers vaccinated, also. The colored lady waited until the scabs had healed on Daddy's or the other children's arms. Then, she and Daddy's mother pulled off the scab, pricked the arm of the colored child and fastened on the scab. The colored children were vaccinated also, without the service of a doctor. I imagine this might have been the only way they could have afforded it.*

> *Daddy used to enjoy telling another story. It was about a*

"mountain man" getting vaccinated in North Carolina. The T.V.A. authorities had said that all their workers had to have a smallpox vaccination. Now, this man did not believe in it and did not want one. However, he did want to keep his job, so he agreed.

The "mountain man" was ready. The doctor vaccinated him. He reached up, took out a hand full of tobacco juice from his mouth and rubbed it on the spot. The vaccination didn't take.

In the late 1800s and first two decades of 1900, the smallpox vaccination was the sole vaccine given regularly in the United States. The sharing of smallpox or even cowpox scabs happened since the early development of that vaccine in modern times, and centuries before. It was a safer method than limb-to-limb sharing of the original vaccine material, and a cheaper way of ensuring that all the children in a neighborhood were protected. This story is the only one passed down from the early generation of Murrays that showed this level of interaction between the village women themselves. It was a progressive step forward in the provision of public health for everyone.

The back of Mary Ellen Murray's cookbook contained pages of traditional medicinal cures. For muscular or rheumatic pains, *Oil of Winter Green Lineament* could be used: *mix 2 oz. Oil of Winter Green with an equal measure of Alcohol, then add 8 oz. of Witch Hazel. Shake well before using. For external use only.*

"When sickness may be traced to the use of unwholesome water in limestone regions, *Blackberry Cordial* is recommended." Mary Ellen's recipe was similar to that of the pharmacist, Joseph Jacob, in 1898 but contained twice the amount of sugar. *Bruise the berries and strain through a cheesecloth bag; to each quart of juice, add a pound of white sugar, one half ounce each of grated nutmeg and ground cinnamon, and one fourth ounce each of allspice and cloves. Boil twenty minutes, skimming well. When cool add half pint of brandy.*

⌁⌁⌁⌁

Isaac Rehert, who farmed further up the hollow, described friendly relationships between people in Rock Run some fifty years later in *Rock Run Hollow: Four Seasons From a Farm Window*. About a man who worked on his farm, he penned:

> *The little settlement where Richard lives is on a narrow winding road that parallels a small branch of Rock Run, cut deep into the underlying granite. The houses are small and close together, the people are extremely friendly with one another, and during the warm months they spend much of their free time on porches or on the open road, chatting together and being neighborly. Everyone knows what everyone else is doing*[6]

Watchful neighbors could help, but the virtues of quarantine were not to be underestimated either. In the early 1930s, there was an epidemic of whooping cough, caused by *Bordetella pertussis*, a truly devastating and prolonged illness for children who contracted it, and it was deadly for their baby siblings. Betty and Patsy contracted whooping cough at the ages of 6 and 2, and they were quarantined at their home on Port Deposit Road that summer, coughing, whooping and coughing again. Mrs. Malinda Brannon next door thought that "Patsy would not make it" — she got so skinny. As soon as possible, the girls were taken to Grandmother Mary Ellen Murray's at 38 Granite Avenue to be fattened up.

Many who survived virulent infection would have marked weakness or impairment of their health. The youngest of William and Mary Ellen's children, Anne, who was born in 1902, was one such youngster and she became a favorite in her family. This may have been a key to her recovery. Her daughter, Anne "Honey" Carney Brown told this story:

My mother attended Jacob Tome primary school in Port Deposit, Maryland. Since she was the youngest in the family, and very well thought of by her four older brothers and two sisters, they would take turns pulling her to school on a sled in the winter or in a wagon in the spring and fall. She was sickly as a child, but was determined to get better. Her brothers and sisters admired her courage and they in turn encouraged her to be able to return to school. She graduated from Jacob Tome School in 1920. She returned the next year to take some secretarial courses. The only place that she was employed was the McClenahan's Quarry.[7]

World War I Service

Illness and poorer nutrition, especially for those who went through the potato famine, would mean that people might not reach their full height or stature. But just how short were the "Short Irish"? My mother says that her grandmother, daughter of the "Short Irish" was tiny. She said, "I was taller than her when I was about six." Grandmother Mary Ellen Murray photographed with Mabelle and her young girls reveal her daughter-in-law towering over her, and the young girls catching up to their grandmother in height. Mary Ellen owned a very diminutive rocking chair. An affectionate greeting for growing children passed down this family, "I'm gonna' push you down! You're growing too fast!" This was always accompanied by a gentle but a friendly, but firm push down on the head.

Two of Mary Ellen's sons, hybrids of the Tall and Short Irish were described on their World War I draft registration certificates as being "short" in height and either of "medium" or "slender" build, both having dark/blue eyes and light/brown hair. Joseph's was completed on June of 1917, when he was 23 years old. He had been working as a clerk in the the Port Deposit Store Company. It must have been a shock to all the family when he set sail for Europe. Joe got an honorable discharge on June 7, 1919, after two years in the army. By the time the war finished, the company store had closed, and Bridget had passed away. Any worries about a job for Joe were left unspoken. For one thing, there was the matter of his feet. "When Joe's boots were finally taken off, his skin and the bottom of his feet came off with them, too." The smell and look of his rotting flesh was horrific. Ewwh. Ohh!! This was like some horror movie.

Joe had been a soldier in the trenches of France serving from 7/8/1918 to 6/3/1919. As part of "Baltimore's Own", he and 3,666 others from the 313th Infantry sailed to France in the summer of 1918, where they were involved in trench warfare in north-eastern France, holding the Allied Line, in Avocourt, Troyon, and during the initial stages of the Meuse-Argonne Offensive, which would be the last battle of the Western front. The Army promoted Joe from Private to Corporal during December of 1918.

Like many others, the enemy gassed Joe with mustard gas. The gas masks they wore did not protect against the burning of their skin and mucous membranes and there was little chance to recover in the trenches. The first cohort from Baltimore sailed home on the *Antigone* in May 1919. With the rotting dead, frostbitten skin from long spells in the wet, cold mud, and the effects of chemical warfare Joe must have needed a period of recuperation.

Nevertheless, within one year, he was back at work, glad to be home and doing civilian work in Perryville. From March 1919, in fact, the U.S. Public Health Service began a comprehensive program to provide a hospital at Perry Point for veterans and patients who required neuro-psychiatric care. There was also a storage depot for hospital supplies for the Army converted from the U.S. Government village. Joe later worked in the store of the hospital at Perry Point, and was no doubt sympathetic to the needs of fellow comrades who came home from Europe suffering from shell shock. Today we call this Post-Traumatic Stress Disorder. It could manifest itself in many ways, but after WWI and WWII, many affected veterans appeared as the walking dead.

Paul, who was Joe's *younger* brother, was drafted on September 12, 1918, within three months of turning eighteen. Although Paul had been a pump runner at the Atlas

Powder Company in Perryville, and was "skinny" at the time, he did not take part in overseas service. In fact, good-natured, family–oriented Paul, who would do anything for you, was considered to be "retired" two years later. Paul later got back to work as a machinist with a construction company in Perryville, but put on weight and suffered from health problems. Paul was a genial realist when it came to life and money. Things were either "not half bad" or "nothing to write home about" to Paul, and if you did him a favor he might say, "Thank you 'til you're better paid." Joe had done enough for both of them, and he, Paul and Jerome stuck together through thick and thin. Paul also found a friend in Miss Anna Bitner, a farmer's daughter from the countryside.

Other sons of Rock Run returned home from WWI as well, including Oscar Griffin, Chester Lewis, Ernest White and a boarder of Janet Thomas's.

Jerome's oldest brother, John William, called "Uncle Bill" got married, but soon after moved to Chicago, rooming with a family at first while working as a salesman, and then later found a new (second) wife! He came back to Port Deposit for funerals, a popular and welcome, but rare guest.

Baseball Fever

51. Jerome with his baseball cap (left) and his baseball uniform (right).
Jerome was wearing his Port Deposit team baseball cap c.1920, when pictured on the front porch of 38 Granite Avenue with his spaniel puppy. His gray and blue-striped baseball uniform at Paw-Paw Museum, was inspected by his great-grandsons, James and Ben in 2010. Jerome favored gray pinstripes for the rest of his life.

Jerome was fortunate enough not to be drafted and spent the early-1920s becoming better acquainted with his sister's friend, Mabelle Thompson from Harford County, while working at Perry Point[8] and following his outdoor interests. This gave him access to a wide network of people and allowed him to pursue one of his greatest loves – baseball. Jerome's place on the "Hill School" team and the honors that ensued were something to be proud of, and his enthusiasm would have been infectious.

Baseball fever was rampant in the early 1900s. Baltimore had two pro teams in 1914. The Baltimore Orioles were a minor league team of the International League, and the Baltimore Terrapins were the new Federal League Team. The O's were having a bad season that year. Fans were deserting them for the Terps.[9] The O's responded in 1914 by signing the young George Herbert "Babe" Ruth, straight from St. Mary's Industrial School in Baltimore, the first pro team to give Ruth a contract. Before the season was out, the Boston Red Sox had poached him.[10] The Baltimore papers published in 1919 and 1920, the *Sun* and the *Baltimore American*, remained loyal to Babe Ruth and declared their hopes about the potential of this rising star of their own.

Jerome loved Babe Ruth, too, and admired to varying degrees his Yankees teammate Lou Gehrig, as well as Harry Heilmann and Ty Cobb of the Detroit Tigers, sluggers as he was. Other talents of the time were "Shoeless" Joe Jackson, "Socks" Seybold, and John Franklin "Home Run" Baker. The Baltimore Orioles' manager, Jack Dunn, fearlessly pursued his own dream team, and "beginning with 1919, his Orioles ran off a string of seven successive championships, the longest pennant run in the history of baseball" winning a high of 119 games in 1921.[11]

Jerome got on one of the semi-pro teams for Port Deposit playing third baseman (without a glove), and being near the top of the line-up when in bat. On Saturday, June 19, 1920, Port Deposit played Elk Mills, the League leaders. He was 22 at the time. On the team were two others from Rock Run. The rest lived in the town, except for the pitcher who was the son of a farmer in Conowingo. Two other teammates were chauffeurs, a matter of convenience for the rest of the team.

That Saturday evening, Jerome was at bat four times, but got just one hit. One was enough. The Special Dispatch, to *The Baltimore American* reported under the by-line "Surprise for Elk Mills" that, "the rejuvenated Port Deposit team played rings around the first place Elk Mills in the Church League at Port Deposit today. Duffy cracked out a homer in the eighth, bringing in Jack ahead of him." William Duffy, 33, first baseman, was an ironworker and next-door neighbor of the Murrays, and, catcher, George Jack, 22, was neighbor of the Bannons and a fireman at the Power House (the hydroelectric plant at Conowingo Dam). The final score was Port Deposit 5, Elk Mills 2! It must have been a jubilant return from the diamond. Around this time, many African-American players from Rock Run played for the town's Black Sox, including fathers and sons of the Griffin, Fields, Stewart, Boddy, Henry, McMullen and Jones families. They initially played on the Canal Field created from the reclaimed log pond, and then moved their home diamond to the wharf behind Washington Hall.

Sisters, Girl-friends and Cousins

52. The Bridge over Rock Run at the Bannons.
It is possible to view the remains of the upside-down railroad tracks that supports the bridge.

A few years later, Jerome began working on the Conowingo Dam, the first of many dams he would help to build or operate. He and Mabelle married in 1926, and started out in Bridget and John's little brown house at 36 Granite Avenue. A next-door neighbor on Granite Avenue, Ellen Carney, was the daughter of an Irish immigrant mother, and she was a dressmaker, who lived on her own after her mother passed away. Mabelle called her Miss Elle Carney, and talked of how Miss Elle befriended her when she moved to Rock Run. Later,

Mabelle and Jerome would help "settle up" Miss Elle's home and property.

During this period, Jerome's sisters were also getting on in life, more or less. By 1920, aged 30, Elizabeth was already teaching at her public school in Fell's Point. In 1925, a teacher friend invited her to a picnic. Some match-making had been planned. A match was supposed to be made between her and Bob Carney, Sr., a young lawyer and government worker. It was not to be. Honey, daughter of Anne Murray Carney, told what happened,

> *There was a picnic someplace between Carney and Hamilton. Eleanor Schaeffer had invited several good teacher friends, including Elizabeth Murray, and Eleanor's husband, whose name was George, invited my father. My mother was visiting her sister Elizabeth, so she went to the picnic, too. I think that a match was supposed to be made between Aunt Elizabeth and my father Bob. Elizabeth and my father were the same age. Anne was 13 years younger [and he fell in love with Anne instead]. I have all the love letters that my father wrote to my mother when she was living in Rock Run. They got married in February 1928 and went to live near Carney.*[12]

Robert Emmett Carney, Sr., was one of eleven children of Thomas and Mary Agnes Carney, the only boy in a family of girls. His father was an Irish immigrant, who started out as a stone cutter in Texas, Maryland, near Cockeysville, a haven of Irish quarrymen; he broke the mold, though, and bought the Eight-Mile House and Post Office, which later put Carney, Maryland on the map.[13] Many characteristics distinguished Bob Carney from the rank-and-file, but perhaps these four exceed the rest: his ability to type 120 words/minute, his role as a front-line war recorder,[14] his exacting mind, and his retraining as a lawyer when he returned home from the war. If any of the Murrays were not entirely convinced about Anne's choice, his love of baseball, the Democratic Party and the Roman Catholic Church ticked all of the boxes. He graduated from University of Maryland Law School in May of 1924 and had an office in the Hamilton Bank Building. He was "quiet, unassuming" and "worked for the good of the community" said his colleagues.[15] Bob wanted a private wedding. Whether this was because of their age difference, or because he feared that interference from either family might prevent him from marrying the woman he loved, he wanted the marriage to remain secret.

Wrote Honey:

> The marriage plans appeared to have been done by letters. On the 15th of February at 7 p.m. my father wrote my mother to say that they would be married on Friday, the 20th of February, 1928. She was to board the train in Port Deposit or Perryville and if he wasn't standing on the train platform in Aberdeen, my mother was to continue to Baltimore. My father wanted to be married at St. Joan of Arc in Perryville by a priest he knew from the service.
>
> He wrote, 'I will meet you at the train in Aberdeen Friday night evening at five o'clock, but don't get off the train unless you see me on the platform. Something might happen and I might not get there, and if you don't see me, keep right on to Baltimore. I would sooner be the one to be disappointed then to have you get off and me not be there.'
>
> My mother finally convinced him to let her parents come and I think Uncle Joe also came. My father told his sisters that he was going on a hunting match in Hershey, Penna. He also told his male friends the same story. When they came back, he said that he had gotten the prize, his wife.

Paul and Joe brought Nana as we called her down every other Sunday for dinner, and their grandchildren, Kitty, little Bobby and Honey were healthy babies. My grandfather (William Joseph) died on Kitty's first birthday in March 1930. Nana or grandmother died the day or two after Christmas in 1939. She was down to see us in November. I remember taking a nap with her.[16]

Anne developed a reputation as a baker. Was it any wonder? Her mother, Mary Ellen, having toiled in the kitchen of the McClenahan family, was also a baker. When William Joseph got home from the quarry, Mary Ellen would trot back and forth in the kitchen, back and forth, trying to get food on the table. If there was nothing else on the table, there <u>had to be potatoes</u>. Jerome's wife later learned that "a meal was nothing without potatoes. Any kind would do."

Once you walked up the steps through the porch and into the door at 38 Granite Avenue, the sweet aroma of baking would hit you. Mary Ellen specialized in pies and cakes. You could carry on straight through and down a step at the back, where there was a dirt floor, a summer kitchen, and there you would find churned butter, and salt-glaze crockery holding goodies. Recipes passed on through the family included *Anne's Saturday Cake* which became famous with the Carney family, as well as her *Butter Scotch Cookies* and Mary Ellen's *Hermit Cookies*,[17] which Mabelle loved making as well. On Saturday afternoons, the *Saturday Cake* would be made, and allowed to cool, and then the icing was made after supper. To 3 squares of Semi-sweet Baker's chocolate, 1 c. sugar, and ¼ c. water were added, and that was boiled and cooked until it spun a thread. "Take off stove. Add 1 T. butter and 1 t. vanilla. Beat until it begins to get hard." If small children gather, allow them to lick the spoon.

By far the most popular cake was the Christmas (and Easter) cake with coconut icing that became so popular, that "Murray girls" generations later are still making it. When someone discovered that Jerome's first cousin, Margaret Wentz Heise, daughter of Aunt Lizzie, also made the white coconut cake, it was tempting to attribute it to Mary Ellen, or even Bridget. Who knows? Perhaps some McClenahans or Watanabes are still enjoying this cake, which traditionally broke the fasts following Midnight Mass (at Christmas) and the Easter vigil.

After work on the Conowingo Dam finished, Jerome got work on the Pretty Boy Dam (on the Gunpowder River in northern Baltimore County), and then on the Safe Harbor Dam, further up the Susquehanna River in Penna. This was when Norman Bannon, Sr., Joe Sice and Jerome's brother, Paul were carpooling. Around this time, Jerome introduced his brother, Joe now in his late thirties to a young woman named Sara Ione, a cousin of Mabelle's, who was living on the Thompson farm in Scarboro. After they married, they moved onto the farm that Uncle Jim and Aunt Bertha lived in as newlyweds. This farm bordered the southwestern boundary of what became Isaac Rehert's property. They had the right-of-way down the farm lane that led to Rock Run stream for their horses, cattle and other farm animals, provided they maintained the lane.

Aside from the bird song and animal sounds, it is the sound of the water from Rock Run itself that you are aware of when higher up in the hill away from Main Street. That sound, and an awareness of the Susquehanna below, promotes healthy living and a sense of peace.

Jerome's girls used to walk up the hill to Joe's farm after visiting Uncle Paul at 38 Granite Avenue. Once Mary Mabelle, aged about six, and Betty, 4, were given charge of two calves. They were to take them to the meadow. These were spirited calves and the little girls couldn't hold onto them. Mary knew what to do. She let go! Poor Betty hung on and was dragged behind hers, breaking her tailbone, which bothered her for years.

When Patsy was just old enough to hold a bucket, she was given the job of going up the hill to get fresh spring water for Uncle Paul. Up at the Bannon's, there was a rickety old bridge. Mary, Betty and Patsy walked out over the rickety wooden bridge and went behind their house, where a pipe coming out of hills brought fresh spring water. This provided excitement and gave them some inside knowledge about Rock Run. It probably also gave them some inside knowledge about their Bannon cousins, Norman, Jr., and Gene, great-grandsons of John Bannon. Gene and Norman belonged to the Nesbit grandparents in the hollow as well, as Mrs. Margaret Nesbit Bannon was their mother. Between the two grannies, there were plenty of eyes watching out for them.

The little Murray girls were not the only ones who were nervous about that rickety old bridge. Mrs. Margaret Bannon was equally nervous. Her great-grandson, Chris Bannon II, a 6th generation storyteller who lives in the Hollow explained:

> My great-Grandmother, Margaret Bannon, wife of Norman John Bannon, Sr. refused to be driven over the rickety old wooden bridge leading to our (then her) house. Instead, Pop-Pop would stop the car at the end of the drive, and Granny would walk over [only] after the car crossed the bridge.[18]

The bridge construction was sound. Norman John, Sr. worked on the railroad and he built the bridge like upside-down railroad tracks, with the rails on the bottom and the wooden ties on the top. It was built at a height of twelve feet, rather than the six foot height of most of the bridges, which washed out in high waters. Not the Bannon bridge!

Two bridge mishaps did occur for the somewhat accident-prone Bannons. One night, Norman John Bannon, Sr. drove his car off the bridge, and had to be hauled out of the creek. The other time Norman John, Jr. fell off the high bridge. Down, down he tumbled … but luckily landed on a mattress that had washed down the creek. Another accident also involved falling from a great height. When Pop-Pop was sick in bed one winter, the television reception was poor after a winter storm. It was Gene this time, who climbed out of the roof to adjust it, only to slide off, down to a cold, soft landing![19]

Provisions

53. Mrs. Jones and family at the Jones' Family Home in Rock Run.
Photograph taken in the 1970s. Courtesy of Rev. John James Abrahams III.

The stores in Rock Run provided a great deal of interest for residents, workers and visitors alike. The Company Store owned by the McClenahan Brothers was a great advantage and imagine how the Irish, who had survived a famine could go into the store and use their script to purchase food from the well-stocked shelves and counters to take home and put on the table. In addition to this and the African Peoples Company Store, there was Reynolds Brothers Hardware Store, which stocked "new hardware", tin, iron and home furnishings. Their ad ran, "They keep constantly on hand Blacksmith's Stock consisting of Bar Iron, Horse Shoes, Horse Nails and Carriage Bolts, &c." Another store was the Rock Run Cash Store run by Steel and Jackson specializing in Missies and Children's Shoes and kid gloves. Patsy remembers John J. Baker's butcher shop in Rock Run where "you reached in large jars and took out as many cookies and crackers as you needed."

Around the time that Patsy and her sisters were walking up the hill to go to the Bannons for clear water, they may have passed their Bannon cousins, Gene and Norman walking down on an important mission. This story of Chris's tells about the facts of their lives, and the way they lived.

My grandfather, Gene Bannon told me that one of his and his brother's [Norman John Bannon, Jr.] jobs growing up was to walk down to the bottom of the holler, to the old mill on Main Street when it turned out scrapple and sausage. They would fill their metal pails with the burnt ends and scraps that were being discarded and take them home to feed the chickens. Pop-Pop said he still remembers nibbling on the still warm pieces, walking back up Rock Run during the cold winter months.

As the milling business wound down, the stone building became a butcher's shop and sausage factory run by Smithsons' son and grandson, Rumsey, Sr. and Rumsey, Jr. Later, it became John Baker's. The Bannons were not beholden to the old mill for all their meat, however.

They also butchered a few pigs each year here at the house. The pigs they butchered would be hung over winter, covered in salt in one of the first floor rooms of the house.

When you got right down to Rock Run, and experienced some of its mystique, you did not want to leave, but our tour of Murray Port Deposit had ended. The richness of the lives of the folks who lived here, and a sense of the prosperity they enjoyed, that came on the heels of hard work, ingenuity, and good fortune would linger with us as we headed back to our Port home on Mockingbird Hill!

Stop Ten

Mockingbird Hill – 339 Tome Highway

54. Mockingbird Hill during its construction in 1928.
This photograph was taken before the company store steps were in place.

Nearly a mile up the steep hill on old Foundry Hollow Road, rising from Center Street (now Jacob Tome Memorial Highway), we finished at the home of 3rd generation and 4th generation Murrays at number 339.

For their wedding, Jerome and Mabelle received rocking chairs – for a porch and a quiet room. If they were to use them, Jerome would need to get on with nest building. He and Mabelle were living in the brown house on Granite Avenue, his grandparents' home and the girlhood home of his mother, and while sunny and cheerful, he wanted more land for a family, a big garden and an orchard. Perhaps he also dreamt of space for his hunting dogs.

In the post-WWI economic upturn, people had a chance to get on the property ladder. The Gordon-Van Tine Company originally advertised their plan-cut homes in the Sears & Roebuck and Montgomery Ward catalogs in the 1920s and 1930s. Jerome cut out the middleman and ordered directly. The Westfield-designed home was said to give the house an air of "comfort and hospitality", and that it would do.

Every option, whether for the heating system, wood frames, storm sashes, plumbing or kitchen could be specified on the mail order form. Jerome received a contract with the Gordon-Van Tine Company dated first of June, 1926 at the time that he and Mabelle were married. Jerome bought the blue prints and materials for the house from the Gordon-Van Tine Company for about $2,500. There was a contract for electricity for $3.03/month and a twenty-year guarantee.

Now all they needed was the land. Jerome and Mabelle were buying a parcel of land from George and Alice Reid, but there was a delay, as Reid's terrace of land running down the road and abutting the Abrahams and Creswell property had to be re-surveyed. Finally, on September 25, 1928, the deal concluded.

I judge that the house was built in 1928. Daddy was working at Conowingo Dam. He worked many overtime hours to get extra money for lumber, etc. Mother's father, Granddaddy Thompson, who was a farmer and a carpenter, was the builder. Two other men came over from Harford County with him: Gene Rocky and Jessie Carr. Daddy and Mom did some of the finishing up. Daddy did all of upstairs and I guess some of us helped. At first it was just one big room.

Note, the foundations and porch posts are Port Deposit granite. Also, the front and back steps. He bought them from the "Old Company Store". The front were the front of the store, and the back the back ones. I love them.

Both Betty and I were born in the front downstairs room, with Dr. Benson and Aunt Icelene helping. She was a nurse from University of Maryland.

Uncle Bill stayed with us when Uncle Paul died. He thought there were so many mockingbirds here. So he started calling it Mockingbird Hill and wrote it on addresses. Later Aunt Ann gave a sign for the mailbox saying 'Mockingbird Hill'. Jerome would end letters to the family with a stick figure of a man and an open-beaked bird, labelled "Old Man of Mockingbird Hill".

The house was designed to let the light in, and the kitchen was designed to "save steps and effort for the housewife"! Proportions of the kitchen and back of the house were redesigned to allow for a nice room for eating most meals, and a big back porch coming up off the company store steps housed an icebox and a laundry room, squeezing the pantry and the cellar steps into a somewhat tighter place. The steepness of the steps, the possibility of a black snake in the pantry, and lack of handrails always brought a frisson of danger while descending to the cellar thereafter.

Jerome, a woodworker himself, ordered the walnut-stained oak option for the floors ($34.40), doors, and trim ($26.95). Maple floors were standard for the kitchen and bathroom. The house would forever retain the wonderful scent of these aromatic woods. Jerome preferred the fragrant and colorful woods, walnut and cedar, that could be sourced locally, for his own woodworking.

Hauling the granite steps and blocks for the foundation was something that Jerome knew he could do, but he gambled and hired a man to do it. Mr. Cameron from the quarry quoted him $1,000 saying, "You can do it yourself but it will cost you more." Jerome figured, "I had trucks and could get help" and decided to do it himself. A man from Colora did the foundation stonework and it cost him double the amount that

Cameron quoted. Jerome received the bill in October 1928 for the work done on his chimney, the porch walls and for the pointing of the walls. For a total of 113 hours of his and his assistant's time, he charged Jerome $2,080 and added "Mr. Murray, you will notice I always give a day on a job like this. Hoping everything is satisfactory."

Photographs of the work crew after the exterior was completed in the autumn of 1928 showed the men on the porch pausing for sandwiches and outfitted in hats, and work aprons. Between them was a well-bundled toddler, Mary, who was born in June the previous year, and, the puppies, jumping up, down and all around. Jerome would value the house for $1,600 in 1930.

The property was on a generous plot of nearly an acre, parceled from the Hope and Anchor farm below. Jerome got on with tree planting as soon as he could break the ground. Orchard trees of apple and cherry on the south side complemented the pear trees in the back. "Pears for your heirs", he always said, and true to this adage, the fifth and sixth generation Murrays benefitted from his foresight. Two hybrid trees were to feature in the shade and fragrance of the porch and drive. Whether it was the hybrid black walnut and English walnut, or a hickory and a pecan tree, which somehow grew into one living organism near the porch, you would know you were at Mockingbird Hill even with your eyes closed. Jerome was later to fasten attachments for a free-swinging hammock under the latter tree, and a porch swing finished off the front.

Mabelle, Jerome and the girls added flower gardens on each side. Sweet peas, seeded from those at 38 Granite Avenue, would rise up near the front porch, while daylilies and Black-eyed Susans would greet visitors to the back door. Golden glow from the Thompson farm was transplanted. Jerome's main pride and joy, and he and his family's greatest efforts, though, would go into a very extensive vegetable garden and berry patch. He considered every space and season.

55. Mockingbird Hill (with Company Store Steps).
Photographed in the mid-1940s when Kitty Carney was visiting.

When the Murrays moved in, there were cows across the road. Country life was interesting. Little Betty, who was born in February 1929 heard people talking about "bull butt", a warning to little girls that bulls could butt you if you entered the fields. Besides the summer of the whooping cough quarantine, family and friends often visited here and to an extent, one could forget the worries that the Great Depression brought. There would always be fruit, vegetables and baked goods to take home. A long, rather unexpected hiatus interrupted the pattern of the seasons for Jerome.

The Tennessee Valley Authority

56. Norris Dam on the Clinch River, Norris, Tenn.
Taken in January 1937, this photograph shows the fully operational spillway and powerhouse. Jerome Murray worked as a mechanic on this project when the Roosevelts visited. Courtesy of the F.D.R. Presidential Library.

After the Conowingo work fell off around 1928, Jerome went to Pretty Boy, and then Safe Harbor, working on the new dams. The Safe Harbor dam opened at the end of 1931. Because there were no plans for new dams within striking distance, Jerome was prepared to travel. He was made for this work.

There were several factors that affected Jerome's decision to move away from his beloved family and home. Besides the scarcity of jobs, he loved working on the dams. He understood the practical need for flood prevention on the Susquehanna and the hydroelectric power it brought. Honed through his mechanical skills and burnished with his knowledge of spillways, cranes, locks and power plants, when Franklin Delano

Roosevelt's New Deal included something that was close to both of their hearts, he was ready.

On April 10, 1933, F.D.R. addressed Congress about the Tennessee Valley.

The continued idleness of a great national investment in the Tennessee Valley leads me to ask the Congress for legislation necessary to enlist this project in the service of the people.

It is clear that the Muscle Shoals development is but a small part of the potential public usefulness of the entire Tennessee River. Such use ... transcends mere power development; it enters the wide fields of flood control, soil erosion, reforestation, elimination from agricultural use of marginal lands .... In short, this power development of war days leads logically to national planning for a complete river watershed involving many States and the future lives and welfare of millions. It touches and gives life to all forms of human concerns.

I, therefore, suggest to the Congress legislation to create a Tennessee Valley Authority, a cooperation clothed with the power of government but possessed of the flexibility and initiative of a private enterprise. It should be charged with the broadest duty of planning for the proper use, conservation and development of the natural resources of the Tennessee River drainage basin and its adjoining territory for the social and economic welfare of the Nation.

This in a truer sense is a return to the spirit and vision of the pioneer. If we are successful here we can march on, step by step, in a like development of other great natural territorial units within our borders.

The President's vision touched Jerome, and after Congress passed the T.V.A. Act on May 18, 1933, Jerome would make his move. His upbringing in Port Deposit: his involvement with the floods and ice gorges, and his work on the dams of the Susquehanna, made him suitable for this role. As Patsy had only been born that February, Jerome agreed that Mabelle and the girls would stay behind. After Jerome left for the Tennessee Valley in his new Chevrolet, Mabelle and the girls kept busy "scaring up things in the kitchen" and getting on with the tasks at home. Mary would be starting First Grade at Tome School that September, and without a car to take them, they made the daily journey on foot. When the Brannon family moved in next door, they walked together.

Jerome first went to Norris, Tennessee, to work on the Norris Dam and he lived in their "dirt bank", the workers' village called Norris Village. Jerome would be home in the summer and at Christmas. Jerome was also a letter-writer and so were the girls. Few of his letters survive, but what he wrote was full of poetry, his usual joviality, expressions of endearment and the stick figure drawings. They reduced feelings of isolation.

"How did you summon the doctor or get groceries?" my sister asked my mother, curious about the practical side of life on the hill. "We had a phone on a stand before going down south and Grandmother would crank the phone and order groceries", she replied. "After the war, we had trouble getting a phone, as there was a shortage."

"How was the house heated?" Fran asked. "Up until 1958", Betty recalled, "the coal furnace was exclusively used. Then there was a big storm, and the Murrays were all out of electricity." Big storms cut off the roads and supplies, and caused the Murrays to rethink the power and heating supply. A wood stove was installed. Jerome used to say, "There's nothing like a kitchen fire", and, Ed Rowland would always say, "There's nothing like the warmth of a stove." So the stove was named Ed, and Ed became an option to the present day.

In the fall of 1934, when Jerome was thirty-seven, his letters home were crammed full of exciting news. The Norris Dam building site at that time covered such a vast area, and nearly obscured the river. Many hundreds of men worked there, although they were just a fraction of the 28,000 T.V.A. workers there were in the year 1942.

On November 16, 1934, the President and First Lady were coming to Norris Dam on an inspection tour. Although the dam was not yet in full operation, the impressive 207-foot spillway was ready. It was a longer drop than Niagara Falls and seemed just as wide. The day would never be forgotten by those who witnessed the first demonstration of the Norris Dam for the man who made history, who took his own courageous steps for the betterment of his country. One witness was Jerome.

The Clinch River had been dammed in preparation and where a giant bucket on a pulley operated by a crane had normally been in operation, a makeshift ride had been rigged up for Eleanor Roosevelt, a pioneer in her own right. In this heavy timber frame, she and about ten others, women as well as men, rather jerkily crossed over the top of the causeway, a vast chasm in all directions under a wide-open sky. Eleanor was no shrinking violet, and she held her own with anyone and everyone. At the powerhouse of Norris Dam, she pressed a button to release the river water, which would fall unleashed past where her husband stood. Down below the spillway, Franklin D. Roosevelt felt the power of the waters of the Clinch River, and was moved. He extemporaneously delivered a speech to whoever could hear him over the sound of the falling water.

My friends, noted his secretary in short-hand,

I am getting a great thrill out of this. I was thinking today that it was only a year ago last January, less than two years ago and before I became President that I came down to Muscle Shoals with Senator Norris and a number of other gentlemen. At that time a very great idea was just beginning to take shape. It was only an idea then and when I think of the very small period of time that has elapsed since then I am very proud to have had something to do with it. But I am a lot prouder of the way you good people are carrying that idea into actual fact. All of you who are working here at this great dam project and all the good people throughout the Tennessee Valley who are working on the rest of this great program some day will be known as veterans - - you will be known as veterans of a new kind of war, the kind of war that is going to improve conditions for millions and millions of our fellow American citizens.

All I can say to you is "God speed the work." You are going at it with a splendid spirit and I am coming back here again some time when you get this work done.

Senator Norris (Nebraska, Rep.) was with FDR when he was visiting the facilities. At one point, the Senator telephoned the office of the Norris Dam project. "Norris here," answered a TVA official. "No, Norris here!" responded the Senator. Aside from the joking, this had been an inspiring day. Norris was the first major project of the T.V.A., and as it was FDR's baby, Eleanor visited it again, twenty-one years later. FDR had died in 1945.

Between the Roosevelt visits, Jerome was to work on the Hiawassee Dam in Murphy, N.C., Watts Bar Dam in Spring City, Tennessee, the Ocoee Dam on the Parksville Reservoir, the Gilbertsville Dam in Kentucky, the Fontana Dam near the Great Smokey Mountains of N.C., and Watauga Dam at Butler, Tennessee. Added to the projects he worked on in the north, this brought his employment on dam projects to ten dams, a truly significant number.

By the time Mary had completed Second Grade at Tome, Jerome wanted his wife and family to move down and live with him in the South. They finally left Port Deposit after the younger girls recovered from whooping cough, and arrived in time for the 1935-36 school year. They rented out the downstairs of their house to a couple, related to a family they knew.

Betty remembers the glass bottles of gasoline that Jerome had in the back of the car. Without reliable gauges, guesswork was required. When the time seemed right, he would pull over and fill up the tank. During the first journey down, they noticed that the green of Maryland had turned to brown. The grasses and vegetation had all dried up with the drought, and dust filled the air in places. Mabelle said on the way, "I just wonder what we are letting ourselves into."

Mary and Betty would be starting school right in Norris Village, where the workers lived. The nearest Catholic Church was in Knoxville, forty miles away. Their lives for the next eight years would revolve around the T.V.A. Projects. They moved the following year to Murphy, N.C. The damming of the Hiawassee River began in 1936, so they could stay in the area for several years, although they did move from Murphy to Hiawassee Village after a year.

Jerome became a mechanic foreman in the summer of 1937, making $1.50 per hour. Promotions came quickly. A year later, he would be Assistant master mechanic, earning a yearly salary of $3,200 per year, and in June 1938 he was Master Mechanic, one of the highest salaried workers, earning $3,500 per year. He worked eight hours a day, six days a week. On Sundays, he took them out in his four-year-old Chevrolet to church and for a drive.

The Social and Economic Division of the T.V.A. carried out a detailed survey in November of '37. Every aspect of their lives was covered. In the tiny Hiawassee Village house they rented, their lighting was by electricity, and they had an iron and a radio, but did not own a phonograph (record player) or a sewing machine. They had a coal heater. During the interview, Mabelle revealed that Jerome had attended 14 years of education, including 2 years of college.

There was also an attitudinal aspect to the survey. The interviewer recorded that Mabelle was "indifferent" to their location. He or she recorded that the Murray family owned a house and lot in <u>Fort</u> Deposit, Maryland. The mistake was probably an unintentional result of different regional accents. Mabelle also had a soft voice. Not everyone knew about Port Deposit and the Conowingo Dam on the Susquehanna River, it seems. On the positive side for the T.V.A., the Murrays had caught the bug. The interviewer recorded that Mabelle cooperated with the survey and that she was indeed an "active booster" of the T.V.A.

Betty started first grade at Norris Village, Tennessee. Then after a year, the family moved to Hiawassee Village, North Carolina, which, like Norris Village, was constructed for the workers, with a village school, store and multi-purpose hall. Betty and Patsy's early school years were in that village school. It was not always satisfactory. The war and the economic depression dominated the news. They moved, and they moved, and the world moved, too.

It was in the Hiwassee Dam Village that something disquieting occurred when Patsy was five, that may have led to a lifelong insecurity when home alone.

In 1938, we were living in Hiwassee, N.C., in a Tennessee Valley Authority village. Being government housing, the houses were small and close together. It was a safe and friendly place, and at that time it was not necessary to lock doors.

One morning, Mother decided to go to the commissary for a few groceries. Daddy was at work. Mary and Betty were at school and Ann had not been born. We had a new bird dog puppy on the screened-in porch. Mother tied the screen door shut with a small rope so that the puppy could not get out.

We had to walk about a half of a mile to the commissary. On the way back, as we were approaching our house, we saw Gloria M. and Jimmy R. sitting on the sidewalk. Gloria was five, my age, and Jimmy was three. When they saw us coming, they began to chant, "We broke your dishes! We broke your dishes!"

It was true. When Mother went in, the kitchen floor was covered with broken dishes. They had climbed upon the counter and thrown the dishes from the cupboard to the floor. Ink was poured on magazines. The butter from the refrigerator had bite marks. Daddy's razor blades were on a chair. It was a mess!

Mother went next door to get their mothers. Of course, they were shocked. I'm sure the mothers helped clean up the mess. I do know they paid for a new set of dishes.

A few days later, Mother missed her good gold watch. She

talked to Gloria's mother. At first Gloria denied having it, but it was in her shoe bag pocket. When she was asked why she did it, she said, "Jesus told me to take it." I was horrified. I knew that wasn't true.

Why did they do it? One thought is that Gloria had seen a movie scene that had someone throwing dishes. Were they jealous of the new puppy? I don't know, but the incident made a good story for later years. I often told it as a bedtime story to my nieces and nephews. They were always shocked at the thought of someone breaking Grandmom's dishes!

Even with a commissary in the village, food provisions could run low. It was around this time that Betty opened her school lunch one day and found a slice of pineapple between two slices of bread. She was appalled at how low she felt they had sunk. Formal rationing would not start until 1942, when grocery shopping needed to be even more carefully planned.

The next year, 1939, would also be a momentous year for the family still living in Hiawassee. They did not go home in the summer because Mabelle was expecting a new baby that September. The school year began abruptly. Patsy started First Grade, and the new baby arrived soon after Labor Day. They named her Ann Carolyn, and she became the darling of her parents and sisters' lives. Before too long, the girls in the first, fifth and seventh grade were miserable in their school. It was a poor school and a mean teacher used a ruler on their backs. They transferred to a Country School in Spring City, Tenn.

In late December, when Ann was just three months old, Uncle Paul, then thirty-nine years of age, sent a telegram. "MOTHER FADING FAST. ADVISE YOU TO COME." What a shock! They packed up quickly and after church and breakfast, they headed north. It was Christmastime. Mother died during their journey. The date was December 27, 1939 and Mary

Ellen Murray Murray, that short Irish bundle of energy, had passed away aged eighty. So ended the life of this amazing little lady who busied herself getting food on the tables of granite dealers and blacksmiths alike.

They stayed at Joe's farmhouse up in Rock Run Hollow. While the funeral was taking place at St. Teresa's, Mary, twelve, was in charge of the little ones, Cousins Lee and Paul, ages 5 and 4, the sons of Joe and Ione, and, her baby sister Ann. Betty and Patsy, ages 10 and 7, were considered too young for the funeral. At least they made it to Port Deposit. Being considered too young to attend as well, their cousins, Kitty, Bobby, Jr. and Honey Carney felt completely left out.

Honey and Kitty used to say they were always glad to see their "dam cousins." The Murray girls were intrigued to hear their cousins swear. They had heard it plenty of times from Sara'n'Ella. Besides, they were proud of their father's work, and understood its importance. Not everyone understood the broad reach of the river programs, as FDR found out, but his campaign was more than just to produce alternative power, or to prevent flooding. He was well aware that if flooding could be prevented, the soil would stay enriched. The T.V.A. program also created fertilizers to add to depleted soils. If food production improved, self-sufficiency would follow. Rich soil could lead millions out of poverty.

Recreation was essential, too. FDR wrote from the White House in January 1940, seven years after the T.V.A. began about all the benefits of the program ending with the recreational facilities that were created, "Recreation in its broad sense is a definite factor in the improvement of the bodies and minds of our future citizens."

Autograph albums were popular in that era, and a good idea, too, for students moving from school to school. In Watts

Bar Dam, Tennessee, in 1941, Betty's big sister wrote,

Dear Betty,
When the golden sun is setting
And your path is no longer trod,
May your name be written
In the Autograph of God.
   Love,
   Your sister
   Mary

Also touchingly, little sister Patsy wrote,

Dear Betty,
Remember M. Remember E. Put them together and
Remember Me.
I love you little, I love you big, I love you like a little pig.
P.S. Be sure to remember Me. Patsy Murray

One autograph from a very young sister, Ann, may have been a drawn face, but they yanked the book away from her hands, as she wrote "Mine."

Most of the autographs were entertaining if not unique.

Dear Betty
Can't write, to dumb
Inspiration won't come
No Ink   Dull Pen
Best wishes Amen
   LOVE
   BOBBIE *Yours till the kitchen sinks.*

One friend who wrote in a wavering hand on the bus chose pure honesty.

I can't think of any nice
pomes to write so I'll just
sign my name

Gordon Koons

And this revealing one written in Norris, Tennessee on April 25, 1936, was from the ever-original Jerome,

Little Betty my curly head Pal,
Is to be Mother Goose and Dance around
   the May Pole
I hope she does not fly north until
I am ready to go with her.

    Daddy

Someone pasted a photograph of Betty dressed as Mother Goose for the school play on her album's black page, amongst others from the dam workers' villages and schools.

Village life and the continual change of schools would add variety into their lives. They became familiar with the southern way of life, learned about the Cherokee Nation, picked up a southern accent, and attended picnics in the fields surrounding the schools or in the countryside with other churchgoers. Once St. Patrick's Church in McEwan, Tennessee, held an Irish picnic, with white and African-American fiddlers in denim overalls performing and dancing a jig to "Danny Boy". Stephen Foster songs would become a part of their repertoire and when Mabelle signed Betty's autograph album on May 10, 1936, she quoted one of Stephen Foster's lyricists, George Cooper.

> *Hundreds of dewdrops greet the dawn*
> *Hundreds of bees in the purple clover*
> *Hundreds of butterflies on the lawn*
> *But only one Mother the wide world over*

The reservoirs created by the TVA projects provided opportunities for recreation. Being a boat builder, Jerome enlisted the help of Mabelle and the girls, and a photograph of Mabelle competently rowing a wooden row boat across Parksville reservoir in a striped cotton dress, told the story of farmer's daughter-turned-riverman's wife more than any words.

Betty clearly remembered how in the seventh grade in Tennessee a neighbor girl told her that the Japanese had bombed Pearl Harbor. "I had no idea where Pearl Harbor was. I had never heard of it before."

> *[Betty] remembers her teacher receiving letters in class from a loved one at war and how she would open them at her desk and read them with tears running down her face. Mom told me about the "tremendous wave of patriotism" that swept the country after Pearl Harbor. She said so many young men- boys, really – quit high school to enlist in the service.* [1]

The Murrays heard that Joe had to register again, but he only was in the army for a year and then was back to work at Perry Point. Sixteen million Americans were to serve in WWII. Schools and communities everywhere were affected.

As part of the war effort, the Murray girls collected metal toothpaste tubes, tin cans and the least scrap of metal on their way to school; they were even encouraged to peel the aluminum foil backing off chewing gum wrappers. We grew up doing the same, and marveled at the war children's commitment, and the possibilities of recycling.

The girls also saved up to buy U.S. Savings Bonds, supervised by Mabelle. The girls bought little pink stamps at school for ten cents and put these in bond books. When the book was full, they got an $18.75 bond, which helped to finance the war effort. It was worth 20 to 25 dollars on maturity.

The newspaper of Hiawassee Dam School in Hiawassee Dam, N.C., *The Kilowatt*, reported in September 1943 that the remodeled school would open. There was the possibility of a school lunchroom with hot lunches, and there were news items about the Art, English, Needlecraft, Photography and Reading Clubs. How poignant to read the headline, *Photography Club concerned with shortages of film*, and, to see that all of the school's sports news fit in a rather small column. "War News" and "Red Cross News" and chatter and jokes about the dam also featured in this monthly paper.

Mary and Betty Murray were listed as the Junior and Freshman Class Vice-Presidents, and the column, "Over The Dam," quipped, "What would the Junior class do without Mary Murray's brain? Or should we say brains?" Another column listed all of the leavers, which was a common occurrence, a few moving to colleges, some to other dam projects, one to the Army Air Corps, and one, a J.R. Roberts, to Navy Bainbridge, Maryland.

Patsy Murray, now in fifth grade, entered the Murray patriotic effort with her poem entitled, *Uncle Sam*. She would have pleased her father, who probably inspired her fervent poem, typical of the day.

Oh! Uncle Sam—he is the man

To slap the Japs

Right off the maps

He'll do it, I know he can.

And when he does it

Old Tojo will have a fit

But it will be too late

Because Tojo has met his fate.

It would not be possible after that to buy metallic, electrical appliances. Mabelle, however, must have acquired a small, portable, foot-powered sewing machine, as the girls had grown out of their clothing. Even with hand-me-downs, Mary, her oldest girl, needed some new clothes. In Great Britain, this was the "Make-do-and-mend" era. Propaganda leaflets from the British Ministry of Information promoted this and the "Digging for Victory" movement to encourage vegetable gardens on the "home front". There was a shortage of food and supplies in America and Britain alike and it was essential to be resourceful.

Textiles developed during the 1920s contained semi-synthetic woven blends, making them strong and hardwearing. Mabelle would create dresses and suits, even coats using new blends of fabric woven with rayon, when they were available. Rayon became a generic name for synthetic fibers made from a cellulose base, and the name replaced "artificial silk". There would be hardwearing woven blends of most textiles including woven wool, cotton and rayon, as well. Jacquard, a woven cotton and rayon blend, was used for dress fabrics at this time. The pallet of the time darkened, and dark brown, rust, green, blue and natural colors were "everyday".

Household coverings and pillowcases could be dressed up with crewel embroidery and Mabelle could free hand embroider beautiful and colorful flowers, using satin stitches, seed stitches and French knots. Seams sewn in purchased material for curtains, linens and toweling would suffice. Women made all their clothing at home, with the aid of pre-printed patterns from the companies, Advance, Butterick, Simplicity and McCalls.

Back Home

57. The Murray Girls, 1949.
Mary Mabelle, Betty, Ann Carolyn and Patsy.

During their southern exile, they lived in tiny, little houses, and thought about their bigger home in Port Deposit, "if only we could ever get back there". As a way of keeping down inflation, the Office of Price Administration did not allow prices to rise. Betty said, "It was a funny thing, you weren't allowed to raise the rent, and you couldn't evict people." Uncle Paul collected the rent from the family in their Port Deposit home, which was $18 per month. He never let on that anything was wrong.

The girls were growing up and Mary was about to enter senior year. It was the last chance for her to go to the Jacob Tome Institute. The Murrays paid a visit to their home in Port Deposit in the summer of 1945 and were surprised to see Bainbridge N.T.C. across the road from them.

In addition to the fact that the girls were missing out on J.T.I., there was the matter of the unexpected situation at the top of their house. "Not all the rooms were originally rented out to the tenants. The tenants rented the upstairs rooms out to the sailors and such." That was that. Their agreement had been broken, and they would reclaim their house. The trip back down south to finish up and fetch their belongings was a short one.

Jerome's brother, Paul, helped get him a job at Bainbridge. Paul worked as a Mechanic there and Jerome would work in the department of Grounds and Roads, eventually becoming Head of the Machine Shop. His job title was Machinist, Leadingman and Quarterman in Public Works. Bainbridge N.T.C. was a massive site, containing over 800 buildings spread over around 1,335 acres. Jerome could put his hand to anything and did.

When Jerome Murray returned to Mockingbird Hill to begin employment in January, his home on the road to Battle Swamp faced a 10-foot tall, chain-linked fence enclosing the United States Naval Training Center Bainbridge. Jerome could have entered the 1200-acre complex at Gate 14, perhaps one mile from his home. At that time, in 1944, each of the four boot camps would process 5,000 men year-round for the war effort. Although the population of Port Deposit was perhaps 1,000, the population of Bainbridge grew during wartime to 20,000 recruits plus 18,000 civilians, including Jerome.

My grandfather witnessed changes at the base over the years, as recruit training was traded for new commands – EPDCONUS, PAMICONUS, and Manpower plus technical schools such as Radioman, Nuclear Power School, Fire Control Technician, and Yeoman. When W.A.V.E.S. arrived in 1951, Camp James was assigned to ladies, and Hunter Hall barracks was the last building erected on the base in 1962, very near to Mockingbird Hill.

Moving back north brought colder weather. Houses were much colder at night back then, and one cold morning in the upstairs room, Betty woke up to find her feet feeling warm and furry. She looked down, and a little mouse had found itself tucked up under her feet. When the roads were cut-off with snow, they would ride gigantic sleds down the hill to church or school, double-decker style, or hooked together in "a train". Patsy said whenever she drove down Rock Run Hollow she often thought of her dad whizzing down there on a sled as a boy on a snowy winter day, past their home and on into Main Street.

As the days lengthened, they could see the drill fields straight across from their front yard and they watched and copied the sailors marching around and singing songs. They remotely observed the flag ceremonies: *Revelry* in the morning, to the sound of the trumpet, and *Taps* at night.

> *Day is done, gone the sun*
> *From the lakes, from the hills, from the sky.*
> *All is well, safely rest, God is nigh.*

When they had leisure time, the sailors would occasionally hit their baseball over the fence and call the girls to go get it. Betty remembers the sailors taking a shine to the sweet and big-hearted Brannon girls who lived next door. Helen Malinda, who held their hands through the fence, was a year ahead of her at Tome. Billy, Leah and Nancy, too, had become more familiar with the presence of the sailors while they were away. They had spent the entire war as "neighbors" to the Bainbridge sailors.

The Murray girls kept their distance, but once Patsy or

Betty caught a weasel stealing the feed from the chickens and whacked it with the feed tray. That brought big cheers from across the road. The sailors communicated in all kinds of ways with the children across the road. Some, including a J.J. Thompson, threw their white caps over the fence to the girls, and others lost their caps when they went quietly AWOL over the fence.

The pull of the dams down in the Tennessee Valley got to Jerome. He moved back down when they closed Bainbridge, just five years after moving north. Betty accompanied him down south while he was seeing about a job. He moved back down south to Camden, Tenn., where he shared a house, rather than live in the village. Jerome would preserve his government pension by working again for the T.V.A.

Visitors

When Mabelle and the girls went to spend that last summer of 1950 with Jerome in Tennessee, Mary Mabelle stayed behind in Port. She was in the middle of a two-year course at Strayer's Business College in Baltimore. During term time, she roomed on Park Avenue with her cousin Jane Ellicott. Jane was a lovely, slightly bashful young woman whose piano playing aided her typing and earlier completion of the course. She also made the best tomato and mayo sandwiches. Like Mabelle, Alma and Ione, Jane grew up on the Thompson Farm with her mother, Icelene, a community nurse, who helped at births. Mary specialized to become a medical secretary and worked with a psychiatrist at Perry Point. This was to become her favorite job.

During that summer, when Mary was out on Mockingbird Hill, Aunt Bertha Foran Murray stayed with her. In her seventies, she concocted a plan for her and Mary to visit some cousins she knew about in Columbia, Penna. It was the family of John Patrick Murray, her husband Jim's older brother, who had run away from home "to live a little" – the same John Patrick who had proved the doctor wrong. He raised a family, including Rhea, John and Margaret, worked a full life in the foundry, even outliving his wife.

The town of Columbia, on the Susquehanna River, had suffered a parallel decline to Port Deposit, after rail replaced river ports and the dams prohibited river trade. The mills, once so prominent in its skyline, were also closing. The Murray family of Columbia was thriving, however. In addition to the iron foundries, they also got work in the silk mills as weavers. Mary Mabelle and Bertha Murray from Port Deposit sat on a porch overlooking the Susquehanna. (They were possibly at the home of Alice McManus Murray, who named her sons, James and Francis, the first and second names of Bertha's late husband.) When Mary's sisters later found out about the cousins in Columbia, they felt indignant. They did not know they had cousins in Columbia, "but Daddy knew it and kept it quiet". John Patrick's disappearance at a young age probably led to a certain amount of silence about him, but warm, loving Bertha did not let that stop her maintaining this family tie.

About this time exchange visits with another aunt, Aunt Elizabeth Murray, the schoolteacher in Fell's Point, began. During her college years, Betty took a Greyhound Bus to Baltimore to visit Aunt Elizabeth very soon after her retirement. Aunt Elizabeth took Betty on a streetcar to Fort McHenry. It was a success, so she did the same with Patsy, when her turn came.

Aunt Elizabeth came out to Mockingbird Hill to stay with Mabelle and Jerome and she spoiled the girls with little luxuries, as did Aunts Sarah and Ella, who came every year at Thanksgiving. Thanksgiving dinner at Mockingbird Hill became a fixed calendar appointment for the extended family.

Another welcome guest was John James Abrahams:

> My first visit to 339 Tome Highway was during the summer of 1952. I had walked the mile-long hill out of Port and felt very thirsty. Knowing Ann, I knocked at the side door. Mrs. Murray was at the back making home-made soap. First time knowing soap other than commercial brands from the grocery stores![2]

Jerome was only down south for a year and came back permanently when Bainbridge was reactivated for the Korean War (1950—1953). He had only about ten years to go until he could retire. He was back north in time for all of the preparations for Betty's wedding in '52.

Home-made

Betty became something of a seamstress having picked it up from Mabelle, and made her own ivory dress and the palest grey going-away suit for her wedding day. The gown had a silk bodice covered with lace and a tiny waist for the slim, athletic P.E. major. A few years later, Grace Kelly wore one just like it for her marriage to Prince Ranier, but with little buttons going down its front. All the Murray girls, cousins, friends, high school classmates and college roommates wore elegant, understated styles. Softly tailored suits like those of Chanel with fascinating details and flattering designs were as home on these women as in their own fashion house in Paris.

Movie star looks did not always come with gowns and high heels. Lauren Bacall popularized fashionable yet functional clothing. Even while working in the garden with blouses and pedal pushers the Murray girls could vie with the stars in fashion and style.

Betty must have told Charlie about the recreational facilities near the dams, and the fresh-water lakes where her family rowed, fished and swam. An envelope addressed to Mr. N Charles Bolgiano arrived at Long Point Farm, Stevensville, Maryland, from Government Services, Fontana Village, Fontana Dam. Postmarked Aug 13, '52 at Fontana Dam, N.C., it contained a color brochure listing off-season daily rates of $6.00 for a cottage for two without cooking, and $7.00 with cooking. It boasted "Fontana in Fall Is Best of All".

A cottage for two would fit the bill for their honeymoon in September, and Charlie would take Betty to revisit the southern beauty spots. They took in Fontana Dam. While in the cafeteria at the village the newlyweds heard, "Well if it isn't Betty Maarr-y?!" It was one of Ransom Price's girls, who had not changed one bit, still with her Southern drawl, charm and all! "How's Mary Maarr-y?" she asked. The cottage for two "without cooking" was the better choice after all!

Later on, after Patsy finished at Towson State Teacher's College (1955) and Ann Carolyn started at the University of Maryland in September of 1956, Mabelle took over the backroom and created a multi-purpose sewing room and painting studio. Together she and Patsy went to art school and produced dozens of striking oil paintings, each with their own style. Mabelle's tended towards bold florals or landscapes of the late Impressionistic school, usually featuring a river or bay, while Patsy experimented with a wide range of painting styles and subjects, including one striking mosaic-styled patchwork of 38 Granite Avenue, her father's boyhood home.

On the floor of this room, were scattered Mabelle's old-fashioned two-pronged hairpins. Little Mimi, her first grandchild picked one of these up and pushed each part into the matching sides of a plug socket. Thwack!! Mimi was jolted off her feet with the shock. Another time, she and Nick, her younger brother by ten months, were standing by the telephone when lightning struck, knocking them both off their feet. The Murrays never answered the phone in a thunderstorm after that.

In the 1960s, a headless mannequin greeted visitors to this room, and a young grandson dreaded the "Yady –No-Any-Head". Mabelle also installed a small black-and-white television to watch soap operas, including "Days of Our Lives" when people thought she was napping there. Later this became the dollhouse room.

Gun Dogs

From when he first bought one as a boy, Jerome enjoyed owning and working with hunting dogs. At first, he got family friendly spaniels, then setters, and then he concentrated on pointers. One of their first dogs was Beppy, then Old Spot down south, the puppy that let the little vandals in, and finally in the end, there was Jigs. Dogs were not allowed in the house, and cats were strictly forbidden on the property. Ann was so disappointed when the kitty-cat she received was not welcome.

In later life, Jerome would call to his dogs penned near the garage to "CIRCULATE! CIRCULATE!" This would get the dogs running around and around, paws up on the garage side, paws up on the chain-fence side. Rattle, rattle, bang, rattle, rattle, bang. Around they went. Jerome was older. Was this a simple substitute for exercise? It was more than that. Bird dogs on the Eastern Shore were trained to circle the fallen game bird. If the bird landed in brush, the dog who could "circle" the area of brush or briars, would eventually locate the best path into the prize.[3] Circulate, boys!

School-teaching

58. Patricia Ellen Murray.
Patsy Murray taught second grade at Bainbridge Elementary School between September 1955 and June 1986.

Patsy graduated with high honors from Towson State Teachers College in 1955. Finding a job would not be difficult for her, although she was looking for a job close to home. She found a job at the closest school, Bainbridge Elementary School, right on the base.

Many people who work with children say the parents are more difficult than the children. In the case of Cecil County, it was actually the administrators. As outlined in the senior thesis of Kyle M. Dixon (2013), *Standing in the Schoolhouse Door: The desegregation of public schools in Cecil County, Maryland, 1954 – 1965*, there were serious problems with the administrators in the local schools. Despite the great strides made in Port Deposit in the late 1800s, the road to equality was rockier than ever. Explained Dixon:

What makes [Cecil] county unique compared to the rest of the Eastern Shore is that it is the only Maryland County [along the Eastern Shore] to sit on the edge of the Mason-Dixon Line. It is in this county a wedge between Maryland, Delaware, and Pennsylvania, where different cultural, legal and societal norms all converge. This is important to note because while the county is defined by a geographic boundary there is an invisible social boundary that exists within Cecil County. There is a huge difference between the social and political attitudes of citizens of Rising Sun and Conowingo on the county's northern end, and the attitude of citizens in Warwick and Cecilton on the county's southern end.

A reluctance to integrate schools on the military base at Bainbridge culminated in the refusal to allow seven African-American children to enter the school in September of 1954. They were blocked entry by the superintendent and the principal who were standing in the schoolhouse door. This was in flagrant disregard to Truman's 1948 executive order to integrate military facilities and Eisenhower's 1952 decision to specify integration in schools on all U.S. bases. The case reached the Supreme Court and after eleven months came a guarantee that come September 1955, all children would be welcome at the school.

One teacher, a brand new teacher at the school, in fact, would welcome all to her classroom door that September. It was Miss Patricia Ellen Murray. Any child entering second grade in Room 15 at Bainbridge Elementary School in 1955 would find an opportunity to learn, to be valued and to have a chance. Miss Murray stayed at Bainbridge for her whole career. Thirty years a second grade teacher and she had the job and her pupils down to a tee.

Whether in classroom, on the playground, and despite "High Karate" cologne battles in the lavatory or fights in the hall, she was in control, more or less. One time, her class line was coming in the school from the playground. As they approached Room 15, two boys started fighting. Miss Murray tried to separate them, tripped and fell in the hall!

In the playground, kickball was one of her favorite organized games, but there was also "free play time". She kept the Strawberry Patch in the back of the school secret for the benefit of her second graders and invented the Four-Leaf Clover Club to keep them busy. If they found a four - leaf clover, she would trade it for a lollipop. About this she said, "Did you know that if you pick two three-leaf clovers, pull off one leaf on each and hold them together, it makes a four-leaf clover? Did you know that if you sneak back in school for paste and paste an extra leaf onto a three-leaf clover, it makes a four-leaf clover? It didn't work!"

Although Miss Murray was not always a particular fan of all her principals, she always raved about Mr. Brubaker, the custodian. Mr. Brubaker was her rock. He was also a retired navy chief, who led the Halloween Parade in his uniform. Miss Murray appreciated her mother's help in making her Halloween costume that first year.

I started teaching the year Great Aunt Ella died. Mother received some old material from her house. She made me a witch costume for school Halloween. The dress part was similar to a choir gown, made of a heavy black material. She used a lot of old white yarn sewn to a type of head band fitted over the head. The hat was a tall piece of cardboard rolled with a brim. Some years I used a rubber mask and some years my regular face. Older classes sometimes said, "I know that is you, Miss Murray".

Mr. Brubaker was always identifiable in his old uniform,

too. At his 90th birthday party, he went in the house and came out in the uniform. He also helped my aunt to organize the gym for the 2nd grade's annual Bainbridge Circus, complete with tight ropewalkers tottering on masking tape on the floor, cowboys and Indians galloping around, trained ponies pawing at the floor and a snake charmer with a rubber snake.

The other classes came to see the Circus, so entertainment value and full class participation was everything. "The best parts were the clown acts. The acts ended with the clowns chasing each other back to their seats in the ring. In a no-hit boxing match, a clown would call out the name of one of the contestants and get him to turn and look. POW." Instead of pulling a rabbit out a hat, Miss Murray's Towson mascot, a black and white fabric skunk, came out of a bag!

Patsy had a maxim for every occasion. About principals, she rationalized, "Don't ask the principal for advice, just use your own common sense and if he says anything, act innocent! If he gives you a stupid directive, say to yourself, "I gotta be here between 9:00 and 4:00, I might as well do that as anything else."

About planning lessons, she said, "There's nothing in the curriculum that could not be adapted to the 'Murray Method'." The curriculum included visits of all her nieces and nephews when they were in the second grade, and a visit of her sister, Ann, a semi-professional clown-schooled school-clown, complete with a Master's degree from Bowie College in Early Childhood Education (1976).

There were "carrots" but there were "sticks", too. These included rummages in a treasure chest as rewards, and visits to the Bainbridge School Museum for children who would not wash their hands. In a chemical jar high up on a shelf in the museum was the Bainbridge Worm.

A student of [Miss Murray's] was in music class. He

sneezed and a big long worm came out of his nose and landed on the floor. She recalls, "The music teacher could only manage to put a paper towel over it." The quick thinking Custodian put it in a jar of alcohol and there it stayed preserved for many years and became a legend. .. "After this, they would get busy washing their hands."[4]

Having made a trip around the world, riding a camel in Egypt, an elephant in India, and attending a tea ceremony in Japan, she brought elements of these cultures to her class. There was an annual Japan Day, including flying carp kites and their own tea ceremony sitting cross-legged on the floor. Patricia Murray, author of that patriotic poem for her school newspaper all those years before when the Japanese were enemies, now embraced the Japanese culture, giving her nieces and nephews Japanese souvenirs – dolls, ivory birds and yens. Every year's vacation to Ocean City included a trip to the Japan House on North Atlantic Avenue.

Summer vacations of course, were "to be lived for". One of her favorite questions was, "What are my three favorite things about being a teacher?" and respond, "June, July and August". During these times, she would be just as busy at Mockingbird Hill, but not too busy to ignore the chance for vacations to Potter County or Ocean City with her sisters' families. There she coined the saying, "When at the beach, always have a high water mark."

Patsy also took long-distance driving or flying vacations with her friends, Kay Maisenholder and Mary Jane Mattingly. Their trips to all fifty states of the United States took in Presidential birthplaces and libraries as well as historical homes, like those of the writer, Laura Ingalls Wilder, who wrote the *Little House on the Prairie* books. She went on adventures to the lands of *Anne of Green Gables* on Prince Edward Island in Canada, and to the Australian outback of

Lucy Walker.

One summer vacation did not start out right. In June, in the early seventies, I was helping my aunt tidy her classroom after school was out. A man from the base who was not acting normally tried to enter her classroom by the outside door. He was completely naked. My aunt heard the doorknob being tried over the whirring of the fans, and said loudly to me, "Did you hear that?" I shouted, "No" and we went on working. Naturally, we had all the windows open, while we worked into the darkening evening. She said again, "Barbie, I think I heard the door."

When the man was spotted, she alerted me; we closed all the windows and flew down the hall, making sure we tripped the burglar alarm. Something went wrong. When she tried to call Mr. Brubaker, who was away, the automatic call to the police did not go through. After what seemed like an age in the school office, the whole of the school drive was filled suddenly with police cars and dogs. The most frightening part was being escorted to her car, and pretending to Mabelle and Jerome that nothing was wrong.

The next day, we entered the school doors again to finish the work we had started. Somebody leaked the news, and some teachers cruelly badgered my aunt over the Public Address system, but one brave and understanding teacher came to talk to her face-to-face and offer support. Her name was Mrs. Irene Nutter. Mrs. Nutter taught fourth grade along the same corridor as did my aunt. She had been a principal at the Port Deposit Colored Elementary School in 1963, but just a year or two before our fateful evening, had endured something that should never have happened. She was refused the chance to become a school principal in an integrated school, although she was more qualified than the other candidates. Her case against the Maryland State Board of Education was a long, drawn-out and high profile case that deeply affected her and the other teachers at Bainbridge. My aunt wrote to me a few years ago to say that Mrs. Nutter should have been given the chance to be a principal. If anyone knew her qualities, my aunt did.

In 1985, after thirty years of teaching, Miss Pat Murray was ready to claim her pension. She began to love Septembers. She really enjoyed teaching second graders, but she enjoyed retirement even more.

Grandchildren's Visits

Mockingbird Hill had not only become a home for the third and fourth generation Murrays, the fifth and sixth felt at home here, too. There would be Girls' Nights and Boys' Nights and Going to Bed by Candlelight, with candles carried all throughout the house to the upstairs bedroom lit by candles including the dazzling light of Aunt Sara and Ella's candelabras, the ones that Blanche Keaveny wanted.

Jerome and Mabelle participated in the visits of the young ones. Jerome once brought a plywood board up to the porch for little tap dancers, and Mabelle was forever getting out her recipes and mixing bowls. Visits became easier when Jerome retired in 1965, after earning his enamel and 24 ct. gold civilian service award pins for 20 and 30 years of service, and finally a 36-year plaque. He had become a veteran as FDR had promised.

As soon as a car tire hit the gravel drive at Mockingbird Hill, Jerome would be out of the door, if not already in one of the rocking chairs, ready to carry the suitcases. For this, he would pay *you* a wage, like a quarter, ask for the tax back, and then give you a dime or nickel. There was always a joke about the tax. It was then, once you were softened up, that he would get you to promise to help him get the "termater bugs", which paid one cent for an ordinary bug, or five cents for a big green tomato bug that really ate up his prize Burpee Big Boys. It was an easy source of income and who did not enjoy working in the large vegetable garden assisting Jerome? We helped lift cabbages, cut spinach, gather potatoes – any and every size – and water the plants. The soil was always rich, brown and soft, perfect for matching our bare feet to his big, wide work shoe steps. Afterwards, after a check of the big rain barrels to make sure there were no snakes, we would clean up, sometimes getting all the way in the barrels.

There was one unforgettable summer night in the upstairs guest room overlooking the orchard. "I remember you and Elaine laughing and laughing upstairs in the room where you used to stay", Patsy said. We had gone upstairs by candle light and the giant Port Deposit lightning bugs spooked us. We thought people were down in the orchard shining flash-lights up! We panicked, "AUNT PAT! AUNT PAT! Someone's shining a flashlight up here!" " Oh", she said, "That's just those old lightning bugs." Giddy and high with the excite-ment, we laughed and laughed, hysterical at our folly.

The next day, things looked fine. We wanted to do "old-time" laundry. I asked to use the ringer; Elaine asked to use the washboard. Things started out well. I got the clothes washed and started to crank them through the ringer. They were coming out fast. Aunt Pat came out to check. "Honey, the water's all going on the floor!" We got that straightened out, and she went down the Company Store steps to help Elaine, who had the harder job at the wash board, but at least her laundry was only flooding the grass. It taught us a thing or two about old-time laundry. We never asked to do that again.

At supper, Daddy, asked Elaine, "do you like potatoes?" Well you know, to an Irishman if you didn't like potatoes, you were nothing!

"No!", little Elaine dared to say to the silent table. "I love 'em!" And to show it, she smacked a whole "smack" of mash potatoes on her plate."

Another time, her brother, Davey did the exact same thing.

In her heyday, my aunt excelled with all ages. Games for children and toddlers included drawing on the skin of a child's hand or back saying, "Draw a magic circle. Somebody dot it with a dot! Which little finger did it? Which little finger did it?" Tickles, like "Bore, bore, bore, bore, stick a fat pig!" were always popular as was hand spelling with the older children. Babies had lullabies, and for fun, the kids were hypnotized during one vacation. There was no limit to the books or crafts on hand, especially when creating nature art, rock painting or sand art. Outdoor games were adopted from traditional southern games, like "Duck, Duck, Gray Duck", "Mother May I?", "Rotten' Eggs" or "Grandmother Hibble Hobble".

While you would always find Jerome on the front porch when you first came, Mabelle would be near the kitchen. The kitchen was only off limits to Jerome when sparks were flying between his Irish temper and her English sensibilities. It was not always clear what the argument was about, but Mabelle was smart enough to ensure she had potatoes on the table at mealtime, just as Mary Ellen had. Mabelle could diffuse any tension with funny comments though. She would say, "Who wants a roll?" ... "Then get down on the floor and roll!"

Sometimes you would arrive to find Patsy giving Mabelle a perm at the kitchen sink. This was only later in life, as Mabelle, in her younger years, wore her hair long, braided and wrapped around her head, as was the style of her generation. Hers was the generation of the hairpins.

When we moved back from the South, our house had not been lived in for a while. Mary went to the pantry for a jar. There was a black snake on the pantry shelf. Mom knew how to get it down. She got cold water and threw it up on the shelf. The snake came down and went on the back porch. Mary and Betty were hitting at it. Maybe they had a hoe or shovel. Anyway, Uncle Paul and Aunt Elizabeth had just driven in to visit. They thought Mary and Betty were dribbling a basketball on the back porch. I didn't see the snake because I got up on the sink.

If Mabelle knew you were coming, she would get out her cookbooks to see if she could find something you would like. This was particularly true if there was a birthday or get-well needed. She was especially busy during September. The September birthday people would get their own batches of cookies. Checkerboards were her favorites and were the very last recipe that she planned.

Inside the upstairs rooms the old Victrola gramophone would be cranked up to hear the music blaring out its front doors, songs from the musical film, *Oklahoma* (1955) on heavy records played with long needles. Vinyl records like "The Devil Made Me Buy This Dress" by comedian Flip Wilson (1970) were played on a more modern record player of the day. After all the laughing, my aunt could calm even the giddiest child with stories, again from the south, like the Uncle Remus stories about B'rer Rabbit and B'rer Fox.

Christmas Days were always special, but my grand-mother also used to host a special Christmas gathering for the Thompson clan in January for Uncle Kemper. Kemper was the fun-loving, younger brother of my grandmother. The run-up to it was always interesting and involved polishing furniture, chandeliers and door handles. Aunt Pat furnished the ideas, we had the elbow grease. Beautiful crystal-glass punch bowls and ladles were readied for the occasion.

The evening would consist of quizzes, slide shows the old-fashioned way, funny readings by Kemper from old etiquette books, and in between the entertainment, a buffet and chocolate fondue kept everyone happy. Laughter and wrapped prizes accompanied everything and it was a chance to find out about relatives you barely knew. One new acquisition was Johnny Glassman, Sr. Johnny married Kemper's daughter, Sara Jean Thompson, in 1971. He had recently returned from a military base in Taiwan, was full of confidence and fit right in.

There was a little blackboard in the kitchen that was a place for marking your territory. "So-and-so was here" would be chalked, then erased, and chalked again. At one of his first parties, Johnny left the message "Kilroy was here" and a cartoon drawing of a man peeking out over a wall. We girl cousins erased it. Johnny crept back in and chalked it up again. We erased it again asserting, "Barbie was here! Patty was here. Elaine was here!" Kilroy came back. We got a little mad. So did Johnny, but not for long. He explained that this comic was popularized during the war.[5] We left it up then, respecting a soldier's way of communicating.

Annual family reunions of the Murray and Thompson clans included rowdy games of whiffle ball. Only a first base was needed, with the telephone pole in the middle of the yard as second base, and a boxwood bush by default being third base. This sensitive boxwood grew to only half the size as its mate. These boxwoods were rooted from the hedge at 38 Granite Avenue.

Once her nieces and nephews became more or less house-trained, Patsy would take them to Williamsburg. The 1963 models, as she called them, all went together. All were treated to a fancy meal at the King's Arms Tavern and a baker's dozen of gingerbread cookies next door.

Experiencing the 1972 Flood

59. Conowingo Dam floodwaters during Hurricane Agnes, 1972.
Courtesy of the Port Deposit Heritage Corporation.

The last significant flood in Port Deposit was on the 11th of September 2011, following Tropical Storm Lee, when the river crested behind the dam at 32.41 ft. (9.88m), the third highest Conowingo River level in recorded history. The town of Port Deposit, 5 miles below the dam, was evacuated following the flooding, as it had also been in 1972, in the aftermath of Hurricane Agnes, which swept up from the Caribbean and reached Baltimore on June 22nd.

To Jerome, who had grown up in lower Port Deposit near the river, worked to build the dam and operate the overhead cranes to open the floodgates, high waters were always a cause for concern. All night radio bulletins on 23rd of June 1972, and the morning of the 24th gave updates on the height of the river as residents worried about the integrity of the dam. To Mabelle and Jerome's 12-year old grandson, Danny, and 11-year old granddaughter, Barbie, who were staying at their grandparents' home on Mockingbird Hill at the time, the events surrounding the flood were the highlight of their summer.

At Conowingo Dam, every one of the 53 floodgates opened up, for only the second time in history, the first being in 1936. Explosives were planted to blow a minor section of the dam if needed, as the waters crested at 1:30 a.m. on June 24, 1972 to within 5 ft. (1.52 m) of the top of the dam. According to the Conowingo Hydroelectric Plant, the record discharge of water from the dam was 1,131,000 cubic ft/sec during Agnes, compared to a minimum discharge on March 2, 1969, when the flow sensor registered just 144 cubic ft/sec.[6]

Aunt Pat's radio alarm clock went off every 15 minutes in the wee hours of that Saturday morning of June 24. Each bulletin gave news that the water level was rising. Being so high up on the hill did not give my brother, Danny, and I any cause for concern. Only when we learned that there was a chance the dam could burst, did we feel an edge to our excitement. Jerome, who was seventy-four at the time, and Patsy, who was on summer vacation from school teaching, took us by car around the back of Port Deposit, to the junction of River Road just north of the dam where we could see the vaporizing water shooting out of the dam. Patsy drove above the quarry where we walked around to see the extent of the floodwaters. Near there we played a baseball game complete with 'ghost runners' on an old abandoned baseball diamond that Jerome used to play on.

Sadly, our fun ended, when our mother, Betty, came to "rescue" us. This visit of the Lancastrians to view the flood was not the first. A steam train full of Lancastrians also came to see the aftermath of the ice gorge in 1910.[7]

At our age, we had no first-hand knowledge of a flood's devastation or the worry of a parent. We only felt our hopes of being marooned with the Murrays somewhat dashed. I did wonder if my grandfather felt a sense of pride that the dam he was so closely associated with had survived such a deluge. He was certainly interested in surveying the floodgates open at full capacity. For me, the high water mark on the old railroad overpass near Rock Run was a reminder of the knowledge that a flooded Susquehanna could submerge cars on River Road.

Peonies

60. Betty and Jerome Murray with the peonies.
In June 1947, Betty graduated from J.T.I., and is pictured here with her father, Jerome at Mockingbird Hill.

It was very sad when Jerome and Mabelle passed away at Mockingbird Hill in 1980, within just a week of each other. Jerome was always one for putting flowers on the graves.

All the Murray grandparents and great-grandparents of mine died in Port, some great-aunts and uncles, too. They are buried in Mt. Erin Catholic Cemetery belonging to St. Patrick's Church in Havre de Grace. Port Deposit had no space for a cemetery and the granite rock shelf it sat on prohibited it. Most of the 'old time' Catholics in Port are buried at Mr. Erin. When Daddy was young, he went with his grandmother and aunts to put flowers on graves. When we were young, he took us and we put peonies there. He took A. Sarah, Ellen and Bertha, also. When all the great aunts died, he and I went. Now, Mary Jane and I go.

Vivid peonies, beautiful, lush and fragrant make a graceful arch around the drive here at Mockingbird Hill, alternating white, deep-pink and pale-pink as you head towards the Company Store steps, the granite steps that now after nearly one hundred and fifty years, and at least a million steps on stone are just beginning to show some wear.

Two most powerful memories are associated with Jerome's peonies. The first memory began with the sharp, pointy tools hung in the garage for all to see, and ended witnessing my grandfather's violent slaughter of these plants with a scythe or sickle in the fall. "Cut the foliage to the ground in the fall to avoid any overwintering disease", says the *Old Farmer's Almanac*. And so he did, and they and their offspring bloom every May or June.

This leads to the second memory. It was a June occasion, although it could be any late spring or early summer occasion - a graduation would do. This the wedding of his first grandchild in the June of 1977, and armfuls of his peonies coming into the house and into my mother's creamware vases, and the gorgeous overwhelming scent of these flowers. And later in the church, in his grey pinstriped suit, seeing his tears fall as the pretty bride came down the aisle — this was a powerful demonstration from a strong man who felt so deeply, and still no doubt does, as to donate his flowers to any event worth a tear or two. Peonies will always be my flower of choice for a graduation, a wedding or a funeral, to bring Jerome's sensitivity to it, except for one thing. I cannot and have not succeeded in seeing a single peony bloom in my garden two years in a row.

Afterword

Whatever forward steps were taken by the hopeful immigrants who came to Port Deposit in the nineteenth century, they were not taken in vain. Many of these were young, poor, and in the case of many of the Irish, malnourished and possibly illiterate as well, such were the counter-effects of the Great Famine. These were the hard workers, whose toil and care giving laid the foundations for generations to come. Though they could have settled in any town, village or city, their eventual choice of Port Deposit, in Cecil County, Maryland, at this particular period in history was fortuitous.

If ever there was a time and a place for a family to rise out of the shanty this was it. The sheer size of the McClenahans' granite quarry operations (as well as the established lumberyards and warehouses) meant that jobs were virtually guaranteed for those willing, and capable of a hard day's work. Food was readily available at the Company Store and housing, shoes and tools could also be acquired in the nearby village of Rock Run. Large and expanding cross-generational families were needed for support in times of need, such as when William Joseph's father died when he was twelve years old, or Jerome's when he was eleven, leaving large families without their main breadwinners.

The free education for Cecil and Harford County residents offered by Jacob and Evalyn Nesbitt Tome from the turn of the century, allowed many of the second and third generations to progress academically beyond the immigrants' expectations. The offspring of William Joseph and Mary Ellen Murray established economic independence through their skilled and/or professional work. Jerome's story in particular illustrated the fruits of his hard-earned prosperity, so that in his leisure time, he was able to pursue his river and land-based interests, including baseball, fishing and hunting. That he was able to find meaningful and enjoyable civilian work on so many different dam projects in the eastern United States was remarkable, a testament to his work ethic, willingness to travel and Roosevelt's T.V.A. program. This opportunity for work during the Great Depression also arose because of the skills Jerome learned in the Machine Shops at J.T.I. His stints on the Susquehanna River dam projects, added to perhaps an innate ability as a son of a blacksmith, were also instrumental in his love for this work. Jerome was blessed with large families from both his mother's and his father's side in Port Deposit, along with his own ingenuity and zest for life. These propelled him forward with greater momentum than enjoyed by prior generations of Port Deposit Murrays.

During the telling of the Murrays' story, the crossroads of the African-American and European migrations in America in the late 1800s and early 1900s became apparent in different ways. The news reports of the quarry strike and witness accounts of the ice gorges and floods added, however, to a growing sense that distinctions in color, race or religion would sometimes blur into the background. The common and beneficent path they chose led to the greatest good for the majority.

A realization of the backbreaking work and the sacrifices that people made for their families, coupled with the inevitable loss of life at much younger ages, was truly sobering for this twenty-first century researcher. The reality of the lives of many in the town, gleaned from the censuses of the times were too sad to repeat on these pages. Their hardships were independent of their financial or social positions. Close-knit communities and extended families were a notable feature of the times, in general, and helped immigrants to integrate into mainstream American life.

The sojourn of the Jerome Murray family into the T.V.A. South provided social and domestic contrasts to the situation back home in Port Deposit. There was a sense of isolation and poverty at times, even though the T.V.A. villages provided much of the same infrastructure that Port would have. As with other families, once third and fourth generation family members travelled for education and work, they blended further into urban or distant neighborhoods. Assimilation would bring advantages and disadvantages, though. Gone were the institutions and people that made a place a home. Patricia, a fourth generation Murray was able to move back and more easily assimilate into the local community, and establish more permanent roots. She then made it her mission to record and archive history for future generations, and became an inveterate storyteller like her father.

From many vantage points, America is yet again, and may always be at a crossroads. Can historical reminders of the lives of previous generations provide markers that can aid in the realization of the bounty we share, and the acceptance of further progress for established citizens and newcomers alike? We must hope so. What questions have we of our elders, and what stories have we, in turn to share?

In its simplicity, this Port Deposit story is an example of how one riverside town survived great change and natural disaster as told through the eyes of one family. Through the Murrays, we witness many instances of heroic individual effort and see the value of the collective community. The retelling of this family's history within the historical framework of the era helps us to understand the social forces that shaped the enchanting riverside community of Port Deposit.

For those who casually drive through Main Street, may you leave with a deeper appreciation for the physical beauty in its granite homes, as well as a respect for the toilers and neighbors who literally gave their lives in this town, while extending a hand to others? In learning from the past generations, it is my hope that we might carry forth the same spirits of generosity and graciousness, and a true enjoyment of life.

May all who are destined to enjoy a day, a week, or even a lifetime in Port Deposit, feel like the Murray, the people "of the sea". Be at your happiest, with a firm foundation under your feet, a rock wall at your back, and the ever flowing, always changing, refreshing water in your view.

Acknowledgements

A poetry book, *Links of Memory*, bears two inscriptions. The first, from Dec. 1912: "From Mrs. C. Newell "Tome School" To Mrs. Mary Murray, Port Deposit, MD, and, "For Jerome P. Murray, Port Deposit, MD, 1946.

Mrs. Mary Ellen Donnelly Murray was Jerome Patrick Murray's grandmother, and the exact reason why Mrs. Newell, gave her this book is unknown. Her daughters must have known, however, that their nephew, Jerome was a poet at–heart, when he was chosen as its next keeper. His daughter, Patricia Murray gifted it to my sister, Margaret Bolgiano Fischer. A gift passing through five generations is a special thing. This gift, the poetry book, expressed an appreciation from school teacher to mother. I would also like to express my gratitude to those who passed on stories from the past and to convey my thanks to the educators who have provided opportunities to generations through the flame they sparked in just a few.

Alice Miller, Charlotte Newall and Nancy Roberts spent decades preparing their own material for print, and greatly added to the subject matter of *Steps*. Historical tales by Andrea Barrett, Frank Delaney, Laurie Halse Anderson, Colum McCann and Colson Whitehead led me to delve deeper, and non-fictional accounts, in particular by Tim Pat Coogan and Cormac Ó'Gráda, to find a broader parchment. Accessible resources from town, county, state, church, university and national bodies have been treasure troves. Some information was retrieved from the databases of Genealogy

Bank, Ancestry and Family Search. I am grateful to the officers of the Port Deposit Heritage Corporation, Glen Longacre, President and JoAnne Luglio Bierly, Secretary, and the staff of the Paw Paw Museum in Port Deposit. JLB and the Rev. George Hipkins very graciously and carefully reviewed an early version, and supplied photographs. The Historical Society of Cecil County provided valuable resources on its website, often the fruit of other researchers' toil, and Carol Donache and Jo Ann Gardner offered further information about the quarrymen's strike, and gave helpful instructions to aid further research. From other institutions, staff members included Kendra Lightner, Archivist technician, F.D.R. Presidential Library; Marie Sypolt, Good Shepherd Parish, Havre de Grace; Ms. Alex Ward, Curator of Dress and Textiles, National Museum of Ireland; and, Terri Kearney at the Skibbereen Heritage Centre, County Cork.

At Apprentice House Press at Loyola University, Baltimore, Director Kevin Atticks DCD led a team of enthusiastic, talented and courteous students to turn my manuscript into a book, including Mary Del Plato, editor; Serena Chenery, marketing advisor; and, Meghan DeGeorge and Jaclyn Oill, book designers. Thank you, Kevin to you and your Acquisitions Class, led by Alexandra Chouinard and Karl Dehmelt, for including this book as one of your academic year projects.

My role in this story was merely as a collector and re-teller of tales from the Murray Storytellers, Jerome Patrick Murray and his daughter, Patricia Ellen Murray, and from many others in the family who contributed theirs. During the drafting of this book, two Murray Girls, Mary Mabelle and Patricia Ellen sadly passed away. Both contributed to the very end, Mary, who with the aid of Retta Grafton, clarified details, and Patsy by providing new material even and a description of the interiors of the old Murray homes. My mother, Betty, good-naturedly endured interviews and questions over many years, thoughtfully commented on all of the stories and provided new ones. My aunt, Ann Carolyn, generously allowed details from her life to be recounted on these pages, as have my Bannon cousin, Chris Bannon II, Carney cousins, Kathleen Buetow MD, Robert E. Carney, Jr., and Anne Carney Brown, and Thompson cousins, Sara & John Glassman.

I am also very grateful to the following photographers: Rev. John J. Abrahams, Dorothea Henrich, Robert Longuehaye and Andrew Miller, and those who offered photographs including Chris and Nina Bannon, Brenda Tipton Knopp and DH. Thank you also to Mary Corbett OBE, Paolo Costantino PhD, Rev. Jerry Daly MSC, Aldo Giannozzi PhD, Niels Hermandsson PhD MCSP and Susan Huff, and my Chevalier Family and Pondfield Crescent groups, for your encouragement and ideas. Cynthia Landrum PhD, an expert on Indigenous Nations Studies at Oregon State University and Clark College gave expert advice and encouragement.

From the first draft, reviewed by Patricia Mary Grafton, many family members have contributed. My sisters, Frances Bolgiano Bidwell and Margaret Bolgiano Fischer have greatly enriched this book through their inquisitive and incisive questions, and editorial comments, and through supplementing the genealogical research of Anne Carney Brown and Patricia Murray. My sister, Mary Elizabeth, shared Mary Ellen's "receipts", and Carolyn Bolgiano Capistrano, her entertaining stories. My father, Charlie, advised me in 2006 to expound on Mabelle and Jerome's life more fully, and he and my brother, Bill, contributed to the descriptions of decoys and duck hunting. My brother, Nick, provided commentary on the natural, military, social and political history contained in this story. All of my cousins and nieces and nephews, including Meghan Patricia Bidwell and Samuel Patrick Bidwell, helped in particular ways, or were, like my brother Danny, my comrades-in-fun with the Murrays. My deepest thanks are bestowed to my beloved sons, James and Ben for their patience during the drafting of this story, and their companionship during summer visits to Mockingbird Hill.

About the Author

Barbara Bolgiano was born north of the Mason-Dixon Line, and summered south of it. A graduate of The Pennsylvania State University and The University of Pennsylvania's bachelor and doctoral programs in microbiology, she now evaluates vaccines as a Principal Scientist at the U.K.'s national laboratory in Hertfordshire, England. After decades of authoring research papers about the molecules that make up vaccines, she has discovered an interest in uncovering and recording human stories. *Steps* is her first book.

Notes

Foreword

[i] www.portdeposit.org.

[ii] Alvin M. Josephy, *The American Heritage Book of Indians* (Rockville, MD: American Heritage Publishing Co, Inc., 1969), 188-219.

[iii] A cousin of Leonard Peltier.

[iv] John Philipps, interview with Cynthia Landrum, Portland, OR, Fall 2015.

[v] Margaret Szasz, *Indian Education in the American Colonies, 1607-1783* (Albuquerque, NM: University of New Mexico, 1988), 52.

[vi] Ibid, 117.

[vii] Helen C. Rountree and Thomas Davidson, *Eastern Shore Indians of Virginia and Maryland* (Charlottesville, VA: University of Virginia Press, 1997), 33.

[viii] Ibid, 131.

[ix] Ibid, 100.

[x] Evan Pritchard, *Native New Yorkers: The Legacy of the Algonquin People of New York* (San Francisco, CA: Council Oak Books, 2007), 305.

[xi] Philip Deloria, *Playing Indian* (New Haven, CT: Yale University Press, 1998), 190-191.

Part I

Early Inhabitants

[1] David J. Minderhout, "Native American Prehistory in the Susquehanna River Valley" in *Native Americans in the Susquehanna River Valley, Past and Present*, edited by David J. Minderhout (Lewisbury, Bucknell University Press, 2013).

[2] Paul A. Nevin, "A Story in Stone: The Susquehanna's Rock Art Legacy" in *Native Americans in the Susquehanna River Valley, Past and Present*, edited by David J. Minderhout (Lewisbury, Bucknell University Press, 2013), 54.

[3] "Valuable Indian Relics Found Near Port Deposit", Patriot (Harrisburg,

Penna.) Dec 2, 1921, 22; "Hunting Indian Relics – Islands near Port Deposit Mecca for those Fond of Historical Search", *Reading Eagle,* Oct 21, 1925.

[4] George Johnston. *History of Cecil County, Maryland, and the Early Settlements around the Head of Chesapeake Bay and on the Delaware River, with Sketches of Some of the Old Families of Cecil County.* (Elkton, MD: Published by the author, 1881), 4.

River and Stone

[1] Alice E. Miller, *Cecil County, Maryland: A Study in Local History* (Elkton: E & L Printing, 1976), 105-132; Earl E. Brown, *Commerce on Early American Waterways: The Transport of Goods by Arks, Rafts and Log Drives.* (Jefferson, N.C.:McFarland & Co., 2010), 4.

[2] Miller, *Cecil County, Maryland*, 106-116.

[3] Ibid.,106.

[4] Ibid., 107-108.

[5] John Smith, *The Travels of Captaine John Smith.* (Glasgow: James MacLehose and Sons, 1907).

[6] A map of the original Susquehanna (or Conowingo) Canal on the eastern side of the river and the Susquehanna & Tidewater Canal on the west bank was redrawn by civil engineer Robert S. Mayo in Jan 1977 from the U.S.G.S. Havre de Grace 1899 map and the B. Henry Latrobe Map of 1801, which was burnt by the British in 1814 and redrawn in 1814. This map showed Upper Ferry (or Creswell's Ferry) route as originating on the eastern side at the center or Port Deposit, across from the Creswell Home and old road to Philadelphia, and crossing to the landing on the western side where the road to Baltimore passes through Lapidum. The other ferry crossings drawn were at Bald's Friar Ferry (1730), and Lower Ferry (1695), which crossed the river under the current Rte. 95 bridge, at the shortest distance between Perryville and Havre de Grace.

[7] Miller, *Cecil County, Maryland,* 106, 120-121.

[8] A Rock Run also extends up the southwestern bank of the river, directly across from this point, into Harford County, the river marking the division between Cecil and Harford counties.

[9] Miller, *Cecil County, Maryland,* 112-113.

[10] Ibid., 114.

[11] Susannah Lawrence and Barbara Gross. *The Audubon Society Field Guide to the Natural Places of the Mid-Atlantic States: Inland.* (New York:Pantheon Books, 1984).

[12] *Into the Earth: Earthquakes, seismology and the Earth's magnetism.* (Milton Keynes: The Open University, 1992), 76-79.

[13] Thomas Leonard Watson, *Granites of the Southeastern Atlantic States.*

United States Geological Survey. (Washington: Government Printing Office, 1910), 59-61.

[14] Edward Bennett Mathews, *The Mineral Resources of Cecil County.* in The Maryland Geological Survey. Cecil County (Baltimore: the Johns Hopkins Press, 1902), 196-203.

[15] Ibid., 197.

[16] Roberts, *Everlasting Granite*, numerous interviews quoted within; U.S.Census of 1860, 1870, 1880, 1900, 1910, 1920.

[17] Nancy Roberts, *Everlasting Granite*, Interviews with Mr. Dominick Cifaldo and Jerome Patrick Murray; Fred Kelso, *Steam, Stone and Wood: 19th Century Commerce in Port Deposit, Maryland* (Oxford, Pa: Henwrt Publishing Company, 1997), 3-4.

[18] Ibid., Interview with Mr. Joseph Rinaldi, Sr.

[19] U.S. Census for Port Deposit or Seventh Election District, various years.

[20] Mathews, *The Mineral Resources of Cecil County*, 199.

[21] Roberts, *Everlasting Granite*, 36-40, 51, 100-102.

[22] Mathews, *The Mineral Resources of Cecil County*, 198-203.

[23] Mathews, *The Mineral Resources of Cecil County.* 198; Kelso, *Steam, Stone and Wood*, 5-6.

[24] Roberts, Everlasting Granite, Interview with Jerome Patrick Murray, February 22, 1976.

[25] The arks weighed down from the granite would travel to "cribs" located further downstream where horse-powered cranes hoisted the granite to larger sea-going vessels. The horses were boarded out on these island homes until the risk of a frozen river halted the operation.

[26] Roberts, *Everlasting Granite*, Interview with Mrs. Thomas Fox, February 12, 1976. "Dirt Bank" homes were "a section near the quarry where the company had built houses for employees." At times, the granite and quarry dust coated the homes and gardens.

[27] Work hours fluctuated depending on the period of management of the quarry, and time of the year.

[28] Rock Run Bard, *Port Deposit in Verse* (Rock Run: June 1st, 1881).

[29] "Port Deposit Does No Work – A Trade and Labor Parade Followed by Speeches and Athletic Sports", Baltimore *Sun*, September 2, 1890.

[30] Alfred Bell was "an excellent horseshoer and was employed in a number of blacksmith shops until he formed a partnership with David Bond," according to his obituary printed in the *Whig* in February 1889.

[31] "The Quarry Trouble at Port Deposit", *Cecil Democrat*, June 27, 1891.

[32] "The Port Deposit Strike – Statement Of The Union Stonecutters Now At Work In M'Clenahan Bro. Quarry. Letter to the Editor, *Cecil Democrat*, July 4, 1891.

[33] A few years later, quarry workers in northern Tuscany in Italy, who were quarrying the famous white Carrara marble, also revolted, but on an entirely different scale. "They earn fair wages, but their work is so hard that applicants at the quarries are few and the overseers must take whom they can get without discrimination concerning anything except muscle and endurance" from "A Stronghold of Anarchists- Italy's Action In Respect To Carrara Fully Justified", *The New York Times*, January 19, 1894.

[34] John Hope Franklin and Alfred A. Moss, Jr., *From Slavery to Freedom: A History of African Americans* (New York: McGraw-Hill, Inc., 1994), 235-236.

[35] Kenneth C. Davis, *A Nation Rising: Untold Tales from America's Hidden History* (New York: Harper, 2010), Chapter V, *Morses's Code*.

[36] When asked questions about their secretive activities, the nativisits were supposed to answer "I know nothing about it", hence they became known as the Know-Nothings. They were active mainly in the 1850s.

[37] Tim Pat Coogan, *Wherever Green is Worn: The Story of the Irish Diaspora* (New York: Palgrave, 2001), 280.

[38] Roberts, *Everlasting Granite*, Interview with Mr. Joseph Rinaldi, Sr.

[39] *Cecil Democrat*, May 16, 1891.

[40] Ibid.

[41] *Cecil Democrat*, September 5, 1891.

[42] Roberts, *Everlasting Granite*, Interviews with Jerome P. Murray and Mrs. Leslie Roberts.

[43] C. Fraser Smith. *Here Lies Jim Crow: Civil Rights In Maryland* (Baltimore: The Johns Hopkins University Press, 2008).

[44] Roberts, *Everlasting Granite*, Interview with Mr. Joseph Rinaldi, Sr.

[45] Rip-rap is a 19th century civil engineering term for "broken stones loosely deposited in water, or on a soft bottom to provide a foundation and protect a riverbed or river banks from scour: used for revetments, embankments, breakwaters, etc." Another use of rip-rap was for a defense of the Eastern Shore of Maryland during the War of 1812; stones lined the shorelines so British boats could not easily land.

Ice gorges and Floods

[1] The width of the river at the Chesapeake Bay end is 713 feet (or 218 meters) narrower than at the Creswell-to-Lapidum crossing proximal to the center of Port Deposit, taking account of Garrett Island on the Perryville side of the river.

[2] "River pushes ice gorge into Port Deposit," *The County Post – Special Edition*, May 3, 1997.

[3] Watson's Island was renamed Garrett Island after it was purchased by B & O Railroad for the purpose of building a bridge. It was called Palmer's Island by the early settlers.

[4] Original account retold in the *Rising Sun Herald*, Feb. 28, 1990.

[5] "The Ice Flood," *Easton Gazetter*, Jan 25, 1873.

[6] A 1910 postcard shows a "Home That Was Carried Two Miles Down The Susquehanna River", and a news report from the Baltimore American that same year told of a Pennsylvania Railroad train station "being crushed like an eggshell".

[7] "Disease Follows Flood," *Baltimore Sun*, Jan 30, 1910.

[8] The McClenahan Granite Company lost a large number of bushels of oats form the second floor of the warehouse which washed away.

[9] "Plan Electrifying of Pennsy Soon – Immense Railroad Power Project May Cost Company $50,000,000," *The Evening Star* (DC) January 8, 1925, 28.

[10] "Suit Would Stop Big Dam Project – Pennsylvania Company Seeks to Halt Power Plans in Maryland," *The Evening Star* (DC) July 14, 1925, 27.

Arrival of the Immigrants

[1] Tim Pat Coogan, *The Famine Plot* (New York: Palgrave Macmillan, 2012).

[2] Ibid, 141.

[3] Terri Kearney & Philip O'Regan, *Skibbereen: The Famine Story* (Skibbereen, Ireland: Macalla Publishing, 2015), 23.

[4] Colum McCann, *TransAtlantic*, "1845—46 Freeman", (New York: Random House, 2013), 40-99; Christine Kinealy, *The Black O'Connell*, irishamerica.com.

[5] Donal O'Kelly, *Frederick Douglass in Ireland*, (Cork: The Collins Press, 2014).

[6] Joel Mokyr and Cormac Ó Gráda. *Famine Disease and Famine Mortality: Lessons from Ireland, 1845—1850*, Northwestern University and University College, Dublin. 30 June 1990.

[7] Coogan, Wherever Green Is Worn, 256.

[8] Steve Donohue, "Charlotte Grace O'Brien", *Africa*, January/February, 81 (1), 2016.

[9] *Maritime Liverpool* (Norwich: Jarrold Publishing, 2003), 10.

[10] Coogan, *The Famine Plot*, Chapter Twelve, "Emigration: Escape by Coffin Ship".

[11] Andrea Barrett, *Ship Fever* (London: Flamingo, 2008).

[12] U.S. Census 1860, 1870, 1880, 1900, 1910.

[13] An "excess mortality rate" is the number of deaths per annum due to a specific condition. The "excess" deaths due to the disease,

environmental condition or natural disaster are above, or in excess
to, those expected for that year.

[14] Roberts, *Everlasting Granite*, 66.

[15] U.S. Census, 1870.

[16] *The Maryland Directory*, 1878.

[17] The Democratic paper from Cecil County, *The Cecil Democrat*, only ran
from 1843 to 1845.

[18] In England and Wales, workers were often supplied with nearby cottages, such as the coal miners' homes in the Pit Village of Beamish
Museum in County Durham, England or the iron workers' cottages
in the Welsh Folk Museum, Cardiff, Wales. Farm workers often were
given cottages, as well.

[19] Speech of Fannie Miller to the Hytheham Club on Jan 19, 1910.

[20] The "Tall Irish" were also known as the "Big Irish".

[21] From the oral tradition of the Bannon and Murray families.

[22] U.S. Census, 1900.

[23] Roberts, *Everlasting Granite*, 90-95.

[24] John Hope Franklin and Alfred A. Moss, Jr., *From Slavery to Freedom:
A History of African Americans* (New York: McGraw-Hill, Inc., 1994),
122-123.

[25] Mark Hughes, *The New Civil War Handbook: Facts and Photos for
Readers of All Ages* (New York: Savas Beatie, 2009).

[26] Franklin and Moss, *From Slavery to Freedom*, 216-217; Eric F. Mease,
"Black Civil War Patriots of Cecil County, Maryland" (Master of Arts
thesis, University of Delaware, 2010).

[27] George Johnston, *History of Cecil County, Maryland* (Elkton, 1881),
312.

[28] John H.B. Latrobe, *The History of Mason and Dixon's Line; An Address
before The Historical Society of Pennsylvania*, November 8, 1854.

[29] Ibid.

Churches and Schools

[1] JoAnne Bierly, e-mail message to author, September 19, 2016.

[2] Guyas Cutas Letter No. 2, 1876.

[3] The 'Banking Building' was labelled as the Cath. Church in Martenet's
1858 map.

[4] Erika L. Quesenbery Sturgill, "St. Teresa of Avila Roman Catholic
Church of Port Deposit, 2016", booklet for the 150th Anniversary of
the Foundation.

[5] Erika Quesenbery and Town of Port Deposit – Port Deposit History

–Year by Year, 2008.

[6] "Tome Pupils Honored – Letters and Caps awarded Those who Starred in Sports", Baltimore *Sun*, June 7, 1915.

[7] "Do You Remember the Rising Sun Baseball Team in 1904", *Cecil County Word Press*, February 12, 2013.

[8] "Jacob Tome Institute – Commencement Seromon to Be Delivered Today", *Baltimore American*, June 10, 1906.

[9] Erika L. Quesenbery, *United States Naval Training Center, Bainbridge* (Charleston, S.C.: Arcadia Publishing, 2007), 17; Franklin D. Roosevelt, Speech in Port Deposit, June 11, 1917.

[10] "Tome School for Girls – Commencement Exercise Will Begin on Saturday", *Baltimore American*, June 3, 1920.

Change of Fortune

[1]Quesenbery, *Bainbridge*, 26.

Part II

Stop One – Old McClenahan Mansion

[1]"A Walking Tour of Historic Port Deposit Maryland" A Booklet. (Hickory Offset Printing:Port Deposit Heritage Corporation and the Port Deposit Chamber of Commerce, 2004).

[2] Jerome Murray witnessed the freshly-killed copperheads while delivering groceries to the home as a boy.

[3] During census listing, the normal pattern was that a married male with a family would be listed as the head of household, even with a parent living with them.

[4] 1867, 1878 and 1906 *Records of Officers of the United States Navy*.

[5] Grace Humphries, "Candlelight Tour" In *Upper Shoreman*, 1977, quoted in Roberts, *Everlasting Granite*, 103-104.

Stop Two – Susquehanna River and the Rail Road

[1]Miller, *Cecil County, Maryland*, 107-111; Brown, *Commerce on Early American Waterways,* Chapter 2. The Susquehanna is Opened to the Chesapeake Bay.

[2] Broadbill is a colloquial term for scaup.

[3] William B. Cronin. *The disappearing islands of the Chesapeake*. (Baltimore: The Johns Hopkins University Press, 2005), 20.

[4] The tidal nature of the lower Susquehanna River at this point is evidence of the interlinking ecosystems of the Chesapeake Bay and the Susquehanna River. During the last Ice Age, the area that the bay

now occupies was the basin and valley floor of the river, until global warming led to the rise in sea level, and formation of the tidal bay, as the Atlantic waters rose at the river's mouth.

[5] Arthur Wilson as told to David R. Craig, "Wading Knee-Deep in the Fish in the Susquehanna", (Baltimore) *Sun Magazine*, April 4, 1976, 53.

[6] Charlotte Newell, "The Life of Jacob Tome", 6

[7] Junction

[8] The Quarry Station was for workers at Keystone Quarry near Mount Ararat, not to be confused with the station at McClenahan's quarry.

[9] William Gibb McAdoo, Jr. served as U.S. Secretary of the Treasury from 1913 to 1918 and was director of the U.S. Railroad Administration from 1917 to 1918, and hence was blamed for problems with the railroad.

[10] The Atlas Powder plant prepared ammonium nitrate powder for the high explosive munitions factory in Perryville for the U.S. War Department during WWI. It opened in May 1918 and closed after the Armistice, which was on 11 November of that year.

[11] Milt Diggins, *Bridging Port Deposit "Off from the World and the Rest of Mankind"*, *Maryland Historical Magazine,* Vol 101 (2) Summer 2006, 202.

Stop Three – Jacob Tome's "Town School"

[1] Carolyn Bolgiano Capistrano, "In My Mother's Box", 2002.

[2] Many versions of the quotation have been used, most famously by Brigham Young and Nelson Mandela.

Stop Four – Gerry "Lafayette" House

[1] There are many historical accounts of this. The name "Head of Elk", was changed to "Elkton" in 1787, when the county seat moved to Elkton from Charleston.

[2] James R. Gaines, *For Liberty and Glory: Washington, Lafayette, and Their Revolutions* (New York: W.W. Norton and Company, 2007), 147; Johnston in *History of Cecil County, Maryland* states that the troops' clothing was renewed in Baltimore.

[3] Gaines, *For Liberty and Glory*, 149.

[4] According to Johnston in *History of Cecil County, Maryland*, Layette stayed the night in an old stone home, the home of Job Haines, which was a short distance north-east of the village of Rising Sun, and about a mile from Harrisville.

[5] "Lafayette and the Virginia Campaign 1781," https://www.nps.gov/york/learn/historyculture/lafayette-and-the-virginia-campaign-1781.htm.

[6] Frank E. Grizzard, Jr. *George Washington: A biographical companion*

(Santa Barbara, CA: ABC-CLIO, 2002), 176.

[7] "The Mitchell Family". Maryland Genealogy Trails. Cecil County Maryland Families. Accessed Feb 12, 2017. http://genealogy trails. com/mary/cecil/families_m.html.

[8] Lafayette's portrait was comissioned by the City of New York and is now part of the Collection of the Public Design Commission of the City of New York; Morse, Willard and Cooper established homes in Paris in the late 1820s where they were part of Lafayette's social circle, David McCullough, *The Greater Journey: Americans in Paris* (New York; Simon and Schuster, 2005).

[9] Auguste Levasseur, *Lafayette in America, in 1824 and 1825*. Vol I.,Philadelphia: Carey & Lea, 1829, 160-161.

[10] Levasseur, *Lafayette in America*, Vol II., 238-239.

[11] Miller, *Cecil County, Maryland*, 118, 122. J.W. Abrahams recalled that Lafayette was taken to the Lyon's Farm above Port Deposit. There were two Lyons families farming in 1830. Andrew Lyon had an estate above Race Street in 1877, and J. Lyon had an estate at the southeast corner of N. Main Street and Rock Run Road (1877).

[12] It was the home of Daniel and Mary R. Megredy.

Stop Five – Downtown Port Deposit, etc.

[1] Erika Quesenbery, "How Port Deposit rallied around its hero Capt. Snow", *Cecil Daily*, March 29, 2014; Register of Officers and Agents in the Service of the United States on the Thirtieth of September, 1871. (Washington: Government Printing Office, 1872).

[2] Erika L. Quesenbery. *A Snowball's Chance: Battery B, Maryland Light Artillery 1st, Snow's, 1861-1854*. (Hickory Offset Printing: Port Deposit Heritage Corporation, 2003).

[3] Miller, *Cecil County, Maryland*, 119.

[4] "History of Port Deposit Read At the One Hundred Anniversary of Naming of the Town", July 4, 1913; Quesenbery and Town of Port Deposit, "Port Deposit History – Year by Year".

[5] JoAnne Bierly, e-mail message to author, September 9, 2016. "It was probably a locally made cannon ball."

[6] This was also the location of Carson's (Pharmacy) Building, as well as Fraser's, and in the late 1800s, Dr. Tate's drugstore was nearby.

[7] Quesenbery, *Bainbridge*, 26.

[8] Guyas Cutas, Letter No. 1; The Still House was near to Heckart's Saw Mill at the south boundary of town.

[9] William Still, *The Underground Rail Road*. (Philadelphia: Porter & Coates, 1872), 684.

[10] Ibid., 553.

[11] Pennsylvania began gradual abolition of slavery in 1780, and slavery

was completed abolished in the state in 1847. The Fugitive Slave Acts of 1793 and 1850 were repealed in June 1864; John Mackenzie, "A brief history of the Mason-Dixon Line", University of Delaware, 2005.

[12] Still, *The Underground Rail Road*, 163, 315, 510, 735; Susan Q. Stranahan, *Susquehanna, River of Dreams*. (Baltimore: Johns Hopkins University Press, 2015),66, William J. Switala, *Underground Railroad in Pennsylvania* (Mechanisburg, Pa., Stackpole Books, 2008).

[13] In 1870, the census information collectors (enumerators) were given instructions to record the color of every person. If a person "had any trace of African blood", "M" for "Mulatto" was recorded.

[14] Working outside the home.

[15] Mease, *Black Civil War Patriots of Cecil County, Maryland*, 2-3.

[16] "History of Port Deposit Read At the One Hundred Anniversary of Naming of the Town".

Stop Six –Old Creswell House, etc.

[1] John M. Osborne and Christine Bombaro. *Forgotten Abolitionist: John A. J. Creswell of Maryland*. (Carlisle, PA: House Divided Project at Dickinson College, 2015).

[2] Eric Foner, *The Fiery Trial: Abraham Lincoln and American Slavery* (New York: W.W. Norton & Company, 2011), 275-276.

[3] Ibid., 277.

[4] Brown, *Commerce on Early American Waterways*, 98.

[5] Charlotte Newell, "The Life of Jacob Tome", 17.

[6] Jacob and Caroline Webb Tome had three babies, who died in infancy.

[7] J.J. Abrahams, letter to author, June 1, 2016.

[8] Baltimore *Sun*, July 8, 1871.

Stop Seven – Middle Town, St. Teresa's, The "Tall Irish" Murray Home, etc.

The *Cecil Whig* reprinted an item from the *Boston Post* in August 1870, entitled "Well Paid Women", listing the salaries of telegraphers, sewing machine operators, teachers, seamstresses and book keepers, who received similar annual pay ($500-1,000).

[2] Mrs. Charlotte Newell was also Tome's biographer. She moved from Port Deposit around this time to the Inner Harbor area of Baltimore, and lived with her son, James, who became a writer and editor of the Baltimore paper, *News-Post*. James Newell, after leaving Tome, went to Princeton University, graduating *magna cum laude*.

[3] Alice Miller, *Cecil County, Maryland*, 121.

[4] JoAnne Bierly, e-mail message to author, July 22, 2016 stating "At some point, my grandfather, Frank T. Bittner, decided to drop one of the "t's" in order to "save ink." Two of his children, Anna and Leo, chose to drop a 't'."

[5] "100TH Anniversary – Port Deposit Is Preparing For An Elaborate Celebration", Baltimore *Sun*, July 4, 1913; "What People Are Doing In Towns and Villages During The Summer", *Baltimore American*, July 1913.

Stop Eight – Rock Run and The "Short Irish" Murray Home

[1] William Kilty, *Index to the Laws of Maryland, from the Year 1818 to 1825*, (Annapolis: Jeremiah Hughes, 1827), 127.

[2] Cecil County Mills, p49.

[3] Race, meaning fast-running narrow stream.

[4] Mease, *Black Civil War Patriots of Cecil County, Maryland*; U.S. Census, 1910.

[5] These distinctions between listed occupations for black and white women also existed in Baltimore City; In Philadelphia, Emilie Frances Davis, a free colored girl" was listed as a "home-sewer", but her *Civil War Pocket Diaries* make it clear, from the wedding dresses that she made, that "seamstress" was a more accurate term.

[6] Coogan, *Wherever Green Is Worn*, 156-159.

[7] Isaac B. Rehert, *Rock Run Hollow: Four Seasons from a Farm Window* (Baltimore: Helicon, 1967), 25.

[8] Roberts, *Everlasting Granite*, JPM interview.

[9] "People of Port Deposit on the Lookout, Ice Gorges Breaking Up", *Baltimore American*, February 24, 1910.

[10] In 1910, Cecil County voted "dry", following the temperance reform movements from the late 1800s. The laws regulated the sale and taxing of liquor.

Stop Nine – Jerome Murray's Boyhood Home

[1] "The Water's Rising", *The County Post*, Special Edition – May 3, 1977, 3-4.

[2] "Iceboat Season Here – Frail Craft Skim over Susquehanna Surface," Baltimore *Sun*, December 19, 1910.

[3] A mess of perch was typically 30-40 per net.

[4] Speech of Fannie Miller to the Hytheham Club on Jan 19, 1910.

[5] This is a suggestion that Andrew Bannon was one of the designated watchmen of the floods, a concept put into action by the post-1910 Ice

Gorge Committee.

[6] Rehert, *Rock Run Hollow*, 104.

[7] Anne Carney Brown, "Kathy Anne Buetow's Grandmother", Summer 2004.

[8] Jerome began his civil service career as a mechanic with the U.S. Public Health Service in Perry Point, Md. from November 1919 to October, 1925.

[9] Bryson, Bill, *One Summer: America 1927* (Croydon: Black Swan, 2014), 156.

[10] James H. Bready. *Baseball in Baltimore: The First 100 Years.* (Baltimore: The Johns Hopkins University Press, 1998), 132.

[11] Bready, *Baseball in Baltimore*, 148.

[12] Anne Carney Brown, e-mail message to author, August 19, 2016.

[13] Margaret B. Fischer, "No Blarney in Carney", *Tap into Sparta*, March 16, 2016. https://www.tapinto.net/towns/sparta/columns/advocating-for-children/articles/no-blarney-in-carney

[14] Cecilia Carney, Correspondence from Robert Emmett Carney from France to Family in Oct 1918) *Baltimore Catholic Review*, Dec 14, 1918, 4; Anne Carney Brown, e-mail to author, February 20, 2005.

[15] Anne Carney Brown, "Robert Emmett Carney", July 15, 2004.

[16] Anne Carney Brown, E-mail messages to author, August 16 and 19, 2016.

[17] 'Hermits' first appeared in Miss Parloa's 1880s era cookbooks. These cookies of sugar, flour fruit and spice were first made in New England and New York. 'Cookies' came into American baking slightly later.

[18] Chris Bannon, Letter to author, August 3, 2016.

[19] Christopher, Nina and Chris Bannon, Conversations with author, November 22, 2016.

Stop Ten – Mockingbird Hill

Carolyn Capistrano, *In My Mother's Box*, September 6, 2002.

[2] John J. Abrahams III, Letter to author, June 1, 2016.

[3] James A. Michener, *Chesapeake* (New York: Fawcett Crest, 1978), 825-826.

[4] Carolyn Capistrano. *Patricia Ellen Murray*, July 18, 2016.

[5] John Glassman's service in Taiwan involved working on C-130s and other cargo planes that flew into Vietnam during that war. Kilroy first became popularized during WWII.

[6] "Susquehanna River, at Conowingo, Maryland." U.S. Geological Survey, http://md.water.usgs.gov

[7] "Sidewalks Cleared But Port Deposit Streets Are Still Blocked With Ice", *Baltimore American*, February 7, 1910.

Bibliography

Anon. [Rock Run Bard], *Port Deposit in Verse*. Rock Run, Cecil County, Maryland, 1 June 1881.

The Anti-saloon league yearbook. An Encyclopedia of factors and figures dealing with liquor traffic and the temperance reform. Westerville, OH: Anti-Saloon League of America, 1910.

Barrett, Andrea. *Ship Fever*. London: Flamingo, 2008.

Bellmayer, Jane. "St. Teresa's celebrates 150 years of hospitality," *Cecil Daily*, July 17, 2016. http://www.cecildaily.com.

Belmonte, Gloria and Jason Belmonte. "Port Deposit Guide," *Cecil County Real Estate*. April 22, 2007 http://activerain.com/blogsview/81263/port-deposit-guide.

Boyle, Phelim P., and Cormac O Grada. "Fertility Trends, Excess Mortality and the Great Irish Famine" University of Waterloo, and University College Dublin, 1982.

Bready, James H. *Baseball in Baltimore: The First 100 Years*. Baltimore: The Johns Hopkins University Press, 1998.

Brown, Earl E. *Commerce on Early American Waterways: The Transport of Goods by Arks, Rafts and Log Drives*. Jefferson, NC: McFarland & Co., Inc., 2010.

Brubaker, Jack. *Down the Susquehanna to the Chesapeake*. University Park, PA: The Pennsylvania State University Press, 2002.

Bryson, Bill. *One Summer: America 1927*. London: Black Swan, 2013.

Capistrano, Carolyn Bolgiano. *In My Mother's Box*. September 6, 2002.

Capistrano, Carolyn. *Patricia Ellen Murray*. July 18, 2016.

Carney, Cecilia. Letter from Robert Emmett Carney to Family from France in October, 1918. *Baltimore Catholic Review*, December 14, 1918.

Carney Brown, Anne. "Kathy Anne Buetow's Grandmother" Summer 2004.

Carney Brown, Anne. "Robert Emmett Carney" July 15, 2004.

Carroll, David H., and Thomas G. Boggs. *Men of Mark in Maryland: Johnson's Makers of America Series, Biographies of Leading Men of the State*. Vol. III, Baltimore: B.F. Johnson, Inc., 1911. Accessed Sep 19, 2016. https://archive.org/details/menofmarkinmaryl03stei .

"Cecil County Mills" http://msa.maryland.gov/megafile/msa/speccol/sc4300/sc4300/000005/000000/000020/restricted/cecil.pdf.

Cecil County: A Reference Book of History, Business & General Information. Published Quinquennially. Baltimore: County Directories of Maryland, 1956.

Centers for Disease Control "Achievements in Public Health, 1900-1999:

Impact of vaccines universally recommended for children –United
States, 1990-1998," National Immunization Program. *Morbidity and
Mortality Weekly Report* 48, 12 (1999):243-248.

Chesapeake Bay Foundation "The Susquehanna River," 2015.
http://www.cbf.org/about-the-bay/more-than-just-the-bay/
susqhehanna-river.

Coogan, Tim Pat. *Wherever Green in Worn: The Story of the Irish
Diaspora.* New York: Palgrave, 2001.

Coogan, Tim Pat. *The Famine Plot: England's Role In Ireland's Greatest
Tragedy.* Croydon: Palgrave MacMillan, 2012.

Cronin, William B. The disappearing islands of the Chesapeake.
Baltimore: The Johns Hopkins University Press, 2005.

Cunliffe, Barry, and Robert Bartlett, John Morrill et. al., *Illustrated
History of Britain & Ireland*, London: Penguin Books, 2004.

Cutas, Guyas. "Port Deposit: Forty years ago and now". Letter No. 1, *Cecil
Whig*, January 30, 1876. Reprinted in the *Bulletin of the Historical
Society of Cecil County*, No 55 (Jan 1988) Elkton.

Cutas, Guyas. "Port Deposit: Forty years ago and now". Letter No. 2, *Cecil
Whig*, February 5, 1876. Reprinted in the *Bulletin of the Historical
Society of Cecil County*, No 56 (May 1988) Elkton.

Davis, Kenneth C.A. *Nation Rising: Untold Tales from America's History.*
New York: Harper, 2010.

Diggins, Milt. *"Bridging Port Deposit "Off from the World and the Rest of
Mankind," Maryland Historical Magazine*, 101, 2 (Summer 2006):
185-202.

Diggins, Milt, *Cecil County*. Images of America series. Charleston, S.C.:
Arcadia Publishing, 2008.

Diggins, Milt. "Diggins Works With National Park Service to Nominate
Two Cecil County Sites For Underground Railroad Listing" *Cecil
County Word Press.* August 8, 2014.
https://cecilcounty.wordpress.com

Dixon, Kyle M. "Standing in the Schoolhouse Door: The Desegregation
of Public Schools in Cecil County, Maryland, 1954-1965" A
Senior Thesis, Washington College, 2013. http://cecilhistory.org/
uploads/3/4/4/9/34490369/desgegration_of_public_schools_in_cecil_
county_maryland.pdf.

Dixon, Michael. "The Water's Rising," *The County Post. Special Edition.*
May 3, 1997. Elkton: White Oak Publishing.

Dixon, Mike. "All's Quiet on the Octoraro Branch Line" *Cecil County Word
Press.* October 20, 2008. https://cecilcounty.wordpress.com.

"Do You Remember the Rising Sun Baseball Team in 1904?" *Cecil County
Word Press.* February 12, 2013. https://cecilcounty.wordpress.
com/2013/02/12/whig-asks-do-you-remember-the-rising-sun-baseball-

team-in-1904/.

Donohue, Steve. "Charlotte Grace O'Brien", *Africa* (January/February) 81 (2016): 4-6.

Douglass, Frederick. *Narrative of the Life of Frederick Douglass.* Boston: Anti-slavery Office, 1845.

Douglass, Frederick. "American Prejudice Against Color" An address delivered in Cork on October 23, 1845. (Cork) *Examiner,* Oct 27, 1845. Documenting the American South, The University of North Carolina at Chapel Hill, 2004. http://docsouth.unc.edu/neh/douglass/support8.html.

Douglass, Frederick. *Life and Times of Frederick Douglass, Written By Himself.* Boston: DeWoolfe & Fiske Co., 1892.

Egan, Timothy. "Immigrants turned away," *International New York Times,* Issue 41,515. Sat Sun, September 3,4, 2016.

Fenton, Laurence. *Frederick Douglass In Ireland: "The Black O'Connell".* Cork: The Collins Press, 2014.

Fischer, Margaret Bolgiano. "No Blarney in Carney," *Tap into Sparta,* March 16, 2016. https://www.tapinto.net/towns/sparta/columns/advocating-for-children/articles/no-blarney-in-carney.

Fischer, Margaret Bolgiano. *Mockingbird Hill, Port Deposit, Maryland.* May 2016.

Foner, Eric. *The Fiery Trial: Abraham Lincoln and American Slavery.* New York: W.W. Norton & Company, 2011.

Franklin, John Hope, and Alfred A. Moss, Jr. *From Slavery to Freedom: A History of African Americans.* Seventh Edition. New York: McGraw-Hill Inc., 1994.

Gaines, James R. *For Liberty and Glory: Washington, Lafayette, and Their Revolutions.* New York: W.W. Norton and Company, 2007.

Gannett, Henry. *A Gazetteer of Maryland and Delaware*, Vol 2. Baltimore: Genealogical Publishing Co., Inc., 1904.

Gibson, Kathy. "Port Deposit: Small town shouldn't be taken for granite," *Cecil Whig,* May 28, 1988.

Gordon-Van Tine Plan Cut Homes: 1931 Book of Homes. Davenport: Gordon-Van Tine Co. https://archive.org/stream/GordonVanTineCoPlancuthomes19310001#page/n63/mode/2up.

Grizzard, Frank E., Jr. *George Washingon: A biographical companion.* Santa Barbara, CA: ABC-CLIO, 2002, 173-180.

Hamersley, Lewis Rudolph. *The Records of Living Officers of the U.S. Navy and Marine Corps.* 1878. Philadelphia: J.B. Lippincott & Co.

Hamm, Richard. *Shaping the Eighteenth Amendment: Temperance reform, legal culture and the Polity, 1880-1920.* Chapel Hill, NC: The University Of North Carolina Press, 1995.

Hamon, Ray L., and Wm E. Arnold. *School Building Survey*

of Cecil County, Maryland, 1948. http://cecilhistory.org/
uploads/3/4/4/9/34490369/school_buliidng_survey_1948.pdf.

"Harriet Ross Tubman Davis" *Archives of Maryland (Biographical Series)*. http://msa.maryland.gov/megafile/msa/speccol/sc3500/
sc3520/013500/013562/html/13562bio.html.

The Heritage Cookbook, Vol II. Port Deposit: Port Deposit Heritage Corp.,
1979.

"Great Migration," *History* website.
http://www.history.com/topics/black-history/great-migration.

"Howard Methodist Episcopal Church Site," *Pathways to Freedom:
Maryland & the Underground Railroad*. Museums and Historical
Sites. Central Maryland. Maryland Public Television. 2016. http://
pathways.thinkport.org/library/sites4.cfm.

Hughes, Mark. *The New Civil War Handbook: Facts and Photos for
Readers of all Ages*. New York: Savas Beatie, 2009.

*An Illustrated Atlas. Cecil County, Maryland: Compiled, drawn and
published from actual surveys*. Philadelphia: Lake Griffing and
Stevenson, 1877.

https://jscholarship.library.jhu.edu/handle/1774.2/34120.

"Interpretive Plan for the Lower Susquehanna Heritage Greenway,"
Maryland Humanities Council History Matters! 2008. http://citese-
erx.ist.psu.edu/viewdoc/versions?doi=10.1.1.114.4217.

"Jacob tome Institute, Tome School for Boys (Bainbridge Naval Training
Center)", Historic American Buildings Survey HABS No. MD-1110.
Massey Maxwell Associates (Washington: National Park Service,
2000).

Johnston, George. *History of Cecil County, Maryland, and the Early
Settlements around the Head of Chesapeake Bay and on the
Delaware River, with Sketches of Some of the Old Families of Cecil
County*. Elkton, MD: Published by the author, 1881. https://archive.
org/details/historyofcecilco00john.

Kearney, Terri, and Philip O'Ragan. *Skibbereen: The Famine Story*.
Skibbereen, West Cork, Ireland: Macalla Publishing, 2015.

Kelso, Fred. *Steam, Stone and Wood: 19th Century Commerce in Port
Deposit, Maryland*. Oxford, PA: Hengwrt Publishing Company, 1997.

Kelso, Fred. *"The Port Deposit Black Sox,"* The Historical Society of Cecil
County. February 12, 1998. http://cecilhistory.org/port-deposit-black-
sox.html.

Kenealy, Christine. "The Black O'Connell," *Irish America* Oct/Nov 2013.
http://irishamerica.com/2013/09/the-black-oconnell/.

Kennedy, Jim. *"Rock Run Landing, gone but not forgotten,"* Sun, July 12,
2012. http://www.baltimoresun.com/ph-re-two-cents-0713-20120711-
story.html.

Kilty, William. *Index to the laws of Maryland, from the year 1818 to 1825.* Annapolis: Jeremiah Hughes, 1827. http://heinonline.org/.

"Lafayette, Citizen of America," *The New York Times*, September 7, 1919.

"Lafayette and the Virginia Campaign 1781," Website. Yorktown Battlefield. Colonial National Historic Park, Virginia, National Park Service. https://www.nps.gov/york/learn/historyculture/lafayette-and-the-virginia-campaign-1781.html.

Latrobe, John H.B. *The History of Mason and Dixon's Line; contained in An Address, delivered by John H.B. Latrobe, of Maryland, before The Historical Society of Pennsylvania*, November 8, 1854 (Philadelphia: Collins, 1854). https://archive.org/details/historyofmasondi00lat.

Lawrence, Susannah, and Barbara Gross. *The Audubon Society Field Guide to the Natural Places of the Mid-Atlantic States: Inland,* edited by Caroline Sutton. New York: Pantheon Books, 1984.

Levasseur, Auguste. *Lafayette in America, in 1824 and 1825: or, Journal of travels, in the United States.* Volume I, Chapter XI, translated by John D. Godman. Philadelphia: Carey & Lea, 1829. https://books.google.co.uk/books?id=WhGc5a5srvYC.

Levasseur, Auguste. *Lafayette in America, in 1824 and 1825: or, Journal of travels, in the United States.* Volume II, Chapter XV, translated by John D. Godman. Philadelphia: Carey and Lea, 1829. https://books.google.co.uk/books?id=pPRIZqUYmoEC.

Longley, Clifford. "The demands of labour must take priority over the demands of capital," *The Tablet*, 16 July, 2011, 5.

McCann, Colum. "1845–46 Freeman" In *TransAtlantic.* New York: Random House, 2013.

McCullough, David. *The Greater Journey: Americans in Paris.* New York: Simon & Schuster, 2011.

Mackenzie, John. "A brief history of the Mason-Dixon Line" University of Delaware, 2005.

MacKenzie, Debora. *"On The Road Again," New Scientist* 3071 (9 April 2016).

Maritime Liverpool: The Guide To Merseyside Maritime Museum, HM Customs & Excise Museum, Museum of Liverpool Life. Norwich: Jarrold Publishing for The Board of Trustees of the National Museums & Galleries on Merseyside, 2003.

Martenet, Simon J. *Martenet's Map of Cecil County, Maryland: from the coast, and original surveys.* [Baltimore: S. J. Martenet, 1858] Map. Retrieved from the Library of Congress, https://www.loc.gov/item/2002624017/.

The Maryland Directory. Baltimore: J. Frank Lewis & Co., 1878. http://

www.newrivernotes.com/other_states_maryland_business_1878_
marylanddirectory.htm.

Mason, Charles. "The Journal of Charles Mason and Jeremiah Dixon."
Abridged. Accessed Feb 19, 2017. www.mdlpp.org/pdf/library/
JournalofMasonandDixon.pdf.

Mason, Charles, Jeremiah Dixon, James Smither, and Robert Kennedy.
*A plan of the west line or parallel of latitude, which is the boundary
between the provinces of Maryland and Pensylvania: a plan of the
boundary lines between the province of Maryland and the Three
Lower Counties on Delaware with part of the parallel of latitude
which is the boundary between the provinces of Maryland and
Pennsylvania.* [Philadelphia: Robert Kennedy, 1768] Map. Retrieved
from the Library of Congress, https://www.loc.gov/item/84695758/.
(Accessed February 28, 2017.)

Mathews, Edward Bennett. "The Mineral Resources of Cecil County,"
In *Maryland Geological Survey of Cecil County.* Baltimore: Johns
Hopkins Press, 1902,195-226.
https://archive.org/details/cecilcounty00shatgoog.

Mease, Eric F. "Black Civil War Patriots of Cecil County, Maryland"
Masters of Art thesis, University of Delaware, 2010.
http://cecilhistory.org/civilwar/measethesis.pdf.

Measuring Worth. The Comparators. www.measuringworth.com.

Michener, James A. *Chesapeake.* New York: Fawcett Crest, 1978.

Miller, Alice E. *Cecil County, Maryland: A Study in Local History.* 1949.
Reprinted as *Bicentennial Edition.* Elkton: C & L Printing, 1976.

Miller, Fannie M. *A short history of Port Deposit, Maryland"* read by the
author to the Hytheham Club at a meeting on January 19, 1910.

Modelling the Earth's Interior from *Into the Earth: earthquakes, seismology and the Earth's magnetism.* Units 5-6 of A Science Foundation
course. Milton Keynes: The Open University, 1992, 76-79.

Mokyr, Joel, and Cormac Ó'Gráda. "Famine Disease and Famine
Mortality: Lessons from Ireland, 1845 – 1850" Northwestern
University and University College Dublin. 30 June 1990.

Morton, Gary. "The 'gem' on the Susquehanna: St. Teresa Church in Port
Deposit, Md., celebrating 150 years," *The Dialog* 51, no. 14 (July 8,
2016), 7.
http://thedialog.org/the-gem-on-the-susquehanna.

Murray, Patricia E. *Stories About My Mother.* 1989.

Murray, Patricia Ellen. *Aunt Pat Remembers.* April, 2013.

Murray, Patricia Ellen. *Stories Daddy Liked to Tell.* January 1989.

Native Americans in the Susquehanna River Valley, Past and Present. Ed.
David J. Minderhout. Lewisburg: Bucknell University Press, 2013.

Newell, Charlotte. "The Life of Jacob Tome." A Pamphlet. Port Deposit,

MD: Jacob Tome Institute Alumni Association, 1948.

Ó'Gráda, Cormac. "Ireland's Great Famine: An Overview. Centre for Economic Research," Working Paper Series, 20014. University College, Dublin. https://www.ucd.ie/economics/research/papers/2004/WP04.25.pdf.

Osborne, John M., and Christine Bombaro. "Forgotten Abolitionist: John A. J. Creswell of Maryland," House Divided Project. Carlisle, PA: Dickinson College, 2015. https://www.smashwords.com/books/view/585258.

Parish, Peter J. *Slavery: The many faces of a Southern institution.* Preston: Keele University Press, 1992.

Pelayo, Jeff. "James Holly (1818-1892), Havre de Grace, MD" *Duck Decoys, Duck Dogs and Duck Guns.* January 29, 2012. http://canvasbackgallery.blogspot.com.

Port Deposit Historic District. Maryland's National Register Properties. Maryland Historical Trust. Posted, 2003-2015. http://mht.maryland.gov/nr/NRDetail.aspx?NRID=474&FROM=NR-MapCE.html.

Port Deposit Historic District. National Register of Historic Places Inventory – Nomination Form. CE-1291. http://msa.maryland.gov/megafile/msa/stagsere/se1/se5/007600/007644/pdf/msa_se5_7644.pdf 2016.

Quesenbery, Erika L. "Port Deposit's Paw Paw Building Restored to a museum of American Rivertown Life," 2003. http://www.portdeposit.org.

Quesenbery, Erika L. *A Snowball's Chance, Battery B, Maryland Light Artillery 1st, Snow's 1861-1865.* Port Deposit, Maryland: Port Deposit Heritage Corporation, 2003.

Quesenbery, Erika L. *United States Naval Training Center, Bainbridge.* Images of America series. Published on behalf of the Bainbridge Historical Association. Charleston, SC: Arcadia Publishing, 2007.

Quesenbery Sturgill, Erika. "Field of Dreams: Port Deposit was once home to all-black baseball team." *Cecil Daily*, February 16, 2013. http://cecilhistory.org/port-deposit-black-sox.html.

Quesenbery Sturgill, Erika. "How Port Deposit rallied around its hero Capt. Snow," *Cecil Daily*, March 29, 2014. http://www.cecildaily.com/our_cecil/article_d9a54c44-1ca3-56a2-b8dc-5ee818375931.html.

Quesenbery Sturgill, Erika. "Susquehannocks – The vanquished tribe," *Cecil Daily*, May 17, 2014. http://www.cecildaily.com/our_cecil/article_75360102-240f-504b-97ae-d7ad37878cb4.html.

Quesenbery Sturgill, Erika L. "St. Teresa of Avila Roman Catholic Church of Port Deposit." Booklet prepared for the 150th Anniversary

Celebration on behalf of Good Shepherd Parish. June 2016.

Quesenbery, Erika L. and Town of Port Deposit. *Port Deposit History –
Year by Year, 2008*. Accessed Jun 10, 2010. http://www.portdeposit.org

Reed, Paula. *Fifty Fashion Looks That Changed the 1950s*. Design
Museum. London: Conran, 2012.

*Register of Commissioned and Warrant Officers of the United States
Navy and Marine Corps to January 1, 1906 Washington: Government
Printing Office, 1906.*

*Register of Officers and Agents, Civil, Military and Naval in the Service of
the United States on the Thirthieth of September, 1867*. Washington:
Government Printing Office, 1868.

*Register of Officers and Agents, Civil, Military and Naval in the Service
of the United States on the Thirtieth of September, 1871*. Washington:
Government Printing Office, 1872.

Rehert, Isaac B. *Rock Run Hollow: Four Seasons from a Farm Window*.
Baltimore: Helicon, 1967.

Roberts, Nancy. Port Deposit Heritage Corporation. *We Called It "The
Everlasting Granite" And, By Golly, It Is*. Havre de Grace, MD:
Hickory Offset Printing, 2002.

Roosevelt, Franklin D. Speech at Tome School in Port Deposit, Maryland,
Jun 11, 1917 Master Speech File. (Box 1, File No. 69); Informal
Extemporaneous Remarks of the President on the Occasion of His
Inspection Tour Of The Tennessee Valley Projects. On the Clinch
River, below the Norris Dam Nov 16,1934-about 4.10 PM. Master
Speech File (Box 20) FDR Presidential Library and Museum, Hyde
Park New York. www.fdrlibrary.marist.edu.

Roosevelt, Franklin D.: "Message to Congress Suggesting the Tennessee
Valley Authority," April 10, 1933. Online by Gerhard Peters and John
T. Woolley, *The American Presidency Project*. http://www.presidency.
ucsb.edu/ws/?pid=14614.

Roosevelt, Franklin D. "Message to Congress. The President Calls
Attention to the Many-Sided Program of the Tennessee Valley
Authority." January 15, 1940. The Public Papers of the Presidents of
the United States.
Quod.lib.umich.edu/p/ppotpus/.

Ruffner, Kevin Conley. *Maryland's Blue & Gray: A Border State's Union
and Confederate Junior Officer Corps*. Baton Rouge: Louisiana State
University Press, 1997.

St. Leger, Alicia. *Gateway to the New World: The story of the origins,
history and legacy of Cobh, a unique Irish port town*. Cobh: Cobh
Heritage Trust, 2000.

Smith, C. Fraser. *Here Lies Jim Crow: Civil Rights in Maryland*.
Baltimore: The Johns Hopkins University Press, 2008.

Smith, John. *The Travels of Captaine John Smith.* Glasgow: James
MacLehose and Sons, 1907.

Snodgrass, Mary Ellen. *The Underground Railraod: An Encylopedia of
People, Places and Operators.* Volumes One-Two. London: Routledge
Taylor & Francis Group, 2015.

Still, William. *The Underground Rail Road: A Record Narrating the
Hardships, Hair-breadth Escapes and Death Struggles of the Slaves
in their efforts of Freedom.* Philadelphia: Porter & Coates, 1872.
https://archive.org/stream/undergroundrailr00stil/underground-
railr00stil_djvu.txt.

Stranahan, Susan Q. *Susquehanna, River of Dreams.* Baltimore: Johns
Hopkins University Press, 2015.

"Susquehanna River Basin Information Sheet," Susquehanna River
Basin Commission. Website. Revised May 2013. http://www.srbc.net/
pubinfo/docs/SRB%20General%205_13%20Updated.pdf.

Switala, William J., *Underground Railroad in Pennsylvania.*
Mechanisburg, PA: Stackpole Books, 2001.

Switala, William J., *Underground Railroad in Delaware, Maryland and
West Virginia.* Mechanisburg, PA:Stackpole Books, 2004.

"Tome School History," The Tome School. Website.
http://www.tomeschool.org/history.

"Improvement of the Susquehanna River, Above and Below Havre
de Grace, Maryland," Annual Report of the Chief of Engineers,
United States Army, to the Secretary of War, for the Year 1891. U.S.
52d Congress House of Representatives. Ex. Doc. 1, Pt 2, Vol II.
Washington: Government Printing Office, 1891.

United States Census Bureau. Table VII. Mortality of the United States
and of Each State and Territory During The Census Year Ended June
1, 1870. Accessed April 20, 2018. https://www2.census.gov/library/
publications/decennial/1870/vital-statistics/1870b-20.pdf.

Verney, Kevern. *The Debate on Black Civil Rights in America.*
Manchester, England: Manchester University Press, 2006, 19, 23

"A Walking Tour of Historic Port Deposit, Maryland." A Booklet. Port
Deposit Heritage Corporation and The Port Deposit Chamber of
Commerce. Port Deposit: 2004.

The Ward Museum of Wildfowl Art. Exhibits. Artists Archive. Salisbury,
MD. https://www.wardmuseum.org/Exhibits/ArtistsArchive/tabid/86/
Default.aspx.

Watson, Thomas Leonard. *Granites of the Southeastern Atlantic States.*
Department of the Interior. United States Geological Survey. Bulletin
426. https://pubs.usgs.gov/bul/0426/report.pdf.

Whitehead, Colson. *The Underground Railroad.* London: Fleet, 2016.

Wilson, Arthur, and D.R. Craig. "Wading Knee Deep in Fish in the

Susquehanna," *The Sun Magazine*, April 4, 1976, p 53.

Winchester, Simon. *The Men Who United The States*. Hammersmith: William Collins. 2014.

Winder, Robert. *Bloody Foreignors: The Story of Immigrants to Britain*. Revised Edition. London: Abacus, 2013.

Wise Whitehead, Karsonya, and Cora D. Gist (eds). *Rethinking Emilie Frances Davis: Lesson plans for Teaching Her Civil War Pocket Diaries*. Baltimore: Apprentice House Press, Loyola University, 2014, p 210.